The Goldmark Case
An American Libel Trial

The
GOLDMARK
CASE

An American Libel Trial

WILLIAM L. DWYER

With a Foreword by Norman Dorsen

University of Washington Press   *Seattle & London*

Library of Congress Cataloging in Publication Data

Dwyer, William L.
    The Goldmark case.
    1. Goldmark, John—Trials, litigation, etc. 2. Canwell, Albert—Trials,
litigation, etc. 3. Trials (Libel)—Washington (State)—Okanogan. I. Title.
KF228.G65D85   1984   345.73′0231   84-40326
ISBN 0-295-96163-5   347.305231

To Vasiliki,
Joanne, Tony,
and Charlie

FOREWORD

GEORGE SANTAYANA'S dictum that those who ignore history are condemned to relive it has achieved the notoriety of a cliché. Like many clichés it survives because it contains much truth.

The Goldmark case brings these thoughts to mind as it beckons us to reflect on the phenomenon known as McCarthyism. The word is (or should be) permanently listed in the Devil's Dictionary. It signifies a particularly irresponsible form of persecution for political beliefs. It also conveys a total lack of due process and fairness whereby unverified allegations, made by rabid and often mercenary ideologues, are used to destroy reputations, careers, and families. Too often these tactics are used against strangers within the gates—recent arrivals to a community who are not of the dominant race, religion, or cultural background.

Most Americans eventually were repelled by what Senator Joseph McCarthy and his allies wrought in the early 1950s and, after viewing the televised Army-McCarthy hearings, gladly assigned him to a purgatory from which he never emerged. But since memories are short, William Dwyer has rendered a high public service in setting down for this generation a harrowing western courtroom drama that will, if it is as widely read as it deserves to be, fortify Americans to resist new attempts to violate civil liberties and debase the political community.

The setting for the Goldmark case was a sparsely populated area in north central Washington, where John and Sally Goldmark moved soon after his completion of naval sevice in World War II. Goldmark was a city-bred easterner and an honors graduate of Harvard Law School, but he chose to become a rancher in remote territory. The ranch prospered with hard work, and the Goldmarks became active in community and charitable affairs. John was elected to the state legislature in 1956 and reelected twice. After six years in office he was the respected chairman of the House Ways and Means Committee.

And then the trouble started. Goldmark was a liberal legislator during a time of suspicion toward liberals. Worse, as a young woman Sally had been a member of the Communist Party for a few years. Although there was no indication of any illegal activity, and she left the Party soon after her marriage, the record of her membership was there to be used. And it was.

Early in 1962, as the legislative election campaign started, a county weekly reported that Goldmark "was running on a platform which advocates the repeal of the McCarran Act, a law requiring the registration of all Communist Party members"; that his son Charles was a sophomore at Reed College, the "only school in the Northwest where Gus Hall, secretary of the Communist Party, was invited to speak"; and that he was a member of the American Civil Liberties Union, "an organization closely affiliated with the Communist movement in the United States." A whispering campaign about Sally Goldmark began at the same time. The libels proliferated through the campaign.

John Goldmark lost the election badly, and he also lost his good name. Rejecting the advice of those who warned that a public trial would cause further harm to him and his family, he promptly brought a libel suit to vindicate his reputation against individuals and periodicals who, he charged, had conspired to ruin him. He hired William Dwyer as his chief counsel.

The trial began on November 4, 1963, and attracted national attention. Witnesses crossed the country to testify on John's character, the threat of Communism to American society, and assorted related issues. In the third week of the trial Lee Harvey Oswald murdered President John Kennedy, and although a recess was taken, Goldmark's friends feared that this shattering event would implicitly support the defendants' claim that an indigenous Communist conspiracy was afoot to destroy American institutions.

The case was tried to a jury of rural westerners. No summary can do justice to the tense and colorful drama that filled the courtroom. No morality play could more sharply etch the roles of parties and witnesses. No novel could more vividly capture the political emotion. What a challenge to the jury of ordinary men and women of Okanogan County! And what a performance by the jury in piercing the super-patriotism of Goldmark's accusers and, with consummate common sense, rendering justice to a man foully charged with disloyalty. One wonders if a single judge, no matter how learned or brilliant, could have matched the jury's distilled personality of the community in rehabilitating Goldmark's name.

As noted earlier, a particularly scurrilous set of charges concerned the American Civil Liberties Union. Herbert Philbrick, a "counterspy" for the FBI and witness against Goldmark, called the ACLU "not just red, but a dirty red." A local newspaper attacked the ACLU as "an instrument of the Communist apparatus." One of the defendants in the trial said that "ninety percent of the ACLU's work was defending Communists." Another defendant said that the ACLU was classified as a Communist front in 1948 by a California legislative committee, although he neglected to mention that the same committee subsequently cleared the ACLU.

The jury's verdict completely vindicated both Goldmark and the ACLU. When he reviewed the verdict and the evidence, the judge found explicitly that the ACLU "was not a Communist front organization." As president of the ACLU, I know that the "communist front" charge is and always has been totally false; yet it was repeated many times, before and even after it was refuted in a court of law at Okanogan.

The drama did not end with the jury's verdict. In March 1964, the United States Supreme Court altered the constitutional rules relating to libel. It held in *New York Times v. Sullivan* that false statements about public officials are protected free speech under the First Amendment unless uttered with "actual malice," that is, with knowledge that they are false or with reckless disregard of the facts. How this Supreme Court ruling for free speech eventually had its impact on the Okanogan verdict provides an ironic but satisfying ending to the story of the Goldmark case.

John Goldmark may have been more valuable to the country he loved because of the calumnies hurled against him and his successful struggle for vindication than if he had lived a conventionally successful life. But what a price this victory exacted, personally and politically. John and his family had to face the shocked reaction of their neighbors when the case broke, and then endure a trial of excruciating tension in which their entire lives were publicized, raked over, and submitted to the judgment of strangers. It is difficult for someone who has not lived through such an ordeal to appreciate what it must mean in human terms.

But the public implications of the Goldmark case are, in the final analysis, at its core. Ugly attacks on decent and patriotic people like John Goldmark were common in the dark days of McCarthyism, and the effect on public discourse and new ideas was disastrous. It could happen again. Indeed, there was more than a faint whiff of politics by slander in some recent accusations against supporters of the antinuclear movement. That is why it is so fortunate that William Dwyer has lucidly recounted the remarkable ordeal of John and Sally Goldmark. Mr. Dwyer began this book in 1966 and did not complete it until 1983. It was worth the effort.

Norman Dorsen

New York University Law School
August 1984

The Goldmark Case
An American Libel Trial

CHAPTER 1

IT WAS a brilliant summer day in 1962 at a far western cattle and wheat ranch. With my family I was visiting John and Sally Goldmark, who owned the place and lived on it. Set on high land in Okanogan County, a remote part of Washington State, the ranch offered a city visitor the chance to exhaust himself with a day's real work and then enjoy the evening in exceptional company. I was a thirty-three-year-old lawyer from Seattle, and I enjoyed the open country, the hot sun, and our friendship with the Goldmarks.

John, a tall and sun-tanned rancher of forty-five, sat down to talk to me in the ranch house. Through the window we saw horses grazing near the house, a tiny lake shrunk by summer drought, grain bins and barns, a rolling plateau beyond them, and in the far distance, across miles of lower country, the crestline of the Cascade Mountains. The wheat would soon be ripe, and it was a season of heavy work.

It was also approaching election time. Goldmark, a three-term state legislator of great distinction and a respected leader of the Democratic Party, was up for reelection. This was what he wanted to talk about.

He showed me an article from one of the county's weekly newspapers. It reported his announcement that he would run for reelection. Then, incredibly, the article went on to make a backhanded attack on him as a communist sympathizer. It said that Goldmark, powerful chairman of the House Ways and Means Committee, was running on a platform "which advocates repeal of the McCarran Act, a law requiring the registration of all Communist Party members"; that his son Charles was a sophomore at Reed College, "the only school in the Northwest where Gus Hall, secretary of the Communist Party, was invited to speak"; and that he was "a member of the American Civil Liberties Union, an organization closely affiliated with the Communist movement in the United States."

The story was startling in the usually decent atmosphere of Northwest politics. John asked me if it was libelous. I answered that it was; the article charged him with membership in a communist-affiliated organization, and insinuated that he was either a communist or a fellow traveler. Either charge would be libelous in the cold war climate of the United States. To call a man a communist, directly or by innuendo, was to brand him a traitor, a renegade, and a criminal.

Goldmark was undecided about what to do, and our talk passed to other subjects. We did not know that we were at the threshold of a long ordeal for him and his family. Vicious rumors, anonymous mailings, and tape recordings would be used in the coming campaign. A public meeting sponsored by the American Legion's "subversive activities" unit would be turned against him. Right-wing Republicans would lead the assault in a Democratic primary, and in the September election Goldmark would lose his legislative seat to a fellow Democrat by an overwhelming vote.

The campaign was to be a classic of political slander. Beginning in a distant region of ranchland and wilderness, it would ignite a libel case of national dimension. The Goldmarks would endure months of anxiety and public revelation. The national press would cover their trial, and people would come from all over the United States to testify in the small county courthouse. "The cast of characters," *Time* magazine would say, "read like the lineup for a movie."

But even more than a courtroom cause célèbre, the Goldmark trial would become an arena of combat between conflicting views of loyalty and government, communism and freedom. The country's recent history—the Depression, the New Deal, World War II, the Hiss case, McCarthyism, the cold war—would be the battleground. The far right's claim that a communist conspiracy pervades American life would meet its first full test in court. Sophisticated liberalism would be pitted against flag-waving patriotism, and the issue decided by a jury of rural westerners. In a trial whose content inflamed people's fear of subversion—and during which the President of the United States would be assassinated by a self-proclaimed Marxist—the American jury system would face a profound challenge.

All this lay ahead as John and I talked at the ranch house. Behind lay a family history which made these events possible.

The Goldmarks were unique in Okanogan County. John was a city-bred easterner with an Ivy League education, an exotic rarity among western farmers. His wife Sally was originally from Brooklyn. Their presence still seemed strange to many of the people among whom they had settled fifteen years earlier.

John had grown up near New York City. His father, an engineer, came of a distinguished family of Austrian Jewish descent. The great Justice Louis Brandeis of the United States Supreme Court was John's uncle by marriage. His mother, Ruth Ingersoll, a descendant of the eighteenth-century clergyman Jonathan Edwards, had died just after the birth of her only child.

As a boy Goldmark was sent away to Quaker schools. Brilliant and versatile, he finished first in his class at Haverford College, near Philadelphia, and went on to the Harvard Law School, where he served on the Law Review and was graduated with honors in 1941.

Goldmark was an athletic, intense young man, restless, curious, and blessed with a remarkable coolness of judgment. In him a scientist's logic meshed with a politician's interests. There was a cutting edge to his personality; demanding of himself, he could be impatient with others. Making money held no attraction for him despite his family's moderate means. He hoped for a career in public service.

World War II had started in Europe, and Goldmark wanted to enlist. Months before Pearl Harbor, he applied for a commission in the United States Navy. While awaiting word he went to Washington, D.C., to work for the agency later called the Office of Price Administration.

On his first night in the capital, at a friend's house, John met a young woman named Sally Ringe. Slender, brown-haired, and vivacious, she was a New Deal employee who worked in programs to aid the poor and unemployed. Sally was older than John but her joie de vivre at once banished the difference.

Sally lived with her disabled sister, whom she supported, and another young woman in a house at Accokeek, Maryland. Getting acquainted, she and John found they shared a love for unspoiled countryside. The Maryland place "was in the only real country around Washington," John recalled later. "It was real farming country." He became a frequent visitor.

The house was a lively meeting place for a large group of friends: New Deal employees, writers, artists, and teachers. By the spring of 1942 John and Sally were in love and planning to marry. Their courtship was filled with the company of friends and the excitement of wartime Washington. There was much enthusiastic talk of politics. In the Depression's wake a wide range of views, some of them radical, was current.

Then Goldmark learned a fact of Sally's life that she had been afraid to tell him. One evening among friends he made an especially harsh remark about communists. "And after that evening was over," John recalled, "she took me aside and she said, 'I think you should know that I am a member of the Communist Party.'" Perhaps, Sally suggested, he would not want to marry her after all.

To Goldmark the news was surprising but not shocking, as it would have been ten years later. Being a communist at the time meant being a radical, not a traitor. John himself was a Democrat who, even as a student, had rejected communism during its Depression vogue. But the Communist Party of the time was large and relatively popular, having attracted thousands of members during the 1930s and the wartime alliance with Russia. To John it seemed that Sally, like many other well-meaning people, had made a regrettable but understandable mistake. He thought he knew enough about her to understand why.

Sally Ringe, the fourth daughter of an immigrant German family in Brooklyn, had grown up in a strict Protestant household. She was christened Irma, a name she dropped in childhood. A girl of immense energy and spirit, she hoped to become a doctor, went to the University of Wisconsin, and got through the first year of medical school. Then she could not go on; the Depression wiped out her family's means.

Returning to New York, Sally was shocked by the mass

7

unemployment, the breadlines, the hardship and despair. Values she had taken for granted all her life seemed to have collapsed. "Unemployment in New York City at that time," she said later, "was a horrible thing, and I was both curious and appalled at my own lack of information."

For the first time, her interest turned to public affairs. Out of curiosity she enrolled in classes at the Workers' School, which was openly run as a communist-sponsored institution in New York. She found a job with an agency that arranged cultural exchange conferences in Latin America. The work took her to Mexico and Cuba, where she saw still worse poverty.

In 1935 Sally moved to Washington and worked first for the WPA, later for the National Youth Administration. She was well liked in her government jobs. "She has a sort of genius for making friends and for creating good atmosphere," one of her supervisors wrote. She was also the kind of young woman for whom injustice was a call to action. Sally could have been a great social worker of the Jane Addams type, for righting the world's wrongs was as essential to her as breathing.

The Depression dragged on—no one knew when it would end, if ever—and Germany and Italy sank deeper into fascism. Sally, like millions of others, looked for answers. The American Communist Party of the time was seeking a mass following. Having begun its "Popular Front" policy in the summer of 1935, the Party openly solicited members throughout the country and portrayed itself as a democratic organization. "Communism is twentieth-century Americanism" became its motto.

Sally Ringe accepted at face value the communists' pledges of full employment and equality at home and effective opposition to fascism abroad. She joined the Party in late 1935, and by the time she met John Goldmark she had paid dues and attended communist study group meetings for nearly six years.

John now answered Sally's confession by saying he wanted to marry her regardless of her politics. He decided not to ask her to leave the Party or to press for details. Obviously she had an emotional involvement; once married, he thought, she would end it of her own accord.

In the summer of 1942 the Navy called Goldmark to active duty as an apprentice seaman. After several months of training he was commissioned an ensign in December, returned to Washington, and married Sally.

John volunteered for bomb disposal, the hazardous specialty of disarming unexploded enemy missiles. The Navy sent him to school in Washington, then kept him on as an instructor through 1943.

As Goldmark predicted, Sally's interest in the Communist Party waned quickly after her marriage. "My husband was not sympathetic with it," she said later. "He was a person with whom I could talk about it. He was both reasonable and logical, and I agreed with him."

Sally quit the Party after a few months of marriage and never went back. "I had absolutely no feeling about having done anything wrong," she said, "except that I felt that I had made a mistake."

Neither of the Goldmarks could foresee how that mistake would injure them years later.

In January 1944 the Goldmarks' first son, Charles, was born. A few days later John shipped out for the South Pacific. Sally moved with the baby back to New York for the balance of the war.

John served in New Guinea and Australia, and then was loaned to the Army during the reconquest of the Philippines. In the Manila street fighting he disarmed Japanese bombs and shells while under heavy enemy fire. When the fighting moved north he stayed on to disarm live missiles embedded in the earth and ruins.

In the hot Pacific nights John lay awake thinking about his future. City life and working for the OPA had both failed to satisfy him, and he felt a growing urge to move west.

From Cavite he proposed to Sally that they take up a new life after the war as ranchers in the Pacific Northwest. "People from there seem less twisted up in tradition, class, and inhibitions," he wrote. The way west "will be a break with both our pasts, but . . . we'll have more happiness following it than clinging to past enjoyments."

Why would Goldmark make such a break? As his attackers would say later, a man of his ability and connections could have joined almost any of the East's leading law firms. Yet it was Goldmark's nature not only to spurn "past enjoyments" but to carve out for himself the fiercest challenges. He had tasted such challenges in the Navy and could not forgo them for a city career. He sought not recognition and comfort but hardship and adventure.

Sally was willing, and when John came home after the Japanese surrender they packed up a few belongings and their son Charles, not yet two years old, and drove across the country.

The Goldmarks knew no one in the rural West. Near the Columbia River town of White Salmon, Washington, John found work as a hired hand for an orchardist. Running farm machinery, stacking hay, spraying the apple trees, he found he liked the work. A second child, a boy named Peter, was born to the Goldmarks in 1946. John spent days off looking for a place of their own. After a long search he bought a spectacular one: a sprawling, dusty, isolated ranch on a high plateau in Okanogan County. He could have chosen a settled farming community. Instead he had picked one of the most rugged and thinly populated regions in the West.

CHAPTER 2

WASHINGTON STATE is divided by the Cascade Mountains, running north and south from Canada to Oregon. The range forms a high watershed—Mount Rainier, the highest peak, surpasses 14,000 feet—and profoundly determines climate. To the west, along the Pacific and the quiet reaches of Puget Sound, the weather is damp and mild and the land was once thick with evergreen forests. Sizable cities have grown up. The largest, Seattle, is the metropolitan center for two million people.

The rain clouds stop at the Cascades, and eastward stretches a dry country of big hills and brown flatlands, wheat and sagebrush, rough weather and isolation. Through it winds the great Columbia River, now slowed by a series of dams including the famous Grand Coulee. There are few cities; the people tend to distrust city power.

Okanogan (pronounced Okan-*ah*-gan) County lies east of the Cascade divide and borders Canada on the north. Bigger than the state of Connecticut, it has mountains, timber, and vast range land. John Jacob Astor's fur company built a fort and trading post there in 1811, at the confluence of the Okanogan and Columbia rivers. But settlement did not begin until decades later, and has remained slow. The early settlers let their livestock overgraze and kill off most of the native bunchgrass, admitting the sagebrush in its place. The Indians were placed on reservations.

Today there are still only about 30,000 people, 2,700 of

them Indians, in the county. The largest towns are Omak, with about 4,000 people, and Okanogan, the county seat, with 2,300. Two-thirds of the region remains forest land, although "forest" here can mean steep hillsides of scattered pine. Some areas are reached only by horseback. Irrigated fruit orchards line the few rivers and spread to the benchlands, but most of the usable ground is fit only for livestock grazing or wheat.

The Colville Indians, holders of a large domain in the highlands, have leased or sold parts of it to ranchers. John Goldmark found a ranch in Indian country about twenty-five miles from Okanogan by a rutted, climbing road.

The drive from town took an hour and ended on a high and almost treeless plateau. Lava rocks, some as big as small houses, jutted through the thin soil. There were groundhogs, hawks, pheasants, coyotes, and rattlesnakes. Anyone who farmed would be a virtual pioneer. But there was still bunchgrass there, and a chance to raise cattle as well as wheat.

The Goldmarks moved in, set to work, and grew to love the hard country. For the first few years they had time only for ranching. They had to learn quickly all that farm-bred people know from childhood about crops, animals, soils, and machinery. The work was endless: cultivating and harvesting; dragging rocks from the fields; stringing barbed-wire fences; putting up hay; tending the cattle through the wildly changing seasons.

In the winter a freezing wind heaped snow in deep banks, often cutting off the ranch from the outside world. Sally wrote to her sister in the East during a storm on New Year's Day, 1950: "Long icicles hang from [the cattle's] nostrils, and their eyes are frozen shut. . . . John makes the decision that while the sun is at its best at noon, with enticement of hay in the wagon, the cows should be brought in to get the protection of the barn and grove and shed, and to be fed by hay, if the blow continues. There are stories of cattle, as to how they run before the wind and never stop. . . . By sundown they are all in, and have all had some hay and now with their bent heads and snow-covered backs, can be seen through two small holes which are unfrozen in the kitchen windows, and finally somehow the day draws to a close, with wood in the house, all the water turned off, no heat in the bedrooms, which are zero, but in which we sleep, dogs in the hay barn curled up, turkeys roosting in the trees in the grove. But one less than yesterday, since one froze to death today. Chickens in their roost preparing to lay eggs which will shortly freeze and be brought in, cracked. Calves in the barn, milk cows milked, and now the last log the fire will take."

With spring came wildflowers of a surprising delicacy. Small lakes filled with melting snow and then went dry in the sun, exposing white alkaline beds. The summers were burning hot and pervaded with a fine dust.

The small frame ranch house was set in a grove of quaking aspen by a seasonal pothole of a lake. There were no near neighbors. From the house one saw for miles over the plateau to blue mountains in the distance; at night an infinity of stars filled the sky.

The Goldmarks improved the old ranch house, and gradually made friends in the county and across the mountains in Seattle. One winter they were snowed in for six weeks. John learned flying, bought a small airplane, and built a landing strip near the road. The family now had easier access to the outside.

Goldmark, remade from a New York lawyer into a western rancher with a weathered face, rough clothes, and a wide-brimmed hat, gained the strengths of a man who works outdoors in all seasons. Taking the bar examination in Seattle, so that he could practice law should the need ever arise, he overheard a fellow applicant say, "Do you suppose that damned cowboy will make it?" He did.

By 1950 Goldmark found time to begin attending political dinners and other events. He joined the Young Democrats, helped found a local chapter, and a year later was elected the organization's state president. Rapidly gaining recognition, he was made a delegate to the 1952 Democratic National Convention at Chicago, where he supported Adlai Stevenson. Back home, he served in the Grange, the Wheat Growers' Association, and the Rural Electrification Board.

In 1956 there was an opening in the state legislature. Okanogan County and adjoining Douglas County formed a huge single district having two representatives and one senator. Representative Wilbur G. Hallauer, a businessman and outstanding public servant from the up-county town of Oroville, was moving up to the Senate. John decided to run for the vacant House seat. "We didn't figure Mr. Goldmark had a chance," the Republican county chairman said later. But he was nominated in the open primary and won office in the general election.

In the biennial House sessions John mastered taxation and budgeting, the bane of state politics. He led the public power forces in several of Washington's recurrent electrical industry fights; worked for better schools and institutions for delinquent children; and brought highways and park expansion to his district.

By his third term in 1961 he had risen to be chairman of the Ways and Means Committee, the most powerful House position next to the speakership. An established leader of the state's Democrats, he was known and respected everywhere. Farmers, lawyers, and college professors were among his friends across the state.

Sally flourished amid the farm wife's endless chores of rearing children, cooking for harvest crews, tending a dusty garden, and helping with the livestock. Still a slender woman given to buoyant high spirits and bursts of social indignation, she became active in the PTA, the County Fair Board, and the Democratic Women's Club. She called herself "more interested in people than in politics," and worked to improve the local schools and libraries. Animated and emphatic, Sally spoke her mind and disdained the rural tradition of womanly reticence—which won her both friendships and resentments.

To both of them Sally's Communist Party experience seemed remote and unreal, an episode outlived long ago. "I wanted to be accepted for what I was," she said later, "not for what I had been."

When the couple came west, there was no reason to make public Sally's past. Ten years later, when John first ran for office, he said nothing about it. By then the subject seemed too awkward to raise, too distant in time, and irrelevant to his own fitness for office. The children knew nothing about it.

The Goldmarks thought they had discharged their responsibility by making full disclosure to the federal government. In 1949 two FBI agents came to the ranch to interview Sally as an ex-communist. She answered all of their questions.

John stayed active in the Naval Reserve. When a 1953 regulation required that officers be cleared for access to secret information, he was called to an interview in Seattle, where he discussed his wife's history with intelligence officers. The Navy granted the security clearance.

December 1956 brought a grim surprise. The federal House Un-American Activities Committee, on a swing through the west, subpoenaed Sally to appear in Seattle. Nothing would

15

be gained by a public recounting of what the government already knew. Sally asked for and was granted an "executive session"—a private interrogation attended only by one congressman and the committee counsel. The questioning was friendly enough and the congressman sent a pleasant letter afterward.

All the agencies seemed satisfied; the Goldmarks considered the subject closed.

In middle age John was a lean, handsome man with a broad smile and graying, crew-cut hair. At once farmer and intellectual, he seemed to have mastered everything from ancient history to flying to quarter-horse breeding. "Renaissance man," he was called by admiring friends.

His idealism, and his need to do things right, drove him to monumental work in government. Many thought him a likely choice for governor or Congress.

But Goldmark's passion for excellence also brought him enemies. Impatient of the foolish and venal, he lacked the statehouse politician's air of genial mediocrity. Some resented him. But those who knew him well knew he was a man of humor and kindness. His friend Emmett Watson, Seattle's most famous newspaper columnist, who learned flying from Goldmark, has written a characteristic story:

"When I first met John Goldmark, I didn't like him much. He seemed prickly and impatient; too questing, too demanding; no time for small talk. It was only later when I grew closer to him that I began to learn the essence of this remarkable man. He had dropped by my house on some errand, and he was talking to my daughter, then a college sophomore, and he began what sounded like a legal deposition. He asked direct, blunt, probing questions about her teachers, her courses, her goals and ambitions. When he left I said to her, 'Well, what did you think of him?'

She said, 'I think he's the kindest man I've ever met.' 'How so?' I asked. 'Because,' she said, 'he was taking a genuine interest in *me*.'"

Stimson Bullitt, the Seattle lawyer, author, and mountaineer, has said of Goldmark: "His aristocratic morality expected more of those who seemed to be better equipped than others, not recognizing that if we fall below an apparent capacity, we merely show that we have been mistakenly measured. His abruptness with grownups' muddled thought or slovenly work was coupled with his tenderness and pleasure with small children."

The Goldmark boys were growing up with a versatility which city life could not have given them. "By giving us life on the ranch," the older son Chuck recalled years later, "John and Sally gave us something very special—the chance to learn things that few people ever learn. How a cow reacts to a cutting horse. What the grass is like in the spring. What the wind sounds like in a blizzard. We were in a place where your life was what you made it. No one else was in control: no one else was able to decide whether you could make it through the next day."

The boys ran farm machinery, herded cattle from horseback, learned to fly the airplane. They went to a one-room country school on the Indian reservation, and later to high school in town.

By 1960 the Goldmarks had lived in Okanogan County for thirteen years. Through hard work they had become true ranchers with a healthy outdoor life, a useful voice in public affairs, and fine children. They enjoyed close friends and a good name with their fellow citizens.

That summer, John again served as a delegate to the Democratic National Convention. He flew his light airplane to Los Angeles, again voted for Adlai Stevenson, and came home to campaign for himself and John F. Kennedy.

17

Goldmark easily won reelection and Kennedy narrowly carried the district, although losing the state. But soon after the new President's inauguration, Goldmark, like many others, was troubled by a familiar political blight: a national resurgence of far-right, McCarthy-style anticommunism.

CHAPTER **3**

TWENTIETH-CENTURY life has battered some of our most cherished beliefs. For generations we held that nature decreed an economy of open competition, with each man free to rise or perish on his merits; that government, a necessary evil, should leave people alone to work out their destinies; that virtue meant adherence to a puritanical code; and that the new country, to safeguard its character against the old world's vices, must avoid foreign entanglements.

When forced into armed conflict—as we convinced ourselves we were in the nineteenth-century wars against Mexico and Spain, and in World War I against Germany—we gained victories, and with them another fervent conviction: that America, being right, was invincible. At the close of World War II, through the luck of geography, we stood as the only major power whose homeland had escaped serious damage. We held more than half the world's manufacturing capacity and a monopoly of the atomic bomb. Our morale was high. It was easy to think the United States could work its will everywhere.

Now these entrenched beliefs are being overwhelmed. Our economic power has slipped while other nations, among them our former enemies Germany and Japan, have surged in productivity. The doomsday weapons are shared not only with our antagonist the Soviet Union but with an alarmingly large number of others. We live in a technological age whose economic power is concentrated in huge business units. Most people live in cities; much work seems meaningless. Government proliferates. Old-fashioned morality has declined, sexual permissiveness flourishes, crime in the streets has worsened.

And in dealing with other countries it has become clear that we are not invincible. At times we may not even have been right. In the decades-long rivalry with communist powers, exactly whom are we fighting, we wonder, and over what, and—above all—why can't we win? We have lost many thousands of young lives in Korea and in Vietnam. Few see the results as glorious.

These changes and uncertainties have imposed enormous pressures, most painfully on those who hold the conventional beliefs most dear. To them, the world has gone wrong. If only we could get back to fundamental virtues, they feel, to isolation, to simple free enterprise, the frustrations and uncertainties would vanish.

But the world is unyielding in its refusal to go back.

From this clash of belief and reality springs a current of extremism. People who see the country as drifting fatally from eternal truths can come to suspect that some powerful enemy is causing the drift. Religious believers in laissez-faire, plagued by taxes and welfare spending, may conclude that the nation is purposely being steered to its doom. And if the United States is invincible, then her failure to win any contest abroad must arise from treachery at home. The results are fear and anger—first at modern society, then at those held accountable for it.

For decades anger in America has erupted periodically against socialists and communists. It did so after World War I in the Palmer raids and the deportation of alien radicals.

20

Following World War II the exposure of communist infiltration in the New Deal, and the onset of the cold war, brought a new wave of fear and the reckless anticommunism of the McCarthy period.

In the early 1950s the Eisenhower administration was above the suspicion of militant anticommunists. The President had come to office with their blessing, and in 1954 Senator McCarthy himself was disgraced because, among other miscalculations, he had attacked administration officials.

But the cold war with its endless tensions dragged on. Eisenhower failed to "win" it. He also failed to retire the national debt or repeal the New Deal. A Supreme Court led by his appointee, Chief Justice Earl Warren, outlawed racial segregation in the schools and imposed constitutional restraints on the police. The Republican president, to the chronically frustrated, proved little better than his predecessors.

Extremist sentiment began stirring again, and burgeoned following the election of President Kennedy and the transfer of power from a Republican administration headed by a general to one made up largely of liberal Democrats. To many the 1960 election seemed to restore the same eastern-urban-intellectual clique that had condoned communist infiltration in the 1930s. They saw socialism in the new government's calls for civil rights legislation, an unbalanced budget, the antipoverty program, and Medicare. They saw betrayal in the Peace Corps, the Alliance for Progress in Latin America, and above all in the acceptance of neutrality as a cold war posture of other countries. They felt threatened by black protest marches and sit-ins demanding integration. Some saw a conspiracy whose agents were everywhere.

Organizations began to flourish on what came to be called

most descriptively the "radical right." The John Birch Society, whose founder, Robert Welch, called former President Eisenhower "a dedicated and conscious agent of the communist conspiracy," gained an estimated 60,000 members. Its tactics paralleled communist methods: it organized semisecret cells, operated under the control of a single leader, exploited front organizations, and infiltrated established political groups.

Anticommunist rallies—a kind of show featuring ex-FBI informants and other "experts"—became popular. The Christian Anti-Communist Crusade, headed by Dr. Fred Schwarz, toured the country, drew large crowds, and raised hundreds of thousands of dollars. Billy James Hargis, an Oklahoma evangelist, attacked the Protestant clergy as communist-infiltrated, formed an organization called "We, the People!" and claimed membership in fifty states. The National Indignation Convention held a meeting at Dallas, attended by 1,800 delegates. One platform speaker joshed another: "All he wants to do is impeach Earl Warren—I'm for hanging him!"

There were others: the All-American Society, the Minutemen (whose members armed to fight a guerrilla war against the communists), the Conservative Society of America, Project Alert, the Network of Patriotic Letter Writers. All believed America's problems were caused by subversion, and that time had almost run out. "Five minutes to midnight"—the hour of communist takeover—was a favorite slogan.

The radical right had some impressive heroes. General Edwin Walker, a soldier with a fine combat record, became one when relieved of command in Germany in 1961 for indoctrinating his troops in the Birch Society view of the nation's leaders. Ordered to another post, Walker resigned from the army in protest and took up a hectic career as an anticommunist speechmaker. Another was Eddie Rickenbacker, the World War I air ace, who favored withdrawal from the United Nations and the erection of a monument to Senator McCarthy.

Fundamentalist religion ran deep in the movement. Believers saw the world in terms of sin and salvation, communism as the devil's way, and anticommunism (a notably vague term) as the force of moral right. "This war we're in," said Senator J. Strom Thurmond, "is basically a fight between the believers in a supreme being and the atheists."

The war would admit of no compromise. Indeed, the devil's strength had been fostered by compromise—by the country's departure from self-reliance, thrift, and uncompromising virtue. The slackening of sexual taboos and the growth of the national debt, no less than "softness" in dealing with Russia, were seen as pushing the country toward the abyss. Even the flouridation of water was perceived as a communist plot.

The intellectual fount of the radical right was Harding College, a school run by members of the Church of Christ at Searcy, Arkansas. Harding produced and distributed great quantities of literature and films through an agency called the National Education Program. Its president claimed the program's materials reached twenty-five million people a year. Harding's best-known product was a one-hour film entitled *Communism on the Map*. The film aimed to awaken Americans to their supposed peril, and its showing became a rallying point and recruiting device across the country. It portrayed a world at the communists' mercy. The following are excerpts from its sound track, which accompanied alarming pictures of alien tyrants and a red tide spreading over the globe:

Communism is strong within the United Kingdom.
. . . Scandinavia, with strong socialist parties in control, could probably offer very little real resistance if the com-

23

munists wished to move boldly for total political power.
. . . all the Middle Eastern nations are progressing into
situations permitting full communist takeover when the time
is strategically advisable. . . . South Americans who should
know say that Venezuela is already a satellite of the Soviet
Union. . . . and with the other communist strongholds
spreading throughout Latin America this largely completed
the southern leg of the encirclement of the United States.
. . . Communists are in the government of Canada, in its
communications networks, in every phase of its national
life. . . . Our electrical industry, our vital communications, our chemical and mineral industries, and in [sic] some
of our food industries—are controlled by the Communist
International, and the orders to the union leaders come to
them direct from Moscow. . . . In the United States today
we have an acknowledged fifth column operating for international communism. It is in a position through its power
in labor unions to paralyze the nation. It wields great power
in the legislative halls of our nation's capital, in the communications networks which influence the forming of opinion and attitudes, and in other vital areas of our national
life. . . . To halt this massive march of communism millions of Americans must be awakened to the facts presented
in this film strip. They must recognize the classic pattern
of communist takeover through bit-by-bit penetration and
subversion.

Communism on the Map frightened people out of their
wits. So did another film called *Operation Abolition*, a
composite of newsreel shots of demonstrations against the
House Committee on Un-American Activities in San Francisco in 1960. Released by the committee itself, the film
portrayed the demonstrations as part of a Communist Party
project to abolish the committee.

The extremist surge was not confined to, or even concentrated among, the economically dispossessed. The historian Henry Steele Commager called it "the first hate

movement chiefly among the middle and upper middle classes." Far-right organizations gained support from prominent businessmen, entertainers, and retired officers, among them General Albert Wedemeyer, Admiral Arthur W. Radford, General Charles A. Willoughby, Ronald Reagan, and John Wayne. Reagan, addressing the National Indignation Convention, denounced the income tax as "spawned by Karl Marx a hundred years ago."

Many of the country's largest corporations began conducting "schools" and "seminars" to educate their employees—and outside businessmen, teachers, and civic leaders as well—to the communist threat. "What is uniquely disturbing about the emergence of the radical right of the 1960s," wrote Daniel Bell of Columbia University, "is the support it has been able to find among traditional community leaders who have themselves become conditioned, through an indiscriminate anti-communism that equates any form of liberalism with communism, to judge as respectable a movement which, if successful, can only end the liberties they profess to cherish."

Communism on the Map was shown and promoted by hundreds of companies including Aluminum Corporation of America, Jones & Laughlin Steel, Goodyear Tire, Minnesota Mining, Revere Copper & Brass, Convair, Texas Power & Light, Schick Safety Razor, Ohio Bell Telephone, and North American Aviation. Leading national business firms paid for Christian Anti-Communist Crusade rallies on television, Project Alert's "School of Anti-Communism," and other far-right activities.

The radical right had little faith in democracy or time for its processes. It saw communism as an absolute evil which must be destroyed by whatever means came to hand. Thus its believers crossed the line of extremism: the conviction that one's enemies are so dangerous, and so hateful, that individual liberties and the time-consuming protections of law and custom must be thrust aside to crush them.

Since the movement's chief impulse was to abandon rational politics, its concrete proposals were few and negative: impeach Chief Justice Warren, withdraw from the United Nations, break diplomatic relations with the communist governments, end foreign aid, abolish the income tax, and prosecute the communists. The latter were defined with wild abandon. Radical-right literature was filled with hatred and talk of vigilante lynchings.

In the Far West, where fundamentalist religion mingled with memories of rugged individualism on the old frontier, the radical right quickly gained strength. The Boeing Company, Washington State's largest employer and holder of a billion dollars in defense contracts, showed *Communism on the Map* to its employees and to numerous outside groups, and sent company executives to the Harding College "Freedom Forums." Dr. Schwarz's Crusade staged rallies in Seattle with the help of prominent local citizens.

The commandant of the Sand Point Naval Air Station in Seattle became a celebrated anticommunist speaker. On the lecture platform he would erect a mast called "Free Enterprise," hoist signs on it reading "Loyalty," "Patriotism," and "Self-Reliance," and then knock them all down with a stick labeled "Communism."

The commandant, like Boeing, was a leading booster of *Communism on the Map*, which was shown to church groups, service club members, and even some public school children. Ninety-two members of the University of Washington faculty signed a letter branding the film "misleading and harmful propaganda," and an "appeal to the emotions of fear, suspicion, and hatred."

Operation Abolition, widely shown at the same time, enlarged the controversy. A group of Seattle clergymen denounced it and the local chapter of the American Civil Liberties Union found it "filled with inaccuracies and distortions." But Congressman Thomas Pelly of Seattle, angered by criticism of the film, said he was "now, more than ever, determined to support the Committee on Un-American Activities."

By late 1961, the far right's growth was alarming. President Kennedy became concerned, and said in a speech at Los Angeles: "[T]he discordant voices of extremism are once again heard in the land. Men who are unwilling to face up to the danger from without are convinced that the real danger is from within. . . . They find treason in our churches, in our highest court, in our treatment of water. They equate the Democratic Party with the welfare state, the welfare state with socialism, socialism with communism."

One of the most successful efforts to equate a leader of the Democratic Party with communism was about to take place a thousand miles to the north.

CHAPTER 4

THE RADICAL right found fertile ground in eastern Washington. In February 1961 a group of citizens formed the Okanogan County Anti-Communist League. "The United States will be Communist by 1973," their press release warned, "unless most Americans wake up to the full extent of Communist infiltration in the U.S. today."

One of the League's founders was Loris Gillespie, a prominent businessman, regional "anti-subversive chairman" of the American Legion, former Republican county chairman, and long-time political opponent of Goldmark and Senator Wilbur Hallauer. Another was Don Caron, a U.S. Forest Service ranger stationed at Okanogan. Caron threw himself into the anticommunist cause. For months he showed *Communism on the Map* to groups around the county; the film alarmed many well-meaning citizens.

In the spring of 1961 Caron began writing a column called "A Discussion of Communism" for the weekly *Okanogan Independent,* published at the county seat. The following are excerpts from his columns: "The communist blueprint for the takeover of America calls for the use of pornography to bring about a wave of degeneracy that will degrade us beyond hope. . . . the Communists are returning to Hollywood. . . . UNESCO has reached deeply into our educational system and has even begun to pervert the English language in its effort to destroy the belief in an independent America. . . . Plans for America call for the initial liquidation of 30 million persons. . . . 'liberals' and 'socialists' under the guidance of communists have been weakening the patriotism of Americans. . . . If we are to survive, it will be because unselfish, courageous, intelligent, dedicated men band together and take direct action against the Communist conspiracy. . . ."

The columns attacked teachers, mental health experts, clergymen, and agencies of the federal government.

Emotional letters for and against Caron's writings appeared. He became what his Forest Service superiors called a "center of controversy"; and on this ground they asked him, in the fall, to give up his column. Caron refused and resigned from the Service.

At once he became a national hero of the far right. Senator Thurmond denounced his "muzzling" by the government. Letters to the editor described him in such terms as "one of the heroes in the front line trenches of atheism vs. Christianity." A Don Caron Committee was formed to raise money for his support. After three weeks of agitation, Secretary of Agriculture Orville Freeman gave the government's view of the affair in a press statement: "Mr. Caron voluntarily resigned from the Forest Service. He was not asked to resign nor was he dismissed. . . . The Forest Service would have made the same request of any employee who had similarly become the focal point of local conflict over any issue not related to his work."

After leaving the government Caron announced that he was taking a full-time job as state coordinator for the John Birch Society. The *Independent* kept on publishing his columns.

Ashley Holden, publisher of the weekly *Tonasket Tribune* in northern Okanogan County, printed the literature of most local far-right causes. For many years political editor of the *Spokane Spokesman-Review,* Holden was known throughout the Northwest as an outspoken ultraconservative. A few years earlier he had retired from the Spokane paper, and now, in his sixties, he ran the small-town *Tribune* under the masthead slogan, "This is a Republic, Not a Democracy—Let's Keep It That Way!" The radical right surge of 1961 fit Holden's long-standing political convictions.

Tonasket was also the home of a Jesuit priest who worked tirelessly to mobilize anticommunist sentiment. Father Emmet Buckley, chaplain of the local hospital, formed "study groups" which met in private homes, listened to tape recordings, and discussed the communist threat. Among the more popular tapes were "Dialectical Materialism," by Fred Schwarz, and "Creeping Socialism," by Ronald Reagan.

The study groups caught on. Businessmen, ranchers, and public officials attended them throughout the district. Many absorbed the full radical-right view of America at the brink of surrender; alarmed, they wanted drastic action taken against the communist conspiracy.

Not everyone gave in to the spreading wave of fear. The Reverend Richard Litherland, pastor of the Okanogan Presbyterian Church, preached two sermons on "How Not to Fight Communism." Acknowledging that his words might cost him friends, he said: "Sincere people are recommending sources of information which I believe are really sources of hatred. . . . I believe that falsehood is not fought with falsehood."

But the sermons provoked attacks on Litherland, and he was soon transferred out of the county.

The new movement found an issue in a proposed affiliation of the Okanogan town library with the North Central Regional Library, to which several nearby communities belonged. The regional system pooled the resources of small local libraries to increase the variety of books available to each. Sally Goldmark had worked on library improvement for years and supported the proposal. The far right mounted a campaign against it, claiming it followed a communist plan of transferring local control to a central bureaucracy. In July 1961 the measure was voted down in a special election. Stanley Pennington, editor of the Okanogan *Independent,* hailed the outcome: "It was a massive victory for residents who were keen enough to detect connotations contrary to everything America has ever stood for. . . . library control is a communist doctrine, rather than one of anti-communism, and was obviously resented by the people of Okanogan."

There were other causes. A public meeting to stamp out pornography was held at the county courthouse; letters to the editor poured in for General Walker; and the public was urged to boycott "communist-inspired" movies such as *Inherit the Wind* and *Exodus.*

But these projects were vague and lacked satisfying results. A better outlet was provided by the campaign to unseat Representative Goldmark.

For years, mostly around election time, there had been vague rumors that Goldmark was a communist. They stemmed from people's difficulty in understanding why he would come to Okanogan. Local boosters who proclaimed the county the world's best place to live grew suspicious when someone actually moved into it. In each campaign Goldmark simply ignored such talk, trusted in the voters' good sense, and won.

A new round of rumors began after John came home from the 1961 legislative session: the Communist Party had picked up him and his wife as "apple knockers" in southern Wash-

31

ington and bought them the ranch; they were not legally married; John would not salute the flag.

One day in October, George Wilson, the Democratic county chairman, telephoned Goldmark and asked him to come to town. The two men met and talked. A pleasant and able man who made his living as a land appraiser, Wilson aimed to keep peace among the local Democrats. He said he had been told Goldmark was a secret communist— not just that, but the Party's leader in four Northwest states. As Wilson later recalled the conversation:

"I told him of what I had heard and I told him that I wanted his side of it and I asked him outright if he was a communist. And he of course told me it was ridiculous. . . .

"I asked him then, 'Well, John, I hear a lot of things, rumors about Sally, now just what is there to this?'

"And in answer he said, 'George, we have disagreed many times on policies but you have always been honest with me and I can be no less with you.' He said, 'Sally at one time did belong to the Communist Party but she has been cleared; she left the Communist Party, has been cleared by the FBI and cooperated with the FBI. We came out here to try to make a new start and hoping that we could.'"

This was the first time Goldmark had told anyone in the county about his wife's past. It was also the first time he had been asked about it; something remains of the frontier tradition of new beginnings with no questions asked.

Wilson seemed satisfied. For several months John heard nothing further.

In 1962 the radical right kept growing. The movement was nonpartisan; Republicans, Democrats, and independents became involved. Hoping to calm his neighbors, John wrote a letter which the *Wenatchee World,* a daily newspaper published in the nearest city and circulated through the district, printed on Lincoln's birthday:

"Like Lincoln, at storm center, our heads must be cool, our minds clear, and our spirit free from hate and prejudice. For only our minds and not our passions can find the road to the survival of free men.

"That is why the divisive voices in our midst are dangerous. We cannot choose our path wisely if we are torn apart by suspicion and fear. We cannot intelligently face real dangers if our minds are obsessed with imaginary dangers at home. . . ."

But the counsel of reason was not to prevail. Others less friendly than George Wilson knew of Sally Goldmark's past mistake. One who knew was Albert F. Canwell, of Spokane, a familiar figure in Washington politics.

Canwell had been elected state representative in the Republican sweep of 1946, and had become chairman of the legislature's Joint Fact-Finding Committee on Un-American Activities, known as the Canwell Committee. The committee held public hearings in 1948 on "communist infiltration" at the University of Washington. It imported professional witnesses, relied on hearsay and opinion testimony, allowed no cross-examination, refused to let counsel for the accused state objections, and had the police eject those who spoke out of turn. In the aftermath three teachers were dismissed, two for being admitted communists and one for dissembling with the university president. There was no proof of biased or faulty teaching; one of the men discharged, a philosophy professor who had been an overt Marxist for years, was praised by his superior as the department's most stimulating teacher. Besides these three, the reputations of many others were damaged by the committee's "exposure" of people who had done nothing worse than associate with communists in the 1930s.

Professor Vern Countryman of the Harvard Law School later reviewed the committee's work in his book *Un-American Activities in the State of Washington*. "The activities of the Canwell Committee and its allies," he concluded, "are clearly more subversive of established legal processes than any activities disclosed by the Committee's investigation."

The committee, however, claimed credit for revealing that "the State of Washington is acrawl with trained and iron-disciplined Communists."

In 1948 Canwell, widely known as chairman, ran for the Washington State Senate. "Those who attack the committee," he said, "are either ignorant or subversive." He was surprisingly defeated by an opponent who made the committee no issue. In later years he ran for office four more times, always as a champion of anticommunism. He won the Republican nomination for Congress and narrowly missed it for the U.S. Senate, but never regained office after his one term in the legislature. He lived in Spokane, running an "intelligence service" and occasionally making the news with attacks on the loyalty of Senator Warren G. Magnuson or of some visiting speaker. In 1958 he published a four-page sheet called *The Vigilante*, promising to make it "a rope of truth and exposure" with which to "hang the subversives"; but it lasted through only two issues.

The radical-right surge of the early 1960s gave Albert Canwell a new lease on life. His garishly printed *Vigilante* reappeared, listing Ashley Holden as co-publisher.

In their January 1962 issue Canwell and Holden published an article headed "Irma Ringe and the Washington State Legislature." It said that an unnamed legislator "has a wife who has a startling past," and that "in the days when . . . notorious Communists were operating high, wide and handsome in the nation's capitol . . . this woman, known in the Communist Party as Irma Mae Ringe, was a member of a Victor Perlo study group." The article questioned whether, since then, her thinking "underwent any drastic change," and referred to "her husband favoring the admission of Red China, a position which . . . parallels another important part of the Party line." Goldmark's name was not mentioned.

Copies of this leaflet appeared in Okanogan County. John saw that his enemies knew his wife had been a communist years before. He could not undo that, and decided to ignore the publication. He thought it typified the kind of smear literature most people would disdain. If the issue was raised by a campaign opponent, he would answer.

In March the famed ex-"counterspy" for the FBI, Herbert Philbrick, whose experiences had been dramatized in a motion picture and on television, gave an American Legion-sponsored speech at Omak. Warning of communist infiltration, he attacked the American Civil Liberties Union as "not just red, but a dirty red."

Goldmark was not mentioned, but he had belonged to the ACLU for years, and was a member of its Washington Committee.

Founded in 1920, the American Civil Liberties Union had worked through four decades to preserve the freedoms guaranteed by the Bill of Rights. Its name was linked with famous causes from the Scopes "monkey" trial to the then-current defense of civil rights workers in the South. It stood for freedom of speech and association for all—including despised radical minorities. In the twenties, and again in the cold war, the ACLU struggled to preserve the rights of radicals against attacks in the courts and legislative committees. As a result it was labeled a "communist front" by critics who failed to distinguish between communists on the one hand and those who supported their constitutional rights on the other.

By the early sixties the ACLU was respected in cities across the country but little known in rural areas such as eastern Washington. There, the few who had heard of it knew chiefly of the attacks on its patriotism.

Another *Vigilante* soon appeared with a second story on the Goldmarks, still not identified by name. "Irma Ringe," it said, "is a real flesh and blood person and is married to a leading member of the Washington state legislature." But most of the issue was devoted to an attack on Senator Magnuson; a cartoon showed him fleeing from a specter labled "Communist Front History."

Through the spring John worked on the ranch. There was little political activity. He did not yet know whether anyone would oppose him in the Democratic primary election in September. Washington State has open primaries—anyone can run for a nomination, and anyone can vote for candidates of either party. Crossover and split-ticket voting are common. For state representative the top two vote-getters of each party win nomination and go on the November ballot; of these four, the top two in the final election win the office. Three times, Goldmark and Horace Bozarth, a prosperous rancher from a pioneer family, had won both the Democratic nominations and their district's two House seats.

The campaign began in July. Joe Haussler, a popular businessman and Okanogan County commissioner, promptly announced he would seek the Democratic nomination for state representative.

When Goldmark announced his own candidacy for re-election, Ashley Holden's *Tonasket Tribune* responded with a front-page story:

> . . . Goldmark is also running on a platform adopted by the Democrats which advocates repeal of the McCarran Act, a law requiring the registration of all Communist party members. He and his wife, Sally, the former Irma Ringe, have two sons, Charles, a sophomore at Reed College, the

only school in the Northwest where Gus Hall, secretary of the Communist Party, was invited to speak, and Peter, a senior at Okanogan high school.

Goldmark is a member of the American Civil Liberties union, an organization closely affiliated with the Communist movement in the United States, and which was classified as a Communist front in 1948 by the Committee on Un-American Activities of the California legislature.

This was the article John showed to me when I visited the ranch. It was the first attack on him by name. The reference to "Irma Ringe" harked back to *The Vigilante;* the rest was a nasty innuendo of communist sympathy.

The state ACLU director sent a letter of protest from Seattle; Holden refused to print it.

In the following weeks Haussler openly ran against Goldmark while Bozarth, the other incumbent, remained aloof. Haussler attacked Goldmark's "high tax record" while his more ardent supporters circulated leaflets linking high taxes with communism.

John heard that a tape recording attacking him was being played in private homes. For a time he was unable to lay hands on it. Living out of town on a ranch, he was less in touch with the voters than were his adversaries.

A dignified-looking publication called *American Intelligence Service* appeared in the district. Its title and typography gave it an official air; it bore a Spokane address and the legend, "A. F. Canwell, Director." The first two issues attacked the ACLU as "an instrument of the Communist apparatus," citing the reports of several state un-American activities committees.

Goldmark pondered how to meet the developing smear campaign. So far, except for the *Tribune* story, it had been subsurface, indirect, and elusive: rumors, leaflets, and tape recordings were vaporous enemies. Haussler was waging a vigorous campaign and saying nothing about disloyalty. The problem was whether to bring the underground charges to the surface. John knew the attack on him would be but one of a hundred competing claims to the public's attention. In the heat of a campaign, trying to answer smears may multiply their circulation and even lend them credibility; the political rule of thumb is to ignore them.

John decided to make no speech on his own loyalty, but to try to reassure his supporters. In the district's towns he and Sally met with his backers in small gatherings and told them of her one-time Communist Party membership, of her cooperation with the FBI, of his lifetime adherence to the Democratic Party, and of why he had thought his wife's past error had no bearing on his fitness for office.

"Their reaction," Goldmark said later, "was not, 'Why didn't you tell us this before?' Their reaction was, 'We can understand how anybody could have been included in this at that time in the history of our country. And we don't like the kind of smear attacks that are going on.'"

His idea was to meet the charges at their own level of private circulation. He concentrated on a strong conventional campaign: making speeches, going to picnics, running ads that stressed his achievements in government. "A Working Legislator," his brochure read. "The Goldmark Record: Schools, Public Power, Highways, State Parks." He placed faith in his constituents' ability to judge him on his record.

But Goldmark underestimated his adversaries. He managed to hear a copy of the tape in circulation; it was an interview of Albert Canwell by an unidentified questioner. Canwell spoke of the ACLU, the Goldmarks' past, and the world communist threat—all to imply, without forthrightly saying, that John was a communist agent.

In August a two-page printed version of the interview came out in the *American Intelligence Service*. Answering the unnamed interviewer, Canwell said he was operating a "non-governmental intelligence service, specializing in security information." He identified the ACLU as "one of the most effective Communist fronts in America" with "some of the ablest left-wing lawyers in the country on its board," and noted that John Goldmark's name was on its letterhead:

> . . . He is a brilliant young lawyer, a graduate of Harvard Law School, a nephew of Justice Brandeis of the Supreme Court. A man with his legal training and background and family connections could probably obtain a job in almost any law office in America, yet he is in the State of Washington doing anything but practicing law, and coupled with the fact that he has usually taken an extreme left position in his legislative activites, I have been interested in the man.

John was married to Sally Goldmark, Canwell went on. "At least that's the name she goes by now. In my acquaintance with her background she was known as Irma Ringe. . . ." He said he had "investigated" Alger Hiss and many others who betrayed their governments in Washington, D.C., espionage cells:

> . . . In the early fifties the research director of the House Un-American Activities Committee asked me to look into the case of Irma Ringe who had been a member of the second highest Communist cell in Washington. . . . I found that she was living in the State of Washington and she was married to John Goldmark; and that John Goldmark was a member of the Washington State legislature. . . . I might add too, that she says she left the Communist Party, and I might accept that in the light that it is given if her activity were such as to indicate a clean break with the party. . . .

39

Sally, he said, had appeared in a private session before the federal committee. "It was a very fair thing to Irma Ringe. And still, in spite of that, she has been very much opposed to the showing of the film 'Operation Abolition,' which is a report of the House Un-American Activities Committee. Such a thing just seems inconsistent to me." Canwell said it was "in 1948 or '49" that Sally testified she left the Party, and "1943" that John got out of the Navy. He was five years late with the first date, two years early with the other. "After that they came out to Washington and he worked for an apple rancher down in White Salmon, which is the first place that I picked up their trail in Washington state. They then came to the Okanogan and suddenly became cattle ranchers."

In closing Canwell warned of "the most critical situation in our history":

> We have one enemy the global Communist Party with its worldwide apparatus which is working everywhere and we are being told by people who know better there is no internal threat in America. That is a dishonest assertion. It is a dangerous one. The Communist threat is world wide. It's both without and within. It's like an octopus—the heart or the center may be in Moscow, but the tentacles are everywhere.

We must take no comfort from there being but a few thousand known Party members in the United States, said Canwell. The "cadre membership" was convenient to the task at hand: "They're hard core, disciplined Communists who are going to go all the way. The weaklings have been weeded out. These people are professionals; they're dangerous; they're out to kill us. . . ."

This masterpiece of innuendo called Goldmark a communist agent without openly saying so.

40

In mid-August the newspapers reported that three local American Legion posts would sponsor a public meeting at Okanogan on the American Civil Liberties Union. The master of ceremonies would be Loris Gillespie and the main speaker Albert Canwell. Handbills were passed out reading, "HEAR THE TRUTH ABOUT THE AMERICAN CIVIL LIBER-TIES UNION—by Al Canwell, One of the Best Informed Men in the State."

Goldmark and Senator Wilbur Hallauer, both ACLU members, decided to attend and ask permission to speak.

A crowd of several hundred gathered at the Legion hall on the warm night of August 23. Most of them were far-right believers.

The meeting opened with a prayer and the pledge of allegiance. Loris Gillespie, a vigorous and emphatic man of about sixty, came to the microphone and introduced himself as the Legion's antisubversive chairman. "I am very proud of the position and am very happy to do what I can to stop the subversive work that is going on throughout our nation. . . . I am very positive in this statement: This is a nonpolitical meeting."

Yet, as the audience filed in, Legionnaires had passed out a new *Vigilante* containing an "Open Letter to Irma Ringe Goldmark," in which Canwell wrote: "I believe it is proper on my part, having knowledge concerning the tactics of the Communist apparatus, to ask if the Communist party, knowning your secret, attempted any pressures to accomplish a left-of-center result in Washington State legislation in recent years. . . ."

Canwell was introduced and came forward to a round of applause. He talked in a resonant voice of the anti-red struggles of three decades, of his friends among the great communist-hunters, and of his hosts' unflagging patriotism.

The House Un-American Activities Committee, he said, was "largely the brainchild and product of the American Legion, a great host of American patriots who have fought this country's wars, who have fought the communists at home, who have fought for good government at all times and in all places, and an organization that has been under constant fire, ridicule and attack by the Communist Party and their stooges and dupes and those who aid and abet them."

The audience was audibly with Canwell as he described legislative investigating committees as our one true weapon against the conspiracy. "The communists know that. They know it is their one greatest threat and so they make that their one greatest target."

The communists were gaining. "They have captured almost half the world by stealth and deception and falsehood and trickery and they have had a lot of soft-headed people doing the job for them. So they have organized fronts and groups and get a bunch of students all worked up about peace, invasion of academic rights and freedoms and so on."

A communist front, said Canwell, "is as deadly as an atom bomb because it does a job that armaments and bullets cannot do. It invades the area of your mind. It conducts a propaganda war; it captures the student mind; it invades the area of religion and teaching."

The ACLU was a front. The Communist Party had "a great deal to do in setting up the original organization." Known communists were in it from the outset. The long-time director, Roger Baldwin, "had somewhere around forty citations and communist fronts, all the worst kind of them."

Canwell brushed aside praise for the ACLU by past Presidents and other dignitaries. "Everywhere I go I get these; they read a letter from General Eisenhower and they read one from Harry Truman and they have a statement from McCloy, I think, and two or three others." Such comments were uninformed. "Now I'm an admirer of General Eisenhower from a little different standpoint. I like him as a person. I know him; he is pleasant and he is just a nice guy. But I don't think he is a competent authority in the area of communism. . . ."

Canwell said he "would like to ask the sixty-four dollar question to the membership of the ACLU, right down the line and see how many of them would answer the question forthrightly and openly under oath—'Are you now or have you ever been a member of the Communist Party?'"

Ninety percent of the ACLU's work, said Canwell, was devoted to defending communists. "Now if anybody can tell me why the well-financed communist apparatus needs an ACLU to carry the ball for them, well I'll put in with them. There's nobody in America better able to defend themselves in court than the Communist Party. They have all the money in the world. . . ."

Cases handled by the ACLU for others than communists were "window dressing." "What good would a communist front be if they didn't do something to confuse people—if they didn't try to make them think that somehow they were doing an American job?"

The Legionnaires had passed out Washington State ACLU letterheads to the audience. Goldmark's name was on them, but Canwell did not mention him. Instead he attacked others in the state group: Professor Melvin Rader of the University of Washington, who helped shield "this monster" Harry Bridges from deportation; Professor Giovanni Costigan, "this joker" who attacks the House Un-American Activities Committee; Benjamin Kizer, a Spokane lawyer once connected with the Institute of Pacific Relations which had sold out China to the communists.

"You know where they are in the program," Canwell said. "They have captured China, for all intents and purposes. They are ninety miles from our shores. They have heavy concentrations in Mexico and Canada. I'd say they are five minutes to midnight in their program."

The ACLU was no ordinary front. "They are operating in the State of Washington and to my notion it's the major communist front operating in the State of Washington at the present time."

Canwell sat down to loud applause. He had talked for three-quarters of an hour. Gillespie had promised "five or ten minutes" for rebuttal, and now recognized Goldmark. John came to the platform and faced the hostile crowd.

"Mr. Chairman, Mr. Canwell, ladies and gentlemen," he began. "I appreciate the fairness of the opportunity to speak on the subject of the American Civil Liberties Union.

"Now we might add another President to this list of those who are disapproved of by the previous speaker because actually, although the ACLU was founded in 1920, the principle which it is set up to defend was laid down before this republic was founded; and it was laid down by the second President of the United States, John Adams, one of the drafters of the Declaration of Independence."

Goldmark told how Adams, then a lawyer in colonial Massachusetts, had come to the defense of English soldiers charged with murdering Americans in the Boston Massacre:

"He did it because he felt that these people were entitled to a fair trial, that they had been incited by the mob, and that it was more important for the patriot cause that justice be done. And this is the basic principle and the reason for the existence of the ACLU. . . . John Adams and those people knew you could not make a revolution in the name of freedom and justice unless justice was for everybody. This is what distinguishes the United States and Great Britain and a few other countries from most all the other countries of the world—why we have been able to preserve a democratic society."

The short talk was ineffective. There were scattered handclaps and hoots.

Senator Wilbur Hallauer walked to the platform. "Now the meeting that we are attending tonight," he said, "I'd like to put it in its true context to you. Today is the date of August 23, 1962. In eighteen days there is going to be an election, a primary election if you please. The chairman of this meeting, Mr. Gillespie—"

Gillespie interrupted. "I'm sorry, this is not a political meeting sir. If you don't mind. I will not give you the time of day to bring this into a political meeting." The crowd applauded.

Hallauer persisted. "I think the date is probably sufficient to fix what I'm trying to say in your minds, and that one of the people who is a member of this organization, ACLU, John Goldmark, is a candidate—"

"All right—just a minute," Gillespie interrupted again. "We have not mentioned candidates here, we cannot do any campaigning from this platform as long as I am the anti-subversive chairman. I have never mentioned any candidate, I am not going to, Mr. Canwell has not, and I assure you, you are not going to from now on."

Hallauer tried once more to speak. "I would like now to take up the subject of the chairman of this meeting and of his political connections . . ."

Shouts of "Throw him out!" came from the audience. A Legionnaire on stage pushed Hallauer and he came down from the platform, nearly falling.

"This is a regrettable occurrence," Gillespie said, "because we have done everything within our power to make this fair."

Canwell returned for questions from the audience.

"Mr. Chairman, I'm Ashley Holden," came a voice from the floor. "I believe there are some one hundred and forty-five members of the Washington State Legislature. Can you tell me why the the only two members in the legislature who are on the Washington Committee of the ACLU are from Okanogan County?"

"That's coincidence," Canwell answered, "and I always say I don't believe in coincidence. . . . I don't know how they select their people."

Gillespie ended the evening by promising "other meetings in which I will have some speakers here to talk about some phase of some communist front so that we will be aware of the insidious menace that is creeping, almost rushing all over the United States. It is up to you and I, as good American citizens, to do that. The only thing that I am going to say is that please go to the polls and vote, and bless you, please vote American."

So ended the nonpolitical meeting.

In the next few days a tape recording of the affair was broadcast twice by the local radio station.

The Legion hall meeting made statewide news. Newspapers carried photographs of Senator Hallauer being removed from the platform. The *Tonasket Tribune* ran a story headed "Commie Front Exposed by Al Canwell in Legion Talk." In the same issue Holden wrote in an editorial entitled "Catching Up With John":

> . . . he has voted invariably with the extreme leftists and has sponsored measures designed to socialize our economy and convert us into a Welfare State. In his campaign at home he has deceived the people with high-sounding phrases, all the while carefully concealing his true political philosophies. . . . But the voters . . . are at last finding out that John Goldmark is not their representative;

that he is a tool of a monstrous conspiracy to remake America into a totalitarian state which would throttle freedom and crush individual initiative. . . .

Don Caron's weekly column in the *Okanogan Independent* had now been appearing for a year and a half. Just before the election he reviewed a book called *And Not a Shot Is Fired,* which claimed that Czechoslovakia had been taken over by secret communist infiltration of its parliament. Caron warned of communists in American state legislatures: ". . . in all countries that have been taken over so far by this parliamentary penetration, it has been at the level of government equal to our state government that the work of subversion has been accomplished. One of the techniques employed by the revolutionary apparatus to implement this is to send the agents whom they want elected into rural areas. . . ."
He did not mention Goldmark.

To the end John's campaign appealed to reason and the public issues. He saw that he should have responded dramatically and early to the misused revelations about his wife, but decided a last-minute public statement would only make matters worse. That he failed to react swiftly perhaps showed a flaw: the champion of reason, he was unable to sense the full power of hatred.
In the final days he felt unsure of his chances. False and damaging things had been said, but he thought his main antagonists were unpopular and might have little influence. The far-right newspapers were not the most respected, and the *Wenatchee World* and weekly *Omak Chronicle* had remained neutral and defended democratic principles. The *World* had even called Holden's first attack on him "a violation of every standard of journalism." He had waged a

strong campaign, possessed seniority and a fine record, and believed he still held the firm support of many leading citizens.

A few days before the election nearly everyone in the district received the *American Intelligence Service* "interview with Canwell" in the mail in unmarked envelopes. The whisperings of a few had grown into a mass attack.

On election day about sixty-six percent of the district voters turned out, compared with thirty-nine percent for the state as a whole. Joe Haussler ran first among the candidates for the legislature, Bozarth second, Goldmark a poor fourth. He lost the primary to Haussler by a margin of three to one. A Seattle daily called it "the state's biggest election upset."

CHAPTER **5**

"THE TACTICS that were used are almost unspeakable and unthinkable," said Democratic County Chairman George Wilson. Goldmark's assailants had gone far beyond "exposing" Sally's past. They had misused that information to paint him falsely as a communist, and had distorted his ACLU membership to the same end.

John had lost not only his political career but much of his reputation. Some now thought him a communist; others, baffled by the summer's events, doubted his loyalty. A dismal air of uncertainty and malaise lay over the late campaign.

Elated over their victory, the far-right forces looked for new conquests. A *Vigilante* issue acclaimed the Legion hall meeting as "the bullet that got Goldmark." Fresh attacks were made on the ACLU, on Senator Magnuson, on "communism" throughout society.

Soon after the election the King Broadcasting Company, an NBC affiliate, made a half-hour television documentary on the campaign and broadcast it from Seattle and Spokane. The film, called "Suspect," struck a note favorable to John. "For whatever motive," its narrator said, "a man's integrity was cruelly dealt with. People were persuaded to let suspicion become an issue, the honorable practice of politics was stained."

But television could not settle the issue. Goldmark felt

there must be no place in politics for character assassination. "You just can't let them get away with that," he said. Although he needed no urging, Senator Hallauer wrote to him that a lawsuit was "necessary as vindication not only for you and your family, but for your friends and supporters."

Goldmark consulted me about bringing a libel suit. With us was R. E. Mansfield, a kindly, humorous Okanogan lawyer of about fifty. A highly able and successful attorney, Mansfield had lived in the county all his life. He knew that representing John would cost him clients and perhaps friends, but gladly paid this price for a cause he believed just. He splendid work and warm friendship were to prove invaluable.

Mansfield and I explained the grave dangers in suing. An unsuccessful libel case can be a disaster; whatever charges the defendant made against the plaintiff may seem confirmed by the jury's verdict, and the damaged reputation reduced to rubble.

We would face an obvious risk of defeat. No libel case in the country had been won by a plaintiff in any way connected with the Communist Party—even through such a remote connection as John had through his wife. Extreme anticommunist sentiment was still growing and might be stronger than ever when we got to trial. Jurors might resent John's having run for office without first disclosing Sally's past. These factors could bring a defense verdict.

There were subtler dangers. To call someone a communist, the Washington Supreme Court had said, "necessarily causes injury to the person spoken of in his social, official and business relations of life. Such words hold him up to scorn, contempt and ridicule, causing such person to be shunned by his neighbors, and in effect charge such a person with being a traitor to his country. . . ."

50

But no one had openly called Goldmark a communist. His detractors had expertly used the old smear technique of talking around the issue and mixing truth with falsehood to imply the victim's guilt without forthrightly charging it. A jury might avoid the harder issues by simply finding the publications too unclear to be libelous.

Finally, the defendants would seek shelter in the "fair comment privilege." Intended to prevent libel laws from dampening debate of public issues, the privilege protected critical expressions of opinion about a public official even if they injured and defamed him, so long as they were made in good faith. Honest criticism of a legislator, no matter how damning, would not support a libel judgment. If the defendants could pass off their publications as good faith expressions of "opinion," even wrong-headed opinion, they would win.

Win or lose, a suit would bring long months of misery to the Goldmark family. Defense lawyers would rake over the past lives of husband and wife for every sign of wrong-doing. Questioning would go on for days in a crowded courtroom. A plaintiff's verdict, if finally achieved, might be for one dollar. If we were lucky enough to win a large award, it might never be collected; of the possible defendants only Gillespie appeared to have substantial property. Mansfield and I would work for no fee except the doubtful one of sharing in any net recovery, but the other costs would be high: depositions, travel expenses, and the like would run to several thousand dollars. Contributions from friends and well-wishers would cover part of the costs, but probably not all of them.

None of this discouraged John. He saw a lawsuit as the only way of vindicating his name and clearing the political air. And he insisted that the trial be held in Okanogan, even though we might be able to move it to Seattle or another city. It would be the first libel case of its kind before a rural jury.

Sally, knowing the pain that lay ahead for her, said she would do her best to help.

We decided to ask damages for all the main libels: the Canwell tape recording, the *American Intelligence Service,* Holden's two attacks in the *Tonasket Tribune,* and the speech made at the Legion hall meeting. As defendants we named Canwell, Holden, Gillespie, and the Tribune Publishing Company. We added a count based on Don Caron's pre-election newspaper article on communist infiltration of legislatures, and joined him, his employer the Birch Society, and the *Okanogan Independent* as defendants. As yet we had little information on who had circulated the libels.

The most delicate problem was how to handle Sally's past Communist Party membership. It was vital to end any remaining speculation or doubt about it, and to take a strong affirmative stand. We must show we had nothing to hide.

To achieve this we alleged that Sally was a former communist, that she had left the Party years ago, and that Canwell's "interview" had injured her reputation as well as John's. While an award of damages to her was unlikely, our immediate statement of her past seized the initiative on a troublesome issue.

We claimed that all the libels were published in the course of a conspiracy among the defendants to defame Goldmark. A conspiracy, in law, exists where people knowingly act together to achieve an unlawful goal. In this case conspiracy might be hard to show—but in trying to prove it we could bring to the jury the whole outrageous story of the campaign.

We filed the complaint two weeks after the election in September 1962. At once the case was seen as a political crucible. The *Seattle Times* ran a series on the late campaign's impact on Northwest politics. "Since Goldmark's demise," it said, "liberal Democrats . . . are openly worried about their political future."

Our opponents promptly formed "defense committees" which raised funds all over the United States. Their mailings called the suit a "plot to gag the free press" and "to crush, once and for all, those who resist the encroachments of Communism." They asked contributions for patriots "involved in litigation by their actions on behalf of freedom."

Three sets of lawyers filed appearances for the defense. They were E. Glenn Harmon, partner in a large Spokane firm; Ned W. Kimball of the small town of Waterville; and Joseph Wicks of Okanogan. Harmon and his firm were established experts in defending libel suits brought against newspapers. Kimball was a well-known trial lawyer, and Wicks a retired Okanogan Superior Court judge of great local renown. The opposition would clearly be strong.

Faced with the job of turning an amorphous underground campaign into a clear picture, we sought to begin at once with pretrial discovery—the gathering of evidence by taking sworn deposition testimony, in the presence of the lawyers for both sides and those parties who wished to attend, and by examining documents. An early start would reduce the problems of drawing the truth from hostile and forgetful witnesses.

But we were thwarted by a quirk of the Washington court system. Okanogan County was part of a huge judicial district having only one Superior Court judge. Washington law allows any party to disqualify one judge automatically by simply filing a paper called an "affidavit of prejudice." The Birch Society, as a defendant, filed an affidavit against the local judge.

Weeks went by while we waited for the State Supreme

Court to find a substitute from outside the district. In the interval there was no judge with power to make rulings in the case.

The vacancy allowed the defense to retreat behind a smoke screen of evasion. Court rules require cooperation in discovery, but the defendants refused to honor subpoenas to appear for their depositions. Witnesses friendly to them vanished, or appeared with counsel and then refused to answer questions. All argued that they need not testify until a judge laid down "protective" ground rules for the depositions; but the ground rules were already clearly spelled out in the rules of court. We were losing priceless weeks.

At last Judge Theodore Turner of Seattle was appointed. A tall, spare man in his sixties, with sparse gray hair and rimless glasses, Judge Turner was noted for his thoroughness and scholarship. Fifteen years earlier he had been a Republican colleague of Albert Canwell's in the state House of Representatives, but we knew this would not affect his fairness or impartiality.

In February 1963 the judge came to Okanogan. The case had been stalled for three months. Thirty-seven motions filed by the defendants were awaiting decision. We asked the court to penalize them for flouting the discovery rules. After hearing argument Judge Turner said the record was "filled with evidence of dilatory tactics" by the defendants, denied or deferred their motions, and ordered them to pay us nearly $2,000 in counsel fees and costs.

The defendants' delaying tactics had gained them time, but now they stood convicted of violating the rules.

The court's ruling broke the well of evasion. We began the long and painstaking job of discovery.

Ashley Holden's Tonasket printing shop, we soon learned, had printed 15,000 copies of Canwell's *American Intelli-*

gence Service attack on Goldmark, enough to reach every voter in the district. Nearly all of these were mailed out just before election day. There was a sizable printing bill. After some small contributions, a balance of $333.94 had remained on Holden's books.

Who had paid it? Holden said he could not remember. From bank records we learned he had received a $500 cashier's check and used it to retire the printing bill. Who had sent the cashier's check? Holden's memory failed again. Through other records we traced it to Luke Williams, the wealthy Republican Party chairman of Spokane County. It appeared that a campaign libel of Goldmark had been financed not by fellow Democrats opposing him in their party's primary, but by a Republican official outside the district.

We took Williams's deposition. A forceful, socially prominent businessman, he protested he had sent the money to help a Republican candidate and never asked what Holden actually did with it. He was enraged at our lawsuit and read a prepared statement calling it "a politically sponsored witch-hunt." But Williams admitted he personally had helped write another attack on John—a "citizens' committee" letter linking Goldmark's "high tax record" with un-Americanism—printed 2,000 copies of it in his own plant, and had Republican precinct workers address them for use in the Democratic primary.

Joe Haussler, the man who defeated John, had publicly shunned "the personal attack" on his opponent. "I did not, of course, enter into it in any respect," he said, "and for that reason I do not know how much it was effective."

But in his canceled checks we found payments to Albert Canwell. At his deposition Haussler admitted that he met with Canwell in 1961, during the latter's "investigation" of Goldmark, and gave him $100. He claimed he wanted Can-

55

well, who ran the Freedom Library Bookstore in Spokane, to use the money to buy copies of J. Edgar Hoover's book *Masters of Deceit* for people unable to afford it. Yet Haussler's campaign manager, an Omak lawyer, had also paid $100 to Canwell, and confirmed that it was for the anti-Goldmark project. And in 1962, after he knew Canwell's attacks on John had begun, Haussler sent Canwell another $100—to buy, he now insisted, more copies of Hoover's book for the needy.

We learned that the libelous tapes and literature had been circulated almost entirely by participants in the radical-right "study groups." Possessed by a mortal fear of communism, these people had gone to night meetings, donated money, and addressed thousands of envelopes to help destroy a "subversive."

For months we put together the story of the campaign. In their turn, the defense lawyers questioned John and Sally for days on end about every facet of their lives. Searching for inconsistencies and weak points, they dredged up the past and pored relentlessly over half-forgotten details.

Sixty-one pretrial depositions running to 4,000 pages were taken in all, and hundreds of documents subpoenaed and examined.

Don Caron countersued the Goldmarks, claiming Mrs. Goldmark had demanded that the Forest Service fire him unless he stopped writing anticommunist articles. As a result, he said, his superiors gave him an "ultimatum" and forced him to resign. At his deposition Caron virtually admitted all this was groundless. Sally had telephoned the Forest Service about Caron's columns but had said nothing about his job, and no one had ever asked him to resign.

Our main goal was to preserve the conspiracy count against the defendants' motion for summary judgment—the pretrial dismissal of a claim for which no supporting evidence can be produced. If the conspiracy claim were stricken, the defendants would argue strenuously for separate trials. If they succeeded in that motion, the case would splinter into bits.

We had no direct proof of conspiracy, but claimed the circumstantial evidence of how the defendants had worked together to defame Goldmark would be enough to take the issue to the jury. This evidence was weakest on the Birch Society. Reports to its Massachusetts home office from four local chapters showed, under the heading "Additional Work Done," entries such as "Arranged for anti-Commie Ralley [sic] at American Legion Hall," and "All members instrumental in defeating Comsymp in primary election." But although many members had distributed the libels against Goldmark, all denied the campaign was a Birch Society project.

After considering several hundred pages of briefs, Judge Turner dismissed the Birch Society from the case and released Caron and the *Independent* from the conspiracy count. The conspiracy claim would go forward against the other four defendants; as to them, the court ruled, "a jury of reasonable minds might find either way on the claim of conspiracy."

All our other claims remained intact.

The judge also dismissed Caron's countersuit, saying that "nothing was done by either Mrs. Goldmark or the Forest Service to interfere with defendant Caron's employment."

We were satisfied with these rulings and eager to begin trial. The *Independent* had recently changed hands and we voluntarily released it from the case. This left as defendants those we believed to be chiefly responsible for the libels: Ashley Holden (and his Tribune Publishing Company), Albert Canwell, and Loris Gillespie. We also retained a smaller claim against Don Caron.

The defendants, who had called the suit a "political trick" which would never get to court, now struggled for a postponement from autumn to the following year. Judge Turner gave them two more weeks and set the trial for November 4, 1963.

We were still unsure what kind of defense awaited us. Perhaps the most effective one would be temperate and reasonable. If the defendants claimed they never meant to call Goldmark a communist but only to publicize facts of importance to the voters, and apologized for any excessive zeal they might have shown, we could be in serious trouble.

There were signs they would take this tack. Canwell, who pictured himself a scrupulous investigator, testified in his deposition that he had no evidence Goldmark was a communist and "would have no reason or desire" to say otherwise.

Then, a few days before trial, the *New York Times* ran a long article on the case. It quoted Holden as saying: "We expect to prove everything we said. Money is coming in from all over the country. I'm getting personal letters from conservatives from California, Texas, New Jersey and other states—from people who have never head of me—saying 'God bless you, keep up the fight,' and enclosing contributions."

Nationwide political turbulence had marked the year 1963. The Cuban missile crisis was a fresh memory and the racial integration battle was at its peak. In that climate, and in rural Okanogan, most of our friends and supporters reluctantly believed we could not win.

CHAPTER 6

THE OKANOGAN River wound through the county seat. Its valley was lined with fruit orchards, giving way to rock and sagebrush on the surrounding hills. The town was a marketplace for ranchers and farmers. Along the main street were feed and implement stores, gas stations, hardware and drug retailers, the offices of lawyers and dentists, and a tall street clock that did not work. The leading hotel and restaurant was the Cariboo, where the Kiwanis Club met weekly and businessmen gathered for drinks. By the railroad tracks, across the river, stood grain elevators and a stockyard where cattle were auctioned every week.

On the morning of November 4, 1963, we walked to court. Tension filled the town, and we knew that much sentiment was hostile to us. The old three-story courthouse, faced with gray concrete, stood on a rise off the main street. Elk antlers decorated the entryway. The halls were drafty and plain.

The third-floor courtroom, reached by a steep climb up the stairs, was of stark simplicity. There was no jury box, merely twelve chairs on a platform at the side. The swinging gate before the witness stand was made of plywood. There was ample room for spectators, but only a small, cramped space for lawyers and litigants between the gallery and the judge's elevated bench.

John, Sally, R. E. Mansfield, and I took our places at

the plaintiffs' table. Immediately in front of us sat the defendants—Holden, Canwell, Gillespie, and Caron—with their lawyers, Harmon, Kimball, and former Judge Wicks. The room was jammed full of prospective jurors, spectators, and newsmen. At the far side a press table was occupied by reporters representing Washington State newspapers, national wire services, and eastern dailies.

The bailiff called the room to order and Judge Turner took the bench. In quiet, precise tones he began the process of empaneling a jury.

The judge outlined the nature of the case and the jury's duty of fairness. "When a case that has had so much said about it, as this one, comes up for trial," he said, "we assume, as I say, most of you have had some notions about it one way or another at some time or other. The test is: Now can you as jurors lay aside any notions you may have had and try the case with fairness and justice to both sides?"

Although there were eighty-five on the panel, it was impossible to find jurors unacquainted with the parties and lawyers. Of the first twelve called to the jury box, six knew Judge Wicks and four knew Mansfield.

Judge Turner again asked: "All of you feel that you could be fair and impartial?" One man answered from the jury box: "I don't know if I could or not; I have rather strong feelings about it in one way. The facts of the case probably aren't as well known to me as they should be, but in reading the newspaper and listening to the reports of it, I deplored the use of a man's family against him. It smacked to me of tactics that were well below . . ." He was interrupted and excused.

The empanelment went on through the day. All who admitted holding strong opinions about the case were excused. Each side used its three peremptory challenges, excusing jurors who possessed the legal qualifications. By late afternoon the job was done; the jurors stood and were sworn.

The jury was a cross section of the county's population. Three men were sawmill workers; two were fruit orchardists; one was an unemployed construction worker and handyman; one was a beekeeper and part-time construction worker; and one was an Indian who worked for the government road agency on the reservation. Of the four women, two were wives of cattlemen, one an employee of the state public assistance office, and one a housewife and former cook at the Cariboo Inn. Two alternates, both mill workers, were sworn in to stand by in case of illness. By local custom the jurors wore everyday clothes to court, not suits and neckties. They looked like any group that might happen to gather at the scene of an accident on a country road.

The next morning I stood to give the plaintiffs' opening statement. We had worked for over a year to reach this point.

The lawyer's job at the outset is to paint a vivid picture of the evidence to come. He must be accurate, for the opening statement is a kind of contract with the jury; the promises of proof must be kept.

The defendants had circulated libels, I said, and these amounted to a charge "that John Goldmark as a state representative who had been elected three times by the voters of this district was in fact a tool and an agent of the Communist Party. We will prove to you that this charge was false."

I traced the Goldmarks' life histories. To many in the courtroom this was the first clear account they had heard after years of curiosity. I told of John's early life in the East and his wartime marriage to Sally; of her New York childhood and youthful radicalism, her years in the Communist Party, and her leaving it soon after their marriage; of John's service in the war; of their move across the country and their life as ranchers in Okanogan County; and of John's work in the legislature.

Then had come the attacks on him by the defendants. I took the jury through the smear campaign, reading aloud the critical parts of each libel—the newspaper articles and leaflets, and transcripts of the speeches and tapes—showing how each of them aimed at branding John a communist in the eyes of his constituents.

"We will show further," I said, "that their reputation was very severely damaged by what was done to them by these defendants, that many people believed as a result of what the defendants did that the Goldmarks were disloyal to their country, that to most other people, if they didn't absolutely believe it, that still a doubt and a suspicion and a shadow was raised in their minds which has been impossible to get rid of. And we will show the importance of this not only to the Goldmarks but to the entire community."

Glenn Harmon rose to give the defense's opening statement. A stout man in his late forties, with silver-rimmed glasses and well-groomed silver hair, Harmon spoke with firm determination. He began quietly, identifying his clients and outlining the issues.

Then, after a midday recess, Harmon switched from moderation to a violent attack. "The evidence presented by defendants will further show," he said, "that from 1951, when he entered politics on the State level, until 1962, John Goldmark consistently refused to tell the public anything about his wife's Communist Party associations with high level communists even when urged to do so by friends in the Democratic Party who found it out.

"The evidence will further show that John Goldmark knew at the time he decided to run for political office that his wife had associated for years with high-level communists

62

and had been interrogated at length by the FBI as a part of the investigation of the Alger Hiss case in which ex-communist Whittaker Chambers told a frightening story of communist intrigue and espionage in Washington, D.C."

Harmon's voice rose. Goldmark, he claimed, had no sooner gone into Washington politics that he was embroiled in a controversy "in which he took a position identical with the position of the Communist Party on the same issues at the same time." He had become a prominent leader of the "left wing" in the legislature. He had "never deviated from following the Communist Party line." His wife had not cooperated with the FBI or the House Committee on Un-American Activities. The evidence would prove, in fact, that she "never got out of the Communist Party."

Everything the defendants had said during the campaign, and more, said Harmon, was true. "When we have produced evidence of those facts, those incredible facts, we will ask you to return a verdict for the defendants, each and every one of them, a verdict holding that everything published by any of these defendants about John and Sally Goldmark is substantially true and that everything published about them by these defendants is nowhere near as defamatory or damning of John and Sally Goldmark as the simple truth.

"We believe you will be compelled to conclude from the evidence presented in this courtroom that John and Sally Goldmark are in fact under Communist Party discipline."

Harmon's words shocked the courtroom. It was one thing to accuse a man of being a communist agent in the midst of a turbulent political campaign where accusers do not face cross-examination. It was another to make that accusation in open court.

The defendants had audaciously raised the stakes of the trial. Their lawyers would not promise such proof unless they were confident they could supply it. Yet only a few months earlier Albert Canwell, the chief defense expert, had testified in a deposition that he had no evidence that John was a communist. What had changed their minds? We did not know, but we knew that if they succeeded even in raising a doubt about Goldmark's loyalty, they would win.

We had decided to call the main defendants as our first witnesses. To show the jury at once their true characters and political makeup would put flesh on the controversy. The defense's opening statement redoubled the importance of doing this while Harmon's promise of proof was still in the air.

We called Ashley Holden to the stand. Surprised, he nonetheless came forward with confidence to take the oath. He was a small, dapper man with a neat white moustache and a jaunty air.

Mansfield, interrogating for the plaintiffs, read to the jury the article Holden had run in the *Tonasket Tribune* when John announced his candidacy for reelection. Then he began to dissect the story's repeated references to communism.

Holden had written that Goldmark's son Charles was "a sophomore in Reed College, the only school in the Northwest where Gus Hall, secretary of the Communist Party, was invited to speak." This was false—Hall had appeared and spoken under the open forum policies of several colleges—and Holden now did exactly what an opposing lawyer hopes for: he dodged for several questions before conceding the point reluctantly.

Mansfield turned to Holden's reference to John's membership in "the American Civil Liberties Union, an organization closely affiliated with the Communist movement in the United States." Why had he said that in a news article reporting Goldmark's candidacy?

A. Well, that had been left out of the release that Mr. Goldmark mailed out and I thought it was important information.

Q. But why did you mention the American Civil Liberties Union?

A. I thought it was important information to the voters—taxpayers.

Holden had written that the ACLU "was classified as a Communist front in 1948 by the Committee on Un-American Activities of the California legislature." He had failed to mention that a few years later the California committee had cleared the ACLU. "I realized," he now admitted "—I was aware of the fact that a later committee of a later legislature had taken a different position on the matter but it didn't influence my thinking any."

As the examination went on Holden grew more combative. He seemed unable to answer forthrightly and would argue and hedge until pinned down.

Q. Mr. Holden, in your article here on July 12, 1962 you have made four separate and distinct references to communism in connection with the story about John Goldmark filing for candidacy for the legislature. Why did you do that?

A. First I want to see if it is correct. I think the story would have been quite incomplete and even incomprehensible without it. You wouldn't have known what it was all about.

Q. What was all about?

A. The references to McCarran Act and Gus Hall. A lot of readers don't know who Gus Hall is.

Q. This is a story about John Goldmark, Mr. Holden, not about Gus Hall. Why four separate and distinct references to communism or communists?

A. To identify Gus Hall; to identify him as secretary of the Communist Party.

Q. What did that have to do with John Goldmark?

A. It was identifying the personality who spoke at this school where his son was a student.

Q. Weren't you really trying to create the impression among your readers that John Goldmark was a communist or was at that time?

A. I don't have any way of knowing what impression the readers would get from reading that, counsel.

Holden had again fulfilled our hopes by refusing to admit his own demonstrable purpose. Within moments he had to retreat as Mansfield pressed on. "I would say if it created any impression at all," he admitted, "it would be the impression that he was soft on communism or sympathetic to communism or communists."

Holden insisted the entire story was true. "Nothing whatever to retract and I wouldn't do it today," he said. "It stands."

Mansfield placed before the witness his editorial headed "Catching Up With John," printed just before the election. Holden had written that Goldmark "has deceived the people with high-sounding phrases, all the while carefully concealing his true political philosophies which make him the idol of the pinkos and ultra-liberals."

What were the "high-sounding phrases"? Holden could not describe any. What were the concealed political philosophies? "His left-wing—leftist philosophies," came the answer. Holden could be no more specific. Who were the pinkos and ultraliberals? "I wouldn't be surprised that Gus Hall would idolize him" said the witness.

Holden's hatred of John was emerging into full view. He had written in his editorial: "[H]e is a tool of a monstrous conspiracy to remake America into a totalitarian state." He tried to hedge on the meaning of this, calling it "simply a matter of opinion," but finally admitted his intent:

> Q. He was a conscious tool of this communist conspiracy?
> A. "This monstrous conspiracy." You can call it whatever you want to.
> Q. You called it a communist conspiracy, didn't you, Mr. Holden?
> A. I said it could be a communist conspiracy, yes. That is what I meant to say.

Mansfield challenged Holden to back up his charges:

> Q. What did John Goldmark ever do that makes you believe that what you have said here in your editorial is true?
> A. His whole record.
> Q. Specifically what has he ever done?
> A. To cause me to form the opinion which I have expressed in this editorial, is that your question?
> Q. To make you believe it is true?
> A. Just his record. I can't be any more specific than that. I am not—

Such vague and irresponsible testimony, coming after the defense's opening salvo, was winning priceless ground for us.

At last Holden cited John's opposition to the "American Heritage Bill" in the state House of Representatives. He could think of nothing else incriminating that had happened in the legislature. "That is one," he said. "You asked for one and I have named it. And we can sit here all afternoon groping around in the dark."

Mansfield pressed for anything Goldmark had done outside the legislature that supported Holden's charge. The response was reluctant and meager. Goldmark had opposed the films *Communism on the Map* and *Operation Abolition*. This, coupled with Mrs. Goldmark's known former Communist Party membership, indicated to Holden that both husband and wife were communists. "That would be sufficient so far as I am concerned," he said. In addition, Goldmark's membership in the ACLU was evidence of communist sympathy.

As the examination went on Holden grew more ill-tempered and evasive. No doubt his lawyers were advising him at recesses to testify more politely and directly, but he seemed unable to take their advice.

In his interview on the television film "Suspect," Holden had claimed that he and Canwell got information about the Goldmarks from the FBI. A written transcript of the film's sound track was now in evidence. Holden tried desperately to avoid admitting his statement was false:

> Q. Let me read it to you again: "Our sources had been the House Un-American Activities Committee and the FBI and other confidential and informative sources in Washington."
> A. That doesn't say the FBI was in Washington. I have talked with the FBI agents in many places, Seattle, Spokane, and I may have talked—I don't recall at the moment whether I talked with FBI agents in Washington, or not.
> Q. What facts did you learn from the FBI?
> A. They were confidential.
> Q. Tell me what facts you learned from the FBI.
> A. Any of the reports of the FBI are completely confidential. Two of the FBI agents came from Seattle over to Tonasket to talk to me about it.

Q. What facts did you learn, Mr. Holden, from the FBI?

A. Absolutely none that weren't confidential.

At a recess Judge Turner spoke with counsel for both sides in his chambers. Holden's testimony, he said, was so evasive as to amount to an obstruction of justice. The defense lawyers promised to speak to their client that night. When questioning resumed the next morning, the truth came out:

Q. . . . Did you or did you not ever receive information about the Goldmarks from the FBI?

A. No.

Q. Never?

A. I did not, no.

Mansfield read the *American Intelligence Service* publication to the jury. In it Canwell said that Sally Goldmark claimed to have left the Communist Party in 1948. The true date was 1943, and the difference was important. In those five years our relations with the Soviet Union had changed from wartime alliance to cold war enmity. Holden now denied noticing the wrong date when checking over the document in his printing plant. "I didn't read it that carefully," he said. At once Mansfield impeached him by showing his testimony on deposition:

Q. You knew at the time that you saw the typescript of this document that that date was wrong?

A. I knew that Mr. Canwell probably without the benefit of his files or his notes—

Q. Answer the question now.

A. Had given the wrong year? Yes, I knew that.

Q. You knew it was wrong but you made no
effort whatever to correct it, is that correct?
A. Why should I?

A transcript of the American Legion hall meeting was in
evidence. It showed that Holden had asked from the floor:
"Can you tell me why the only two members in the legislature who are on the Washington Committee of the ACLU
are from Okanogan County?"

Q. You wanted to call to the attention of
everybody in the hall that John Goldmark and Mr.
Hallauer were present in the hall and that they were
members of the ACLU which Mr. Canwell had just said
is a communist front, isn't that right?
A. Yes, that is true.

We turned Holden over for cross-examination by his own
counsel. Harmon tried to bring out the temperate side of
his client's personality. Holden testified that like all reporters he must rely on imperfect memory; that he knew
Goldmark to be a "liberal" from years of covering the state
legislature; and that he had not acted under any plan with
the other defendants.

But the cross-examination could not redeem the impression Holden had made. In three and a half days on the stand
his hatred of political opponents and irresponsible use of
the label "communist" were established.

We followed up by calling Holden's co-defendant, Albert F. Canwell.

Now in his fifties, Canwell was a slight, mild-appearing,
sandy-haired man with a habitual half-smile on his face.
He had an air of secretly knowing the worst about everything. His mournful voice recalled that of his late hero,

Senator Joseph McCarthy. We knew Canwell was determined to appear a scientific investigator who patriotically sacrificed his private life to serve the anticommunist cause. A good speaker, he had succeeded in selling himself as an expert during the 1962 campaign in Okanogan County.

I began by showing that Canwell had never lived in the county and had received money for coming in to attack Goldmark with the tape, the *Intelligence Service,* and the Legion hall meeting:

> Q. How much money did you get altogether to finance your work concerning the Goldmarks?
> A. My best guess would be five or six hundred dollars. I know it wasn't—you mean—I don't say it was directly aimed at the Goldmarks but during that period of time or with some relationship to this there may have been five or six hundred dollars, I don't know.

Questioned about his personal history, he said he had left school at an early age—"I suppose I was around sixteen—sixteen or seventeen, I don't know—" and had gone to work "doing a little bit of everything." He said that as a young man in the 1930s he had traveled through the Midwest as a "free lance journalist," covering such events as the great strikes in the automobile industry.

"Was there some paper that was publishing what you wrote?" I asked. "No," he answered. "My recollection is that those were very lean years, like Sally was talking about."

Canwell had reviled but never met Mrs. Goldmark, whom he now referred to as "Sally." I asked him: "You mean Mrs. Goldmark?" "We won't split hairs," he replied. "Irma, Sally, Mrs. Goldmark—whatever it is."

When World War II approached Canwell had taken a job in the identification bureau of the Spokane County sheriff's office, and remained there for the duration. During the war, he said, he became troubled about "communists in the legislature." In 1946 Ashley Holden, then political editor of the leading Spokane paper, urged him to run for the House. He was elected and became chairman of the state un-American activities committee. After that, he had run for office three more times, without success.

Q. Now we understand that you operate a non-governmental intelligence service?

A. That is what I call it.

Q. What does that mean?

A. It means that I specialize in information having to do with the internal security field, largely to do with communism and other subversive activities.

Q. Do you have an office in Spokane?

A. Yes, I do.

Q. How many hours a day do you spend at this non-governmental intelligence service?

A. Well, it varies. But I am there usually all day and much of the night.

Q. All day and much of the night. How many days a week?

A. What?

Q. How many days a week?

A. Well, it varies. Sometimes it is seven days a week.

Canwell said he had been carrying on his full-time intelligence work for fifteen years. But only two years earlier he had given under oath a different version of his occupation. I placed before him a personal bankruptcy petition he had filed in Spokane in which he had listed his occupation as "farmer." How could he work full time at the intelligence service and be a farmer? "It isn't easy, but I am," Canwell answered. In fact his family's main source of income was his wife's late father's estate, which apparently was not liable to Canwell's creditors.

The intelligence service was not a commercial success. Canwell got only a few small contributions. "I would be receptive to much more than I receive," he said.

Yet he claimed to work intimately with the FBI and other investigators throughout the country, and he maintained files on a vast number of people. Among them, the questions brought out, were Senators Magnuson and Jackson, Governor Rosellini, and former Governor Langlie. Goldmark was far from being alone under Canwell's scrutiny.

Canwell strove to appear cool and reasonable, but time after time his extremism betrayed him. I asked him about his *American Intelligence Service* attack on the ACLU:

> Q. And what you are saying here is that the American Civil Liberties Union stands for the overthrow of the United States Government?
> A. Some of the key figures in it, people who manipulate and operate the thing.
> Q. Does the Communist Party stand for doing away with the free enterprise system?
> A. Yes.
> Q. And are you meaning to say that the American Civil Liberties Union stands for that?
> A. I have never known any of their members who didn't.

While pretending to support the Bill of Rights, he said, the ACLU in reality opposed it. "Yes, they fraudulently say they are protecting [it] while they are providing free propaganda to the world that you can't obtain justice in the courts in America."

> Q. Do you realize in your description of this organization you are talking about membership and board members of the ACLU who are, for example, judges of the Superior Court of this State?
> A. Yes.

Q. And you realize you are talking about people who hold or have held very high positions of respect and trust from the American public?

A. Yes.

Q. And you are talking also about a great number of conservative businessmen?

A. Yes.

Q. And none of that makes any difference to you?

A. No. They should have better sense than to be mixed up in an operation like this. And I cannot provide immunity to such an operation just because they are able to get some well-meaning but simple souls involved.

Canwell had written that John "could probably obtain a job in almost any law office in America, yet he is in the State of Washington doing anything but practicing law." This, he now testified, was "one of the many imponderables in this case." I asked him, "Do you think Okanogan County is a good place to live?" "Wonderful place," Canwell answered.

Q. Have you ever been in New York City?

A. Oh, yes, just recently.

Q. How would you say this place would compare with New York City to live?

A. I would prefer this.

Q. Do you think it strange that he would feel the same way as you?

A. No.

The libel said Goldmark "has usually taken extreme left positions in his legislative activities." I challenged Canwell to name any "extreme left" stand John had taken. In reply he cited Goldmark's opposition to the "American Heritage Bill," which had failed to pass the legislature:

Q. So that means that a majority of the Washington State House of Representatives, according to you, were taking an extreme left position?

A. The majority is usually responsive to able leadership. I think of John as being an able leader of the legislature.

Q. "John" you mean Mr. Goldmark?

A. Mr. Goldmark, yes. I have never questioned his talents.

Q. So you think he was responsible for getting the majority to defeat this, what you call "The American Heritage Bill"?

A. I would say that he would have a responsibility because of his leadership in the legislature. What took place in committee rooms and in the corridors I don't know.

Q. You really don't know who was in charge of the battle on that bill, do you?

A. No, I don't.

Q. And that is the only particular thing that he did in the legislature that you can point out to back up your statement?

A. That is the one I think of now.

Again the defense had failed to support its charges.

Canwell had been losing composure as the questioning went on. A three-day weekend intervened. When court resumed I asked for his response to our subpoena of his income tax returns, which might show his sources of money for printing and circulating the libels.

Q. Now you were also subpoenaed to produce your copies of your federal income tax returns for the years 1956 through 1962. Did you produce those this morning?

A. As I testified before, there are none.

Q. Did you file an income tax return for any of those years?

A. No.

Q. And you haven't filed any, even late since our last deposition?

A. No. I am in conference with the Revenue Department now. We are trying to straighten it out. I don't believe that I owe the government anything, however.

Canwell's stock in trade, his patriotism, fell short of impelling him to file the federal tax returns which burdened every juror.

We had also subpoenaed his file on the Goldmarks, a stack of notes and news clippings about half an inch thick. It was incomplete, he said; some documents had been mistakenly thrown out by a janitor. "I have a feeling that he did get some very, very important material and I rather imagine that some of the Goldmark material was there because I no longer can find it." Canwell himself, he admitted, had burned one page of notes after receiving the subpoena because it contained "confidential information" on other subjects. He claimed to have retyped and kept the entries about Goldmark.

I returned to the *Intelligence Service* libel. It implied that Sally Goldmark had remained a communist despite her statement that she left the Party years earlier. Asked to support this, Canwell cited two facts: her nondisclosure of her past membership, and her opposition to the federal House Un-American Activities Committee's film, *Operation Abolition*. I set out to show that the film's opponents included respected people from all walks of life. As we hoped, Canwell responded by attacking the critics.

Q. Didn't you know that the National Council of Churches opposed that film?

A. I also know that the National Council of Churches is badly infiltrated with communists.

Q. You think that the National Council of Churches opposed that film because it is infiltrated with communists?

A. Yes.

When Sally Goldmark testified before the federal committee at the Olympic Hotel in Seattle in 1956, Canwell, who had no position with the government, was in the building. He knew she had been summoned. Her testimony was transcribed promptly and someone on the committee staff— Canwell said he could not recall who—showed him the transcript in the hotel. He made notes from it, and six years later made public the information by twisting it into an attack on John. The committee itself had never released the testimony.

Q. You took it upon yourself to make it public when they had not?

A. Yes, I think it was well timed when it was done.

Before trial Canwell had insisted that nothing he said was meant to charge John with being a communist. Now he had to reconcile his pretrial testimony with the defense's opening statement to the jury. We wanted to draw out the accusation clearly to cut off any escape routes based on arguments over what the alleged libels had meant to say.

Q. What is this language about, "These people are professionals. They are dangerous. They are out to kill us." Why did you put that in an article about the Goldmarks?

A. I was describing the five or ten thousand hard-core members of the Communist Party who have remained through all the purges and exposures and investigations and everything else.

Q. And you claim the Goldmarks are among these people?

A. I did not so claim there.

Q. Do you claim that; do you claim that the Goldmarks are communist agents?

A. I would have to qualify that. I would say that they are either communist agents or under the discipline of the Communist Party.

The answer was what we had sought.

"One cannot overestimate the danger," Canwell had written in the *Intelligence Service*. "These agents are everywhere. They are in key positions. They are in the ministry of the churches, they are in our educational system, they are in the scientific field, they are at the highest levels of government." Who were these agents at the highest levels of government? Canwell evaded. At last he named four men: William Wieland, a current State Department official who "filed false information on the Castro situation"; and Lauchlin Currie, Owen Lattimore, and J. Robert Oppenheimer, none of whom was then with the government at all.

Q. . . . Now J. Robert Oppenheimer is a physicist, isn't he?

A. Yes.

Q. And what is his position with the government?

A. I do not know. I know he is consultant and advisor. I believe the White House had him to dinner not long ago.

Q. He is a communist agent?

A. I believe he is.

Q. Now Mr. Oppenheimer is not with the

government. Mr. Canwell. Can you name us a communist agent at the highest level of government?

A. No, I don't think I will speculate in that area. The conclusion is, obviously, if they were not, some of the mistakes that we make in the Department of State would be made on our side once in a while.

Q. You think the fact that the Department of State makes mistakes means that it is full of communist agents?

A. When they all run counter to America's security interest I would say that that is evident and obvious.

This answer laid bare the defendants' logic: where misfortune occurred, communists must be at work.

Q. A lot of these mistakes are made by the Secretary of State himself, aren't they?

A. I would suppose.

Q. A lot of them I imagine have been made by Secretary Rusk, the present Secretary of State?

A. Yes, too many of them.

Q. And you claim he is a communist agent?

A. I have no way of knowing. I know of his association with the communist front, the Institute of Pacific Relations. I know that he was an advisor to the President in the firing of MacArthur. I know that his actions would indicate either a very great lack of knowledge or that he was doing these things deliberately. I would say that he is a most unfortunate selection for Secretary of State.

Q. Do you claim that he is a communist agent?

A. I said that I have no way of knowing.

Q. You think he might be? You suspect him, don't you?

A. I wouldn't put it that way. I wouldn't know whether he is a fool or knave. It makes little difference.

I turned to his Legion hall speech against the ACLU.

Canwell insisted this was nonpolitical and had nothing to do with Goldmark. But his latest *Vigilante,* published just after John's primary election defeat, suggested otherwise:

> Q. In that *Vigilante,* on page four, you wrote as follows: "This particular legislator happened to be a prominent member of the American Civil Liberties Union and exposure of the true nature of that organization by the American Legion and Canwell was probably the bullet that got Goldmark."
> A. That is correct. That is a subsequent observation to what happened.

We played for the jury the tape recording of the American Legion meeting. Canwell's long attack on the ACLU, John's brief response, Hallauer's expulsion from the stage, Gillespie's exhortation to "vote American," came through clearly. The crowd's ugly mood could be sensed.

Canwell now admitted knowing that neither the United States Attorney General nor the Subversive Activities Control Board had ever listed the ACLU as a communist front. This made no difference to him. "No, there are many fronts that are not on the list."

I placed in evidence a certified copy of John's Navy service record from the Pentagon files. It showed his wartime service and recent promotion to commander.

> Q. Did you know at the time you wrote and said the things that you did about Mr. Goldmark in 1962 that he was a commander in the United States Naval Reserve?
> A. Yes.
> Q. And did you know that he had been investigated or must have been investigated by the Naval Intelligence Department with the aid of other federal authorities to get his security clearances?
> A. That was one of the things I was concerned about. I knew if he had told the whole truth he would not be commissioned in the first place.

MR. DWYER: I move to strike it out as not being responsive.

THE COURT: It will be stricken out; jury will disregard it.

Q. Do you know that Mr. Goldmark in his commission as a commander must have been investigated by the Naval Intelligence with the aid of other services?

A. I assumed he had been.

The fact of John's clearance by Navy Intelligence was now before the jury.

I turned Canwell over for cross-examination. At once he seemed to regain full composure. He enjoyed the limelight and talked in a fluent, temperate way under his own counsel's questioning.

"I have been devoting all of my time to this opposition to communist activity which has not been remunerative," Canwell said. This was why he had filed no tax returns. "My best knowledge is there is not income to report there."

He described a career of selfless patriotism. "Well, for some fifteen years at least I have gathered and accumulated technical information in the field of communism. During some of that time I have maintained contacts with people inside the Communist Party—informers. I have made records and obtained information. I have supplied information to any responsible person who asked me for information. . . .

"I have lectured or spoken to groups—high school groups, colleges, universities, service clubs, American Legion groups—almost any place that I have been asked to talk wherever I could possibly do that. I have in general tried to operate that type of a service where people who were concerned about communism could get accurate and technical, complete information on the subject. . . ."

The effort consumed him. There was time for nothing else. "I could never stop. There are times when I tried to or tried to devote more time to my personal income but I just not—have not been permitted to do so.

"When I have tried to stop people have come to me, sometimes agents of the government, the military and others asking me for information that perhaps only I would have. And I have done the best I could to supply that information to be careful and accurate about it, to do what I was called upon to do. And I have felt at all times that was my responsibility as a citizen because of what I knew in the field. . . ."

The trial had become a source of education and entertainment. Classes of school children and their teachers came to watch, and local citizens and other visitors often filled the courtroom.

Calling Holden and Canwell as plaintiffs' witnesses had worked exactly as we hoped. The chief accusers had failed to back up their charges. No doubt they would appear again, better prepared, as defense witnesses; but we thought nothing they might do could quite redeem this first performance.

On evenings and weekends my wife and two small children and I used what brief time we could spare to become acquainted in the county. We became friends with our landlords, Al and Marjorie Ridpath. An independent Republican who ran an oil distributing business, Ridpath rented us his basement apartment knowing the gesture would cost him customers. We met others in the valley and found an increasingly warm welcome.

After two weeks of trial the atmosphere seemed to shift in Goldmark's favor. An Okanogan grocer, who felt strongly about defaulting debtors, spoke to me of Canwell as he rang up a purchase. "It's interesting to learn that one of the defendants is"—he groped for a word—"despicable."

CHAPTER 7

STATE SENATOR Wilbur Hallauer was a robust, plain-spoken man who seemed to radiate common sense. On the stand he told of his friendship with John, dating from the 1952 Democractic National Convention. "We talked politics many times after that," he said. "I tried to interest him in becoming active in politics in the district and in the state to the extent of becoming a candidate." Since then Goldmark had earned a fine reputation throughout the state. Hallauer had seen the libels and described their impact: "These were very venomous things and they certainly damaged John's reputation. They created doubts in the public's mind that he was unable to overcome."

Mansfield asked the witness his connection with the ACLU. "I happen to be a member of that organization and I am proud of it," Hallauer testified.

We called the third defendant, Loris Gillespie. A wealthy orchardist and businessman, Gillespie was in his early sixties but looked younger. Bald, bespectacled, and quick of movement, he virtually bounded forward to take the oath. On the stand he answered all questions with a strenuous showing of politeness.

Before trial Gillespie had professed amazement at being a defendant; disclaimed any connection with Holden's or Canwell's attacks; and, in short, claimed he did not know what we were talking about.

I now brought out that before trial he had sworn that in John's fifteen years in the county Gillespie had never heard anyone call him a communist or communist sympathizer. On the television program "Suspect" Gillespie had said: "I don't know of anyone that was running that wasn't a good American."

Then I turned from these public utterances to what he had said in private conversations over the years, and Gillespie—knowing some of the evidence we had found—struggled to cover his tracks:

Q. But this isn't the same thing you have been saying in private about the Goldmarks, is it?

A. Oh, it is possible that in person to person talking that I have—may have been rather indiscreet, I will say it that way, without sufficient knowledge. I will grant you that, Mr. Dwyer.

Q. You have been telling other people that the Goldmarks are communists, haven't you, for many years?

A. No, sir. No, sir. No.

Q. And is it your testimony now that you have not told other people in this county in the past that John Goldmark was a communist?

A. I did not say that, sir. I said it was possible that I could have been indiscreet at times.

Q. How could you be so indiscreet to call him a communist when you said, "I don't know of anyone who was running that wasn't a good American?"

A. In just an individual conversation, Mr. Dwyer, it can happen a hundred times with almost any human being. And it wasn't done with any thought of damaging him. It was a matter of conversation, if I did say. Now, if I—I honestly do not recall if I said it and if I did—and it is possible—it wasn't done with the idea—it was more of a conversation piece or just talking with people. So I honestly cannot tell you.

Bank records showed that in July 1961 Gillespie had made out a check for $200 to himself as commander of a local American Legion post and then endorsed it to Ashley Holden. Holden had deposited it with the notation "Washington, D.C. trip expenses." The next day Holden and Canwell had flown to Washington where they "investigated" the Goldmarks. Gillespie emphatically denied that he had helped finance the trip or even known of it. The money, he insisted, was a contribution to Canwell's general patriotic work, and the timing was coincidence.

Q. But you have known him for fifteen years?
A. Yes, sir.
Q. And you say that every time you see him he asks you for money?
A. Yes, sir.
Q. And that was the first time in fifteen years that you gave him some money?
A. Finally have to give in once in a while.

Also in 1961, we brought out, Gillespie had enlisted Joe Haussler, a county commissioner, and Stanley Pennington, editor of the *Independent,* in an anticommunist study group. That fall he had driven the two men and Haussler's lawyer to Spokane, where all of them met Canwell at his office. Canwell had provided certain information about the Goldmarks; Haussler had paid him $100; and Haussler's candidacy and the smear campaign followed in the succeeding months.

In early 1962, he admitted, Gillespie had distributed several hundred copies of the *Vigilante,* but only as a favor to Canwell. He had meant to harm no one.

At the Legion hall meeting in August Gillespie had been master of ceremonies—but only because other Legion officials asked him to, he said. He insisted the meeting had nothing to do with politics or with Goldmark.

Q. There was an election coming up in just a few days?

A. Yes, sir.

Q. And at the end of the meeting you urged the people to go out and vote American?

A. Yes, sir.

We excused Gillespie from the stand. His pose of astonished innocence was before the jury. At hand was a series of witnesses who would demolish it.

Josephine Pardee, an attractive librarian from Wenatchee, recalled a conversation with Gillespie in 1956. He had said "that he thought Mr. Goldmark was pink or red or a commie. He made some comment, used one of the slang expressions for a communist." The timing placed Gillespie among the first to slander Goldmark.

William Barnes, a talkative, friendly Okanogan undertaker, had known Gillespie for years. Their friendship did not deter him from telling what he remembered. In 1961 Gillespie had said at a dinner party: "We have irrevocable proof that the Goldmarks are communists." In August 1962, at the peak of the election campaign, Gillespie told Barnes that the Goldmarks' marriage had been "forced" by the Communist Party.

Donald McIntosh, a feed and implement dealer, recalled that Gillespie had told him in 1961 that he had documentary proof that Sally Goldmark was a communist.

Nick Cain, a widely known orchardist, described a conversation with Gillespie in the summer of 1962: ". . . He came to my home one evening with his hired man and knocked at the back door. And I answered the door and Mr. Gillespie said 'I have come to dispel a horrible lie about you that has been going around Okanogan and Omak'. So I invited him in for coffee and asked him to tell me about this. . . . I said 'What is this horrible lie about me that you are concerned about?' And he said 'I have understood from some people in the Omak-Okanogan area that you had the Goldmarks to your home some time ago.' And he said 'Certainly, that is not correct, is it?' . . ." Gillespie went on to tell Cain that the Goldmarks' marriage had been forced by the Communist Party.

Defense lawyer Joseph Wicks, the retired Superior Court judge from Okanogan, cross-examined Cain. Wicks was a remarkable man. A Cherokee Indian from Oklahoma, he had gained a legal education, moved to Okanogan County years earlier, risen to a judgeship, and then retired. Tall, rangy, and handsome, with bronze skin and flowing white hair, he spoke in a confident, booming voice. Through most of our case he sat eyeing the jury or the witness, and handled the cross-examination only on a few local residents. Now he attacked the "forced marriage" statement head-on:

> Q. Have you made any particular reading or done any particular reading or study of the activities of communists in this country?
> A. No, sir, I haven't.
> Q. So you wouldn't be familiar with the statement, or the fact, if it is a fact, that they do have forced marriages among the communists in order to protect their operation; you wouldn't be familiar with that, would you?
> A. No, sir, I wouldn't.

We called Dr. Joseph Fischnaller, a tall, gray-haired physician who had practiced for years in Omak until his retirement. In 1961, he testified, Gillespie had approached him and asked him "to contribute to a trip by Mr. Canwell to the East to investigate the Goldmarks further."

Gillespie could no longer claim he did not belong in court.

For days we had lived in the defendants' murky world.

The results were good but the atmosphere oppressive. When we devoted a day to evidence about the ACLU, it was like opening a window.

Robert Winsor, a young Seattle lawyer, came to the stand. Winsor had been state ACLU president and knew the organization intimately. We aimed to explain the ACLU so clearly that no one could mistake its true nature. It had only about 75,000 members nationally and was little known in eastern Washington.

Winsor named some of the 1,600 members in the state. Among them were a former United States senator, a Federal Communications Commissioner, an immediate past president of the state medical association, and numerous lawyers, doctors, and businessmen. An elected board governed the organization. Two Superior Court judges had recently filled the office of state president before going on the bench.

Every year, Winsor explained, the ACLU had a state convention. The speaker the year before had been Arthur Flemming, president of the University of Oregon and former Secretary of Health, Education and Welfare under President Eisenhower. Flemming spoke on why the University of Oregon had allowed Gus Hall of the Communist Party to speak on campus.

I asked Winsor the ACLU's purpose. He ably explained the Bill of Rights—the first ten amendments to the U.S. Constitution, adopted in 1791, supplemented by the Fourteenth and Fifteenth Amendments after the Civil War. The ACLU's role was to secure these rights in daily American life. "For whom?" I asked. "For everybody," Winsor answered. "We don't care whose rights. We don't care who it is—who is being denied the right of speech, the right to worship God as he chooses. We don't care who it is that is having his rights trampled upon or restricted in some way; it is the issue that we are interested in."

Winsor brought these concepts to life by describing typical ACLU projects in Washington State. A Red Cross employee was fired when denied a security clearance by the Army. He received no hearing, or even an explanation. The man happened to be a decorated Korean War veteran. The ACLU provided a lawyer; the Army at length ordered a hearing; the man was cleared and restored to duty.

A local judge had sentenced a witness to jail for contempt because he thought the man was lying. The ACLU contended the witness should receive a trial, as with any other criminal charge. The State Supreme Court agreed and freed the prisoner.

It was proposed in Congress that committee hearings be held to investigate the John Birch Society. The ACLU opposed the idea; the Society, like any other group, should enjoy its constitutional rights free of government intrusion.

Dave Beck, president of the Teamsters Union, was brought to trial for tax fraud in an atmosphere inflamed by hostile newspaper publicity. ACLU lawyers asked a postponement until public feeling could abate. "We are not interested in knowing whether or not a man is guilty or innocent," Winsor said. "He is entitled to fair procedures. . . ."

> Q. Has the ACLU taken issue with the House UnAmerican Activities Committee?
> A. Yes.
> Q. And on what ground?
> A. We have taken issue with them from the very beginning on one ground. That is, that Congress, that the committee's direction by Congress gets them into the matter of investigating ideas and beliefs. It gets them beyond the area where they have the right to legislate. . . .

But should radicals who would destroy the Constitution enjoy its benefits? Yes, said Winsor. "If we don't give freedom of speech to those whose opinions we don't like, the next thing it will be taken away from people whose opinions we like quite well. And then eventually ours will be gone."

Q. Does the ACLU support the ability or right of the communists or the Nazis or anybody else to commit any espionage or anything of that nature against the United States?
A. Absolutely not.
Q. Is the American Civil Liberties Union affiliated with the Communist Party?
A. In no way whatsoever.

The cross-examining lawyer will usually get a strong witness off the stand quickly to avoid his doing more damage. Harmon took the opposite course with Winsor—not through ignorance of trial tactics, but as part of the defense campaign to destroy the entire "communist-liberal" position as the defense saw it. The result of the far-ranging cross-examination was only to strengthen Winsor's testimony.

Fred Haley, the tall and serious president of a Tacoma manufacturing firm, described his years of ACLU membership. Sam Fancher, an engaging lawyer from Spokane, told of his presidency of the small ACLU chapter in his native city. He added that Canwell, his fellow townsman, had a bad reputation in the community where truthfulness was concerned. Defense counsel committed the classic cross-examiner's mistake of asking too many questions:

Q. . . . You don't particularly like Mr. Canwell, do you?
A. I don't like the character assassination that I have seen him carry out for years.
Q. Is it your view that Mr. Canwell has been carrying on character assassination for years?

90

A. Yes, it is.

Q. And has all of this had to do with the field of communism?

A. Oh, the people he attacked were not communists.

Our last witness of the day was the Reverend Francis Conklin, a Jesuit priest, lawyer, and teacher at Gonzaga University. In early middle age, a dark-haired, open-faced man dressed in his black clothing and clerical collar, Father Conklin answered my questions with calm authority.

His prime field of study for fifteen years, he said, had been the philosophy of communism. He had taught the subject at Gonzaga, published articles on it in learned quarterlies, and outlined a course on it for use in Jesuit universities throughout the United States. Not content with academic work alone, he had helped mine workers in Idaho break away from a communist-dominated union.

If given the chance to invent a perfectly qualified expert witness, we could not have improved on Father Conklin.

He had looked thoroughly into the ACLU and concluded that it was not only not a front but was one of the most important organizations standing against such doctrines as communism. "Once a state no longer respects the individual rights of citizens," said Conklin, "then that state is a totalitarian state. And the Civil Liberties Union has consistently over the years fought hard, long, bitter struggles to defend the individual rights of individual citizens. And that is why I regarded it as one of the strongest bulwarks against communism or any form of totalitarianism in this country."

Q. Now in all of the studies that you have made of the ACLU, either as a writer or a teacher or student or a lawyer or a law teacher, as you are now, as a member of the ACLU have you ever seen any sign of any communist connection with the ACLU?

A. I have never seen anything. I heard these allegations in the late forties and fifties and I investigated them as thoroughly as I could and concluded that they were completely false.

If the jurors were affected like the audience, our ACLU day was a success. Several spectators who had known little of the organization now spoke of wanting to join it.

CHAPTER **8**

I
T WAS November 22, 1963. At the morning recess, in an office down the hall, one of the reporters made his daily telephone call to his editor. In a moment he rushed out with the news that President Kennedy had just been shot in Dallas.

Dismay and confusion spread through the courthouse. The lawyers entered the judge's chambers, and I asked Judge Turner to recess the trial. He agreed and called the jurors into the courtroom.

"Members of the jury," he said, "we have just received a report that the President has been shot. It is possible that he has been killed. We know very little about it yet. But it is—this is terrible news. And since we know so little, I feel that it would be best not to adjourn for the day but to recess until 1:30. I think this news is overwhelming and I think we should not attempt to proceed with the trial until we know a little bit more."

Soon we knew the President was dead, and met again to excuse the jury until after his funeral.

For three days a group crushed by sadness waited in the Goldmarks' rented house in Okanogan. The young President's loss, the horror of his assassination, seemed to say "No, it is impossible" to every hope for justice and reason.

Who was Lee Harvey Oswald, whom the police identified as the murderer? We watched as fragments of his sorry life came over television. He had lived in Russia; he supported the Cuban revolution; he called himself a Marxist. The next day a Dallas lawyer was shown leaving Oswald's cell after an interview. He announced to the country that the suspect insisted on having an American Civil Liberties Union lawyer—because, Oswald said, he belonged to the ACLU himself.

I checked this by telephoning the ACLU national office in New York. The records showed that a short time earlier Oswald had indeed sent in a membership application and a two-dollar contribution. Membership was open to everyone; nothing else was required for him to join.

A worse blow could hardly be imagined. That the mentally ill Oswald happened to be a left-wing rather than a right-wing extremist, that he had reached out to the ACLU, was fortuitous. But the defense had portrayed communist conspirators all around—"out to kill us," in Canwell's words. We had called this a delusion and asked the jury to keep faith in freedom of speech and association. Now the defense's "internal menace" seemed to have sprung grotesquely to life.

Messages of consolation arrived from friends who thought our cause was lost. Goldmark had the right, under the rules of court, to dismiss his lawsuit voluntarily at any time before he rested his case and bring it on for trial again many months later before a different jury. By taking that course he could lessen the damaging impact of the Kennedy assassination on his chances. But he and Sally rejected that alternative at once. The issue in Okanogan should be decided then and there.

The witness on the stand when the President was shot was Edna Larchar, Sally's older sister, who had come out from New York. A gray-haired, dignified woman with a warm smile, she told of the Depression and Sally's attraction to communism. Mrs. Larchar had been a welfare worker in the early 1930s: "I was very distressed because I was seeing every day people who were in a dreadful state. And Sally was very—she was a very impulsive, very warm-hearted, very energetic person. She still is. And she wanted to do something about it. And I—we discussed the Communist Party. Everyone discussed it at that time. . . ."

The two sisters had argued about politics. "I objected strenuously to the hysterical fanaticism that I thought communism demanded." Mrs. Larchar had thought Sally naïve. "And she was very determined that—well, I was her older sister—and I wasn't going to tell her what to do. That is what it amounted to." Sally was then about twenty-five—"unmarried and very young for her age, I thought."

But no one in the family knew until much later that Sally joined the Communist Party in the mid-1930s.

Mrs. Larchar's husband was an overseas General Motors executive. They were living in the Philippines with their two children when World War II broke out in the Pacific. Captured by the Japanese, they spent three years in wartime internment camps.

Mrs. Larchar had never met John Goldmark, whom Sally married during the war. In 1945 the Americans, reconquering the islands, bombarded Manila. Mrs. Larchar and the children, all three of them wounded, made their way through the rubble of the city to the camp where Mr. Larchar had been held. Then, she testified, "a young man dressed in fatigue uniform with another American soldier walked up and said to me, 'Are you Mrs. Larchar?' and I said 'yes' and he said 'I am your brother-in-law, John Goldmark.' This was February 15, 1945."

Goldmark was in the vanguard of the advancing American forces. In the following days he managed to come to the camp several times, or to send a friend, bringing food and greetings.

After the war the Larchars and Goldmarks were at opposite ends of the country. The sisters corresponded. In 1950 Sally mentioned in a letter that she had belonged to the Communist Party for several years while still living in the East. This was the first the Larchars had heard of it.

On cross-examination Harmon hammered at the theme of secrecy. Not even her sister had known of Sally's communist affiliation in the 1930s. Edna Larchar gave a simple explanation: "I am sure she knew that I disapproved of it and didn't want to discuss it with me."

Peter Asher came to the stand. A New Yorker with an Ivy League education, partner in a Wall Street law firm, he might have aroused resentment in a western country jury, but his easygoing manner and genuine modesty made him immediately likable.

Asher had met Goldmark in the spring of 1944 in Australia. Both were volunteer members of a Navy "mobile explosives investigation unit." When the Americans invaded Luzon, Asher and Goldmark were there to collect new Japanese ordnance specimens and write intelligence reports on them. After several days on the beachhead they were separated, and then met again in the battle of Manila.

> Q. What were you doing at that time?
> A. We were in the front lines as the First Cavalry was advancing through the ruins of Manila. We were—it turned out that the Japanese had laid a great many types of explosive obstacles in the streets, shells, mines, even depth charges, and the First Cavalry had no one to deal with this type of explosives so that Mr. Goldmark and I were getting rid of this stuff so that the American tanks and armored vehicles could advance.

Asher was shot in the chest during the street fighting.

John was the last person he spoke to before being evacuated.

> Q. What did you tell Mr. Goldmark?
> A. I told him he ought to get out of the area.
> Q. Did he do it?
> A. Not to my knowledge, no.

Goldmark could have left instead of continuing to disarm explosives. "We simply were doing this work because the Army engineers hadn't shown up and we had been requested to do the work by the Army field officers. Our job at that time, our orders, were to collect new specimens of Japanese ordnance for our Naval commanders."

Asher, badly wounded, was awarded the Silver Star. After weeks in a hospital he rejoined the mobile explosives unit. He and Goldmark were assigned to clean out unexploded shells and bombs on the island of Cavite. We placed in evidence a photograph Asher had taken of a lean young mean, stripped to the waist, shoveling dirt under a hot sun. It was Goldmark, "looking for unexploded bombs in a crater which we thought was a bomb crater on Cavite." Former servicemen on the jury might sense the caliber of an officer doing this work.

I concluded with Asher: "Did John Goldmark ever say or do anything in your presence to suggest to you any communist sympathy on his part?" "Absolutely no," he answered.

Again Harmon cross-examined about secrecy. Despite their long friendship, John had never told Asher that Sally was a former communist; Asher knew nothing of this until he read a news article about the 1962 campaign.

Now came our last two witnesses on the ACLU. Ray Moore, a Seattle stockbroker whose parents were well-known residents of Okanogan County, testified he had belonged

97

to the ACLU for years and agreed with "I would say ninety-nine percent" of its positions. His testimony had both local and bipartisan appeal; he was a former King County Republican chairman.

John Pemberton, national executive director of the ACLU, had flown from New York to testify in his organization's defense. A youthful-looking Minnesota lawyer with blond, crew-cut hair, Pemberton was a Quaker who had given up an established law practice to become the ACLU's full-time chief of staff. In a pleasant, calm voice he answered my questions.

During the war he had been an ambulance driver for the American Field Service in the Middle East and Asia, and had set up an ambulance service for the Chiang Kai-shek forces in China. Here was one more note in a counterpoint theme we were building. Many parties and witnesses on both sides of the trial had been of service age in World War II; on our side most of the men had seen distinguished service, many of them overseas and in combat; on the defense side, where outspoken patriotism prevailed, the majority had never served at all.

Pemberton had been a teacher, a practicing lawyer for twelve years in Rochester, Minnesota, and a Republican county chairman. A dedicated civil libertarian, he accepted appointment as the ACLU's national director in 1962, and moved to New York.

Many countries have high-sounding constitutions; few enjoy real liberty. Pemberton said the ACLU's purpose "is to protect and advance the kind of liberty and rights that are guaranteed by the Bill of Rights and the United States Constitution." He described a sampling of ACLU projects over four decades.

Pemberton named some of the people currently on the ACLU's board or national committee: Ernest Angell, a renowned New York lawyer; John Haynes Holmes, minister of the New York Community Church; Gerard Piel, publisher of the *Scientific American;* Edward Bennett Williams, the famous criminal lawyer; Francis Biddle, former Attorney General of the United States; Pearl Buck, the novelist; Frank Dobie, author and historian; Palmer Hoyt, publisher of the *Denver Post;* Karl Menninger, chief of the well-known psychiatric clinic; Thurman Arnold, a famous lawyer and former federal judge; Melvyn Douglas, the actor; Robert Hutchins, former president of the University of Chicago and head of the Center for the Study of Democratic Institutions; Elmo Roper, the public opinion expert; Thornton Wilder, the playwright; William L. White, a noted journalist; and Arthur Schlesinger, Jr., historian and assistant to the late President Kennedy.

Pemberton had brought with him a collection of letters and telegrams about the ACLU, received over the years, which could be inspected by anyone interested. Among them were communications from President Eisenhower, President Kennedy, Adlai Stevenson, and Governor Nelson Rockefeller.

I kept the examination brief and pointed. The ACLU's philosophy might need further explanation to the jury, but we hoped our opponents would provide it through another all-out cross-examination attack against a strong witness. The attack came at once: "Mr. Pemberton," Harmon demanded, "are you now or have you ever been a member of the Communist Party?"

    A. No.
    Q. Are you now or have you ever been under Communist Party discipline?
    A. No.
    Q. Mr. Pemberton, the ACLU, as I understand it, as a matter of principle vigorously defends the right of

any and all persons, including communists, to refuse to answer both of those preliminary questions I asked you, isn't that right?

A. That is correct.

Q. And why did you agree to answer them instead of standing on your constitutional right to refuse to answer?

A. Because I have no objection to answering them in a court of law.

The defense was still failing to distinguish between protecting a person's rights and sharing his views. Didn't the ACLU maintain that a man's use of the Fifth Amendment in refusing to answer as to communist membership should never raise an inference against him? Yes, answered Pemberton; invoking a constitutional right can raise no inference of guilt. Didn't the ACLU also advance the view that communism represents no internal menace to the United States? "It has not taken that position nor the opposite," said Pemberton.

Harmon turned to loyalty oaths for teachers, on which the ACLU view could easily be misunderstood.

Q. . . . So that the position of the ACLU would make no distinction between a member of the Communist Party and anybody else—if they are otherwise qualified they should be permitted to teach without being required to take a loyalty oath?

A. The position of the ACLU would make no distinction based upon their membership in the Communist Party.

Q. Well, what about the civil rights of the parents of the students and of the students themselves, or don't they have any civil rights in this field to be protected?

A. I think the right of the parent—and I am a parent myself—is to have a competent teacher. I personally do not see how the person you described, subject to the discipline of an outside organization, could have the honesty to be a competent teacher, but I think the persons who employ the teachers of my children ought to be looking for that honesty and that competence and not looking at loyalty oaths in order to select their teachers.

A disciplined communist, Pemberton said, would probably take the oath and the slight risk of a perjury conviction that went with it. Those who refused such vaguely worded oaths were not communists but conscientious teachers who were concerned not with prosecution but with principle.

Pemberton was leaning forward and talking earnestly, as though he wanted not only the jury but counsel and the defendants as well to understand him fully.

> Q. Mr. Pemberton, do you agree that the government has a right to control my right to possess a dangerous instrumentality such as a switchblade knife, let us say?
> A. Yes.
> Q. Actually when the state or the federal government or the local government tells me I can't possess a switchblade knife it is interfering to some extent at least with my civil rights, isn't that a fact?
> A. No, I don't consider that one of your civil rights. It is interfering with your freedom of action.
> Q. Well, it is curtailing my right to defend myself with a particularly dangerous weapon, at least?
> A. Yes. I didn't classify that as one of your civil rights.

> Q. . . . . such laws outlawing possession of switchblade knives are perfectly proper, aren't they?
> A. Yes.

Q. And the ACLU doesn't oppose such laws?

A. The ACLU does not.

Q. Well, in your opinion, which is the most dangerous, a switchblade knife in the hand of an irresponsible teenager or a deadly ideology such as communism in the hands of a secret communist teacher?

A. The switchblade knife, because to say that a deadly ideology is the most dangerous is to lose all faith in the people to judge between right and wrong and is to assume that the only way we can protect people from making errors is to keep erroneous opinions from being expressed. I don't think the people are that weak.

Here was the clash of beliefs underlying the campaign and the trial. The plaintiffs were committed to the open society and its corollary, faith in the common man's ability to think and choose. Our opponents demanded a retreat to the imaginary safety of an authoritarian society. Would the jury understand?

Harmon pressed on. Did the ACLU defend cases involving communists? Some, said Pemberton, but the number was a small percentage of the total. Did the ACLU favor unrestricted travel to communist countries? And urge the right of returning travelers to say whatever they chose? Yes, said the witness. The nation's political system rested on "a faith in the ability of people to judge for themselves when that speaker is telling the truth and when that speaker is not. And every time we are so afraid one speaker is going to misinform or will issue propaganda that we cut him down, we exhibit lack of faith in that ability and we deprive ourselves of one of the means of distinguishing truth from falsehood, the ability to hear both sides and choose for ourselves which is true."

Q. Well, does that assume, Mr. Pemberton, that the average person has some expertise or enough knowledge about communism to recognize ideas as soon as they begin to be peddled?

A. No, this is based not upon expertise but common sense, not that the average person will identify them necessarily as communist ideas but he will recognize them as bad ideas, and this is where our faith is placed.

The cross-examination went on half again as long as the direct. At last Pemberton was excused. He left behind the memory of a superbly articulate account of why libertarians believe in constitutional freedom for all, even the despised minority. Any jury, in any state, would have been impressed.

Court adjourned for a four-day Thanksgiving recess and we drove up the long, rutted road to the Goldmarks' ranch. We spent the time at work, but a few days in the country gave a welcome change. The evenings brought good music and warm conversation in the house, and moonlight on the strange, snow-covered plateau outside.

We reviewed our position. We had done much to discredit John's accusers and make clear their political extremism and irresponsibility. We thought we had made a stunning case for the ACLU.

Chuck Goldmark had made a fine appearance on the witness stand while home on a vacation from college. A tall, slender, light-haired young man of nineteen, he had been serious and perfectly calm before the crowded courtroom. Chuck's testimony that his parents had never taught him anything of a procommunist nature was plainly believable.

We had called to the stand the last of the defendants, Don Caron, the ex-forest ranger who was now state coordinator for the John Birch Society. Just before the election he had published a newspaper column warning of communists infiltrating rural areas to run for election; but the column had been part of a long series on communism, and had not mentioned Goldmark. Our case against Caron was weakest. He was a tall, quiet man in his thirties with thinning red hair and a mild manner which contrasted strangely with his startling words.

We had proved John Goldmark's good reputation, and the damage done to it by the libels. The court allowed twelve witnesses per side on this subject; ours were chosen to achieve a balance between local people and witnesses of statewide stature who could prove John's reputation in the larger community. We had called government officials, housewives, business people, and farmers. Joe Dwyer (no relation to me), a cattle rancher and state director of agriculture, testified that Goldmark's reputation "was excellent, the very highest." Charles Hodde, an eastern Washington farmer who was chairman of the Washington State Tax Commission, said John's good name "was at its height when he left the '61 session; he had obtained his greatest eminence and greatest influence." The libels had raised "a lot of doubt and suspicion," said Anne Nelson, an orchardist's wife. "You feel it in the people you meet, people who used to back Mr. Goldmark."

But we knew the jury's fear of communism, the hate campaign, and the tragic assassination of President Kennedy left many pitfalls ahead.

After the holiday we called our last reputation witnesses. State Representative Slade Gorton, a Republican, had come over from Seattle. An outstanding young lawyer thought to have a brilliant political future, Gorton was willing to tell the truth as he saw it about John regardless of what it might cost him with the right wing of his party. "His reputation was excellent," he said. "It was not questioned." The defense in cross-examining tried to place John on the extreme left. "[H]e was a leading member of the liberal group of the Democratic Party," Gorton answered, "which included the great bulk of the Democratic Party in the legislature." State Representative Tom Copeland, a Republican farmer from Walla Walla, gave similar testimony.

Mrs. Arthur Skelton, a bright, pleasant, middle-aged housewife, had been state president of the Parent-Teachers Association. Among groups concerned with child welfare, she testified, John's reputation had been high throughout the state. "Mr. Goldmark was what I would call a conservative in this area. . . . he was more concerned with seeing that children had a chance to become independent, that they have adequate guidance, that their families were strengthened to the point where they could become good citizens."

A strange interlude followed. The defense had surprisingly allowed us to place in evidence the entire television film "Suspect," even though the only parts of it technically admissible as evidence were statements made on the sound track by two of the defendants, Holden and Gillespie. The defense's condition for waiving any objection to the remainder was that we make available as witnesses the television men who had made the documentary. We had gladly accepted this condition and shown the film to the jury. In telling the story of the 1962 campaign it contained out-of-court statements favorable to Goldmark. One farmer said of the American Legion hall rally that if those who staged it "were on Mr. Khrushchev's payroll he would undoubtedly increase their salary. If he didn't he would be pretty ungrateful."

In court now was Robert Schulman, a highly able journalist and commentator with the King Broadcasting Company in Seattle. The documentary had been his idea and mainly his creation.

Schulman, testifying as our witness, said he had heard of the huge 1962 voter turnout in Okanogan following a reported campaign to connect John Goldmark with communism. He gathered a crew together and came to the county. They investigated, interviewed many people on film, and went home to edit their work into the finished product. He had brought with him to Okanogan courtroom all the "outtakes"—the raw film omitted from the final product. They were on hand for anyone who wanted to look at them.

When I turned Schulman over for cross-examination, it became clear why the defense lawyers had passed up their chance to keep the television documentary out of evidence. They saw the film as one more symptom of a conspiracy to misinform the public, and believed they could turn it to advantage by showing bias and unfairness.

Wasn't Schulman himself a member of the ACLU? Harmon asked. He was. So was Stimson Bullitt, then the president of King Broadcasting Company. Shouldn't both sides be represented in a documentary? Yes, answered Schulman, "a fair and balanced presentation in my judgment is essential." Hadn't he started out with the preconceived notion that the ACLU was not a communist front? Schulman answered that he had indeed been skeptical of such a charge. "However, as a journalist, and this is not easily accomplished at any time, as a journalist when a thing is questioned then you have got to make yourself go out and test your own idea even more strongly so that you to the best of your ability can be as sure as possible that this is the truth."

Had Schulman run two of Joe Haussler's answers together, leaving out an intervening question? He did not believe so.

106

Harmon pressed his attack on the filmmakers' research. Schulman, a balding man with thick glasses, a determined jaw, and the strong voice of a television newsman, became nettled and defended his work with eloquence. He had checked with federal government sources, he explained, to verify Goldmark's Navy security clearance and the ACLU's legitimacy. The office of Attorney General Robert Kennedy had confirmed that the ACLU had not been characterized by any responsible organization as a communist front.

Sally Goldmark had spoken in the film of joining and later leaving the Communist Party. Had Schulman simply taken her word for all this? Not entirely. He had verified with the government her statement that she cooperated with the FBI. Harmon was enraged at this answer.

> Q. Mr. Schulman, in the transcript itself it says in essence that the FBI doesn't give out such information. Do you mean to tell me that they confirmed to you something about her cooperation and the nature of it?
> A. No, I did not say that. They confirmed that she had been cooperative with the FBI. Beyond that they would not go.
> Q. What did they tell you?
> A. That is all.
> Q. Who told you that?
> A. My recollection is that that came either from the Attorney General's Office or from the agent in charge of the Seattle office—one of the two.

We had fallen heir to a priceless bit of testimony. Before the trial, FBI agents in Seattle had confirmed to me the fact of Sally's cooperation. This meant not merely that she had submitted to interviewing but that she had answered truthfully in their opinion. But the FBI refused to let its agents testify in a private lawsuit of this nature, and we could not compel their appearance. Schulman's testimony about what the FBI told *him,* had we offered it, would have been excluded as hearsay. Now the defense had inadvertently brought it out—a windfall for us.

The groundwork had been laid, and it was time for the plantiffs themselves to take the witness stand.

CHAPTER 9

SALLY GOLDMARK came forward with her quick, light step and took the oath.

The pressure that had weighed upon her for many months was at its height. She felt responsible for John's injury; the past error she had tried to outlive had returned, after all, to wound her husband.

I questioned Sally about her early life. She was tense at first but her natural vivacity soon came through. She told of growing up in Brooklyn, studying at the University of Wisconsin, and returning to New York to work when the Depression struck. It was there that she first became attracted to communism. "The unemployment problem in New York City was very severe," she testified. "It was something that was faced every day every place. And I was very concerned about why this thing had happened. . . ."

Sally was then about twenty-three years old. "I really felt at that time that the whole capitalist system had broken down as far as being able to provide gainful work, wages, to people." The Communist Party claimed it could bring economic justice and resistance to the spread of fascism. She took night courses at the Workers' School in Manhattan, but did not join the Party in New York. In 1935 she got a New Deal job with the WPA. Before she moved to Washington a friend told her to expect a call from someone who would ask her to join the Communist Party.

Sally settled in Washington with her roommate, another young woman who worked for the New Deal. Soon afterward Charles Kramer, an Agriculture Department official, sought them out and asked them to join the Party. He seemed "a very nice person, very well spoken, very interested in things that were going on." Sally and her roommate agreed to join, and began attending the meetings of a small group which convened once or twice a month at members' houses.

What happened at the meetings? "We talked about current events; we were given literature to read; we would discuss this. We would discuss our interests, jobs, and what we were doing." They did little else except to pay sizable dues, five to ten percent of their salaries.

Victor Perlo, another New Deal employee, led the meetings when Kramer was absent. The meetings were devoted mainly to talk and argument. Sally agreed with much, but not all, that the communists said.

Her New Deal jobs concerned unemployment problems and recreation for the poor. She had no access to classified information. In her communist group, Sally testified, she heard no discussion of espionage, nor of overthrow of the government, nor of any other unlawful project. Her membership had no effect on her work. Yet the affiliation was secret; no one outside the group, not even her sisters, knew of it.

In late 1941 Sally met John Goldmark. "And I came to respect him very highly as a person," she testified, "in his character, and I admired him a great deal." After he proposed marriage she told him of her secret membership.

> Q. Did you know at that time what his views about it were?
> A. Yes, I knew he was opposed to communism.
> Q. And what was his response to what you told him?

A. Well, I think it was the next day or the next evening he said he had thought about it for a long time and he felt that he loved me and that in spite of that he wanted to marry me and that he had complete faith in me as a person. And this meant a great deal to me.

They were married when John finished his Navy training in December 1942. Over the next few months she went to progressively fewer communist meetings, then lost interest entirely, and finally told Kramer she would attend no more. She dropped out of the Party and never went back.

After the war the Goldmarks moved west, and the new ranch life consumed her for several years. "I have no memory of doing anything but working very hard." The ranch was without electricity at first, and the two boys were very small.

In the spring of 1949 two FBI men came to the ranch house.

Q. And what did they want to know about?
A. They had come to see if I knew anything. They asked me if I had been a member of the Communist Party. And I told them I had been. They came to see me if I knew Mr. Alger Hiss.
Q. Did you?
A. Or Mrs. Hiss. No, I had never met them.

Sally told the FBI all she could remember about her communist associations in Washington.

Seven more years had gone by peaceably. Then Sally was subpoenaed to testify before the House Committee on Un-American Activities in Seattle. She was granted an executive session, appearing before only one congressman and the committee's chief counsel. At the defense's request we had obtained a transcript of her testimony from the committee in Washington. I placed it in evidence and read it to the jury. The congressman, apparently satisfied, had thanked Sally for her testimony and promised to write to her sons.

Sally told how, as the boys grew older, she was able to work in civic affairs. She was active in the Grange, the PTA, the Four-H Club, and the County Fair Board. She had never announced her past Communist Party membership to the people of Okanogan. "I had done something in good faith many years ago," she now testified. "I had my reasons at the time. I had changed my mind completely. I wanted to live a very constructive life. . . ." Since moving west she had never heard from the Communist Party or anyone representing it.

Her husband, Sally testified, had never had any connection with communism or with the Party or any front organization.

> Q. Has he ever expressed any sympathy for any such thing that you have ever heard?
> A. No, none.

Harmon began the cross-examination with what amounted to a threat: ". . . I am sorry that I am compelled by the necessity of this lawsuit to ask you questions which pry into your past, which examine your motives and which question both your veracity and your loyalty. You do understand that I have no choice but to play my part in this lawsuit just as you have no choice to play your part?"

Sally was upset, and at first her answers showed it.

> Q. What is your name, Mrs. Goldmark?
> A. My name is Sally Goldmark.
> Q. Isn't your real name Irma?
> A. Yes, I was christened Irma, but I haven't used this name for many, many years. It is a distasteful name to me and I hate even to use it. I am sorry.

Harmon launched a painstaking review of her past life. He probed for details about her college years, her jobs in New York, her life in Washington. He jumped from one period to another and back again, heedless of time sequence. What was she being trained for during her years in the "Perlo-Kramer cell"? Nothing, Sally answered.

> Q. You didn't have a Communist Party card then at any time during that eight-year period, did you?
> A. No.
> Q. Well, isn't it a fact that that was the hallmark of the communist underground rather than the communist open party?
> A. I don't know if that was the fact. I just know I joined the Communist Party on my own volition and say so and I left them under the same condition.
> Q. Well, you do know that you were not in the open Communist Party?
> A. I do know that, yes, certainly.

Sally's temperament was poetic and passionate, not precise. She was a strong witness in her obvious sincerity and concern for other people; her weakness was recollecting details. Eager to give the essential truth of every situation as she saw it, she was impatient of smaller points. Her committee testimony several years earlier had been given hurriedly, in tense circumstances, and with little chance of preparation. There were inconsistencies.

Sally had testified once, Harmon brought out, that the wife of a certain cell member did not belong to her communist group, another time that she was introduced as a member of it. She testified once that she saw Charles Kramer in New York in 1943, another time that she did not. On one occasion she said she lived at Chevy Chase when she stopped paying Communist Party dues; later she said it was Bethesda. In her deposition she said she had lived in

New York with the young woman who later arranged for her to be contacted by the Party in Washington, but at trial she said this was an error. Once she said that a certain New Deal official was the first man she asked for a job in Washington, another time that he was not. None of these inconsistencies was important in itself, but the total effect could be damaging.

Harmon turned to the campaign-year coffee hours where Sally had told friends and supporters of her past.

> Q. Did you tell any of these meetings the nature of the communist cell that you had belonged to, Mrs. Goldmark?
> A. No, I didn't go into any detail. I told them why I had joined the group, why I had left.

Had her communist group been essentially a study club? "That was its major function," Sally answered.

In her pretrial deposition Sally had refused at first to name those she had known as Communist Party members. She had finally done so on condition that the knowledge be limited to the lawyers, who, as officers of the court, were obliged not to misuse the information. Harmon now brought this out. "I was more than willing for you to do any discovery which you can about anything in my whole life," Sally explained. "But I was very anxious in my own mind that people that I would name to you would be harassed, intimidated and be cruelly torn apart in their family and community life as I had been. . . ."

In court there was no privilege which would entitle Sally to withhold her former associates' names. In reply to Harmon's questions, she gave them. The newsmen in court agreed to print no names except those of Kramer and Perlo, who had already been publicly identified; the others were not newsworthy and their publication could only cause needless harm.

Harmon asked if Sally's group discussed "the historic mission of the Communist Party to destroy capitalism in the United States." No, she said.

> Q. Well, were there any discussions of the fact that that was the Communist Party line?
> A. To destroy the United States government?
> Q. Yes.
> A. I think that their position was that eventually they would overthrow it to have some type of communist regime but it was an entirely theoretical thing.
> Q. Well, of course, it would have to be theoretical until it was an accomplished fact, Mrs. Goldmark?
> A. Yes, but there was no activity in any shape or form to make it an accomplished fact.

This part of the communist teaching had been only "a remote tenet of the old doctrine," Sally said. "And I didn't go along with it and it wasn't of any immediate consequence in the situation in my group."

Did she still maintain that she had not been a traitor, had done nothing wrong?

> A. Yes. I think I made a mistake.
> Q. Well, did you feel the other way, that perhaps you might have been doing your country a service by working in the Communist Party for its ends?
> A. I thought in the beginning that way. I thought I was being a big help. I was mistaken.

Had she been fully committed to the Party? "I would say that I was not totally committed, no, as a person."

Hour after hour the cross-examination attack went on.

Hadn't Sally been taught that she was free to lie whenever it would serve the Communists' purposes? "No, I was never taught that." Was it her position that the voters had no right to know of her past membership? She did not think it was pertinent, Sally answered. "This did not involve the legislator who was a candidate; it involved his wife."

Harmon focused on a particular day: July 4, 1936. How had she spent the holiday? She did not remember. Did she dine that day at Herzog's Seafood Restaurant on a balcony overlooking the Potomac River? She did not recall. At last the reasons for these questions emerged: Harmon accused Sally of having dined that day with Mr. and Mrs. Alger Hiss. She denied it: "I don't know these people personally at all," she answered.

The defense, it appeared, must have evidence which it believed would connect Sally with Hiss, the former State Department official who had been convicted of perjury in denying that he had passed secrets to the Soviet Union. Hiss was almost universally seen as a traitor; a connection with him, however fleeting and unimportant, could be devastating.

That evening we helped Sally search her memory again about her life in Washington. She remained positive she had never known Hiss or his wife.

The next day Harmon leaped ahead a quarter century. Why had Mrs. Goldmark opposed the showing of *Operation Abolition*? "I was not opposed to showing the film," she answered. "I was opposed to showing the film without some further explanation." Why had she written to radio station KPQ in Wenatchee to protest a public service feature called "Know Your Enemy"? "It was a series of broadcasts which I thought were not factual, valid, charging that the National Council of Churches was a communist organization or a communist front. I thought that this was not true. . . ."

Sex—another communist weapon, in the defense's view— entered the cross-examination.

Q. Did you ever discuss in your cell the views of the Communist Party in the United States with respect to what was referred to as "free love"?
A. No, I never heard of such discussion.
Q. Never discussed? Isn't it true, Mrs. Goldmark, that at that time in the Communist Party in the United States that the communist position with respect to sex was that there wasn't anything particularly objectionable in free love, including sexual relations between unmarried men and women?
A. I have no such knowledge. We had no personal discussion of this nature whatsoever.

Had Sally told John's political supporters that she had associated with two Party members, Kramer and Perlo, who "had been engaged in communist espionage activities during the same period of time?" She had not known of such a thing. "I knew they had been so accused," she answered.

At last Harmon released the witness. In redirect examination Sally explained a passage, which the defense insisted on misreading, in her testimony before the House Committee on Un-American Activities. It had occurred when the committee counsel argued momentarily with her statement that the cell had no action program.

Q. Now in your Committee testimony, page 33, the questioner said "You see, we have got top espionage people here in the cell" and you answered "Yes, I know." What did you mean by that; what did you mean?
A. I knew they had been accused of something like that.

Q. Did you know anything more than that?
A. No.
Q. When did you learn [of that]?
A. Sometime in the early fifties.

Sally would not make a breast-beating apology for having been a communist. "I don't like to use the words 'make amends' because I don't think one can always do that," she said. "But I certainly have tried consciously to make up for what I considered to be a wrong and a mistake."

The Okanogan weather was at its worst. A freezing fog hung low over the valley, blotting out the sun. We walked over snow and ice to the courthouse.

John Goldmark came to the stand knowing that he would be the most important witness. If he failed, all our work would be in vain. We had decided that R. E. Mansfield should question him; the closer we could tie John and his cause to the county, the better.

In a clear voice that carried easily to the back of the room, John told of his New York family, his childhood, and his eastern schooling. The jury was watching him closely. A farmer wearing a suit does not look like a city man; he looks like a farmer dressed up for an occasion. John, sixteen years a rancher, looked that way.

Q. How did you come to be a rancher, Mr. Goldmark?

A. Well, like a great many of my generation the war broke me loose from the path of life I had maybe started in, in a way, and I began thinking of new things. I was thinking about farming and I had become tremendously interested in the West. I had read some books that gave me some of the history of the exploration of the West, the pioneers, the country, the traditions of the West. These things all appealed to me.

118

John told of volunteering for the Navy at the outset of World War II, of taking an OPA job in Washington while awaiting his call to active duty, and of meeting and marrying Sally.

From the Philippines, John said, he wrote to his wife of his decision to become a farmer. When they made the move after the war he was twenty-nine years old. In his enthusiasm he bought the ranch on the Indian reservation before Sally saw it. "She wanted to see it," he testified, "and I said, 'All right, we will go back and look at it.' We got up here. There had been a snow and the wind had blown; the roads had drifted shut. So we didn't get to see it. She didn't get to see it until the first of March."

They moved up with their two sons, the younger of whom was only a few months old. John was ignorant of ranching, but luckily there was a hired man named Robert Wilson. "He did everything. He was probably one of the reasons that I was able to survive as a rancher." From Wilson, John learned about cattle, grain, machinery, plumbing, and electrical work.

> Q. Do you have any assets that are not involved in your farming operation?
> A. No.
> Q. Is this the way you make your living?
> A. This is the way I make my living.
> Q. The only source of your income?
> A. Yes.

When we adjourned for the day, John's quick and firm answers, his deep integrity, had already begun to tell. The next morning Mansfield returned briefly to his life in the East:

> Q. . . . did you following your marriage to Sally

discuss with her her membership in the Communist
Party?

A. Very little.

Q. Did you at that time ask her to leave the
Communist Party?

A. No, I didn't, Mr. Mansfield. I felt that she
was sure to leave it and that it was a kind of a situation
where if I put pressure on her or tried to persuade her it
would be less effective than if I simply left it to her best
judgment.

He told of obtaining his Navy security clearance in 1951,
when he was "invited to visit at the district headquarters in
Seattle and spent the better part of a day talking with officers from Naval Intelligence."

Q. At that time and in that connection did you
make a disclosure to them concerning Mrs. Goldmark's
former membership in the Communist Party?

A. Yes, I did. They started asking me questions
and it reached a point where I could see that full
frankness would make it important to state what I knew
about Sally and I did. And their subsequent questioning
indicated that they were well aware of what information
the government had about my wife.

John described his work as a legislator, and real issues
emerged from the fog of generalities spread by the defendants. He had drafted bills which compensated Okanogan
County for taxable land flooded by the pools of new down-
stream dams on the Columbia; helped to save a program of
psychiatric aid for troubled children; doubled the number
of parks in his district, with the help of Hallauer and others;
worked to raise rural schools to the higher standards pre-
vailing in the cities; sponsored economies in the public assistance program; and defended public power from several
attacks. All this was not ideology but the practical work of

120

government. John explained the bill which the defendants repeatedly invoked in charging him with a procommunist voting record:

Q. There has been some testimony in this case heretofore concerning the American Heritage Bill. I wish you would tell the jury what that is and when it was considered and the legislative history of it, please?

A. The American Heritage Bill was offered in the 1961 session, provided for setting up a commission to advance the study of American institutions, history and so forth. It did not provide an appropriation. It provided that this commission could accept money from private groups. I am not sure if it would have been constitutional for that reason. But in any case from the way in which the sponsorship came and the background at that time of agitation with "Communism on the Map" and other things, I was concerned that this commission would become a means of expressing an extreme view about our American heritage, of attacking anybody who doesn't agree with the people who were supporting the commission.

When the bill came up on the floor of the House I attempted to test this concern of mine and I offered an amendment to make this commission which was to administer the study of Americanism consist of the presidents of our five state institutions of higher learning and the State Superintendent of Public Instruction. The supporters of the bill beat down my amendment. And I therefore did not support the bill on the floor of the House. I think it did pass the House but I think about thirty others voted with me against it. That was why I opposed it.

Goldmark expected there would be an attack on his loyalty from the time he learned that a far-right movement was starting in Okanogan County. During the 1962 campaign, he said, he told supporters "the facts about Sally's connection with the Communist Party. I told them they could tell that to anybody who raised the issue. I was trying to meet this issue on the level on which it was being raised which was the level of private conversation primarily."

Q. Would you then describe the nature of the campaign for re-election that you did pursue?

A. I tried primarily to base my campaign on what I thought were the problems facing this legislative district in the State of Washington and to set forth what stands I took on those issues, what experiences I had to deal with them. I was aware of all these rumors and things and I did try indirectly to answer them in my campaign leaflet.

Mansfield ended the examination by taking phrases from the libels to ask John the truth of every charge against him. The answer came with quiet conviction.

Q. Mr. Goldmark, in the Washington State legislature did you invariably vote with the extreme leftists?

A. I don't think—no, I don't think I invariably voted with anybody. I don't think—well there weren't people there that I would consider extreme leftists.

Q. In the legislature did you sponsor measures that were designed to socialize our economy and convert our government into a welfare state?

A. Certainly not.

Q. Did you in your campaign for the legislature at home deceive the people with high-sounding phrases while concealing your true political philosophy?

A. I certainly did not.

Q. Have you ever belonged to a Communist Party front?

A. No.

Q. Are you or have you ever been a tool of a monstrous conspiracy, a communist conspiracy?

A. No.

Q. Were you sent to the Okanogan County country, a rural area, by communists to run for the legislature?

A. Certainly not.

On cross-examination Harmon attacked at once by trying to tie John to his wife's former communist affiliation.

Q. I assume that during that time you came to know your wife and her thoughts and ideas as well as any man can really ever understand any woman, would you say that is correct?

A. You have stated it as sort of a hesitant proposition and on that basis I would certainly agree.

Q. Do you think it is possible that your wife could have remained a member of the Communist Party for all of these years that you have been married to her and keep that—or under Communist Party discipline— and keep that a secret from you?

A. I think it is not possible. She is not that kind of a person.

Harmon again launched a detailed search of the past, shifting unpredictably one time period to another. John had known Kramer and Perlo in Washington, but Sally never told him they were among her fellow communists until their names appeared in print in the 1950s. How often had Sally attended communist meetings after their marriage? "I have no knowledge at all," John answered. They lived outside Washington and she often stayed late in town for one reason or another.

Harmon tried an attack on Goldmark's ability as a rancher. How much was invested in his place? About $60,000 at the start, John said, and about $30,000 since. How long had it taken him to learn the ropes? "To learn to where I didn't feel that I needed somebody to lean on took me ten years or more." These facts, the defendants apparently believed, showed that an outside sponsor must have been involved.

The defense had promised to prove John became embroiled in a controversy over communism immediately on entering politics in 1951. Harmon asked about the Young Democrats' platform the year Goldmark became president.

> Q. Isn't it a fact that that particular platform advocated amendment of the Smith Act and repeal of the McCarran Internal Security Act?
> A. I really couldn't answer that question positively. My general recollection is that the position was that some features of both of those acts and some of the political atmosphere of the country at this time, particularly with reference to Senator McCarthy, was causing a climate in which free speech was being endangered.
> Q. And you took an active part in the debate over those planks of the platform, did you not, Mr. Goldmark?
> A. I remember making one speech. As I recall it had to do with free speech. And it was approximately to the same effect as the talks that Congressman Jackson and Congressman Mitchell had made to us at the dinner preceding that debate that there was a real problem of free speech at that time in this country.

The more Harmon probed into the past, the more clearly John's candor and intelligence came through. When Sally was subpoenaed by the Committee on Un-American Activities, did she ask to be heard in a private rather than an open session?

> A. I think she did. And I would like to explain it.
> Q. Yes.
> A. —a little if I could. Her first concern was in what position this would put her with reference to the

FBI and so she went and talked to them first. And I
think the general feeling was that the less publicity the
better.

Q. At least you mean this is what she told you
the FBI told her?

A. I was there at that meeting.

In 1949 two FBI men had walked several miles through
snow to see Sally at the ranch. John sat through the first
of her several interviews with them. Until then he had known
"very little" of his wife's Communist Party activities. Had
it not occurred to him the FBI believed she had belonged
to an important underground cell in Washington? No, he
said.

Q. Well, you knew at that time, did you not, Mr.
Goldmark, that Alger Hiss, Charles Kramer and Victor
Perlo, among others, had been named as members of an
underground cell in Washington, D.C. during the 1930s,
did you not?

A. No, I don't think I knew that. I knew that
Hiss had been accused of something and that this was a
very big, dramatic case. I knew that Perlo and Kramer
had had their names in the news but I don't think I knew
details.

Harmon leaped ahead to the 1962 campaign. To the defense John's foreknowledge that an attack would be made
on him was sign of guilt.

Q. . . . what made you think there would be
such an attack made on you?

A. I have studied a lot of American history, Mr.
Harmon, and I was particularly aware of the fact that in
the early '50s there was a tendency to use an issue of
communism against anybody who was at all liberal. And
when I saw this I recognized it as a revival of this

attempt to discredit everybody you disagree with by calling them communists.

    Q. . . . What made you conclude that there would be or might be an attack on you on the subject of communism in the next election? Was that it?

    A. Simply the fact that I am a liberal Democrat.

Harmon attacked John's opposition to the 'anticommunist movement," taken as another sign of communist sympathy. Why had he opposed *Communism on the Map*? "My conclusion was that it was full of a tremendous number of factual errors. And that based on those factual errors it attempted to build an entirely false picture of the world, to scare Americans and make them distrust their own government." Had he not charged in speeches that the anticommunist movement is similar to fascism and Nazism? "I have charged in speeches that this is totalitarian, that it is like communism and fascism."

"Are you a member of any church organization?" Harmon asked suddenly. "No," John answered. Mansfield objected to this as irrelevant, and was sustained; but the answer had been given.

Did Goldmark wholeheartedly support the "citizens' rights" planks of the 1962 Democratic platform? Yes; he was at the convention where they were adopted. Did he know that the delegate who wrote them had been publicly identified in sworn testimony as a member of the Communist Party? "I haven't the slightest idea," John answered.

The barrage of questions went on. In early 1962 the Methow Grange considered a resolution asking the legislature to outlaw the Communist Party. John appeared at the meeting and spoke against it.

    Q. Did you tell the people at that Methow Grange

meeting that your wife had been a member of the
Communist Party for years?

A. No.

Q. Did you make any reference at all to that
subject—your wife and communism?

A. No.

John summed up his talk to the Grange. Any espionage
threat the communists might pose could be handled by the
government intelligence agencies. As a domestic political
force the communists were negligible. "And then I told them
some of the things in the world where I thought communism as represented by Russia and China was a great danger
to us and some of the things that the United States was
trying to do to offset Russian and Chinese influence and
how they could contribute and help out with such things.
I think I mentioned the Peace Corps among other things. I
tried to suggest what I thought were more constructive ways
in which they could help to protect this country from the
total menace of communism."

Q. Told them that they were all wrong in their
belief that communism was a serious internal menace to
the United States?

A. A serious internal menace that could be
combated by vigilantes, yes.

Q. Well, what have you done in opposition to
communism since you came to Washington?

A. Mr. Harmon, I have done the most I possibly
could to support what I think is the opposition to
communism which is the development of the United
States as a free country in which political discussion
between the two major parties can be carried on without
hatred and suspicion. . . .

The defense saw communism permeating John's views.
But wherever they probed, he responded with a clear ex-

planation. Challenged on his opposition to the House Un-American Activities Committee, he said: ". . . in a great many cases people were identified who had left the Communist Party, who had no particular connection with anything important. And yet these people were in effect publicly punished by being identified. Now this isn't just my view, this is a position taken by Justice Black of the U.S. Supreme Court that the effect—the overall effect of the committee's activities has been to publicly punish people without the right of the judicial process, without the rights that they have when they are tried."

Harmon's best points were scored on John's persistent silence about his wife throughout his political career. Senator Hallauer had urged a public announcement early in the campaign; John had made none. Another friend had warned Goldmark that his enemies were going to print a charge that Sally had been in the Communist Party; John had thanked him for the information without bothering to tell him whether the charge was true or false.

On redirect Mansfield tried to put this point to rest. "The first question," said Goldmark, "is did I or did Sally and I have a duty to disclose without being asked her former Communist Party membership to various people.

"Now I feel we did have a duty at least when asked to disclose it to these agencies of our government that were concerned with security matters. And we did, to the FBI, to the House Committee, to Naval Intelligence.

"The further question is whether we had a duty to tell the public generally without being asked. I felt that since we had told the people in government whose primary concern it was, since it never had any effect on the way I thought or any positions that I had in public affairs, since it would cause Sally pain, and since I felt that the FBI was not anxious to have an informant publicized, I felt that it was not up to us to volunteer this to the public.

"Another question is whether or not my political opponents had a right to bring out the fact that Sally had been a member of the Communist Party a long time ago at any time as part of a political campaign.

"On that I felt it was partly a question of taste. They did have a right to bring it out but they did not have a right to say falsely that she had been a traitor or that I was under communist influence."

To justify a later instruction to the jury on pain and suffering as an element of damages, we had to elicit testimony that the libels had hurt. On this John was incapable of anything but understatement. "Mr. Goldmark," Mansfield asked, "did you personally sustain real suffering as a result of the libels and slanders sued on in this action?" "It was a very painful process for me," John answered. "What is your observation of the same matter with respect to your wife?" An objection was overruled. "My observation was it was very hard on her." He would say no more on the subject.

John had come through superbly as a witness, gaining stature every hour he was on the stand. I announced that the plaintiff rested.

Our case in chief, except for the blow of President Kennedy's assassination, had gone well. Yet the defense was doggedly insisting on Goldmark's guilt, and the memory of Harmon's shocking opening statement remained.

Now a question hung over the courtroom: how would the defendants "prove" their charge that the Goldmarks, whom Mansfield and I knew as devoted friends, were in fact secret communists?

CHAPTER 10

THE DEFENSE began with Russell Will, the county sheriff, a large, ruddy man with the look of an ex-athlete. A Democrat, Will had run on the same ticket with John in past years, but worked against him in the 1962 primary. Now he testified to having visited the Goldmarks' house at Olympia during the 1961 legislative session. At dinner an argument arose over *Communism and the Map,* then being widely shown. "I remember I brought up Cuba and Korea and the San Francisco riot," said the sheriff. But "Mr. Goldmark, supported by Mr. Klein [another legislator present], never felt that there was any external or internal threat of communism. And it was certainly not for me to argue with them."

Wicks asked whether Mr. or Mrs. Goldmark had said anything about what would happen to the sheriff if he did not go along with their views on legislation. Mrs. Goldmark had made a remark, Will answered. What was it? "That she would put me in a cocoon." "That she would do what?" "That she would place me in a cocoon," said the sheriff.

This odd statement attributed to Sally, although unclear, sounded like a threat. The defense had shown the jury that the popular county sheriff was on their side. Wicks sat down.

Cross-examining, I brought out that Will had taken one or two drinks during his evening in Olympia. It followed that the puzzling "cocoon" statement he thought he recalled might simply reflect a misunderstanding.

At that point the standard cross-examination would have ended. Doubt had been cast on observation and memory. The rule of thumb is to ask an adverse witness only those questions to which a favorable answer seems certain. But the sheriff struck me as honest, and I decided to venture onto the ice.

> Q. You took no part in any campaign which accused Mr. Goldmark of being a communist, did you?
> A. No, sir.
> Q. Even though you were opposing him in that election?
> A. Yes, sir.
> Q. Did you know such a campaign was going on? ,
> A. Yes.
> Q. Pardon?
> A. Yes.
> Q. Were you asked to take part in it in some way?
> A. Yes, sir.
> Q. And you refused, didn't you?
> A. Yes, sir.

So far, so good. The sheriff in rejecting an invitation to take part in the smear campaign had impliedly rejected the libels themselves. The next questions were directed to his natural pride in working closely with the FBI.

> Q. Now you are the chief law enforcement officer for the State of Washington in this county, are you not?
> A. Yes, sir.
> Q. And you are in charge among other things of enforcing the laws against subversives?
> A. Yes, sir.
> Q. And in that connection, or in connection with

your law enforcement work generally, do you cooperate with the FBI?

Q. Definitely, yes.

Q. How many years have you been doing that?

A. Seven.

Q. Seven years. And both you and Mr. Goldmark have lived here in the county those whole seven years, haven't you?

A. Yes, sir.

Yet, the sheriff testified, he had never heard or seen anything purporting to connect Goldmark with communism until the 1962 campaign. We had gained more ground.

One can often sense a favorable rhythm in the answers of an adverse witness. I decided to risk one more step: with luck, the sheriff might agree with us on the very issue the jury was to decide. "You don't believe it to be true that Mr. Goldmark is connected with communism, do you?" I asked him. "I have no proof, sir," he answered firmly. "And you have never seen any, have you?" I followed up. "No," said Will.

The sheriff had become, in effect, our witness. He was surely familiar with all that had been said and written against Goldmark in the campaign; and he had now told the jury that to him it was "no proof."

Loris Gillespie resumed the stand to deny having made the attacks on John our witnesses attributed to him. This put him in a weak position on cross-examination. Was Miss Pardee mistaken, then, in her testimony? Yes. Was Mr. McIntosh also mistaken? Yes. And Mr. Schulman as well? Yes. And Mr. Hamilton? Yes. With his stream of "sirs" and demonstrative politeness he insisted he had no connection with any attack on Goldmark.

Next came a series of witnesses who believed Goldmark had tried to disarm the country in the face of communism.

Five local citizens, most of them ranchers, testified to what John had said at Grange meetings in early 1962. He had, according to them, opposed a resolution to outlaw the Communist Party; resisted another resolution urging the right of federal employees, such as Don Caron, to oppose communism in their spare time; said Gus Hall should be allowed to speak to students anywhere he wanted; urged the recognition of Red China; and scoffed at the notion that communism posed a real threat to America. There was open resentment of his education. "Mr. Goldmark is a brilliant speaker with a wonderful education, which I don't have," one farm wife testified, "and I would hate to try to comment on what he said more than just to say what my impression was, is all I would say."

One rancher testified that for years Goldmark's reputation was that of being "soft on communism." Another claimed John had said "that we should not be concerned with communism and that we should let it be up to the government to be concerned, that we was not qualified." A local man who had devoted his spare time to working for the anticommunist cause testified that, although a Democrat, he had been asked to leave a gathering of Goldmark's supporters during the 1962 campaign. The sinister implication was weakened by his admission that he was a member of the Birch Society, and an opponent of Goldmark's, at the time.

Joe Haussler, a trim, affable man who had defeated Goldmark in the primary election, testified that the television documentary "Suspect" had unfairly implicated him; the film's editors, he said, had run two of his answers together and left out a qualifying sentence. His desire to disassociate himself from the libels won further ground for us. In 1961 he and his campaign manager had visited Canwell in Spokane. After they returned there was a meeting of some of the local Democratic leaders. "It was the consensus of the meeting, wasn't it," I asked him, "that there was no question about the loyalty of Mr. or Mrs. Goldmark?" "I think that is right," said Haussler.

A silver-haired, stout, dignified old gentleman came to the stand. He was Dr. Alfred O. Adams, a Spokane physician and veteran Republican state representative. There had always been rumors about Goldmark in the legislature, Dr. Adams said; his reputation for loyalty was "questionable." The judge allowed him to characterize John's voting record. "It was towards the left," Dr. Adams said. Was he suggesting, I asked on cross-examination, that Goldmark was a communist? "No, sir," he answered.

But three more state legislators appeared for the defense. Margaret Hurley, a Spokane Democrat, had been one of a small group who joined the Republicans to form a majority coalition in the House of Representatives. She spoke of John with obvious dislike. Goldmark had been "extra liberal," she said; by 1961 his reputation was "questionable." But she went too far. Those on the "left," she said, "promote extensions in government control, fiscal irresponsibility, embarrassing those who uphold morality and patriotism and things that are decent." How many legislators of that stripe were there in the House? "Too many," said Mrs. Hurley.

Elmer Huntley, a farmer and Republican state legislator, told of "rumblings in the corridors and men's lounge at times as to actually whether [Goldmark] was rather socialistic." Did these discussions raise questions about his loyalty? "I am sorry to say that they did." Such testimony could be damaging; we must show that these rumors were nothing more than the small talk of disgruntled opposing legislators.

Q. Did Mr. Goldmark ever do or say anything
over there, Mr. Huntley, that were really any different

than other people of liberal, Democratic persuasion did or said?

A. No, I don't think he did.

Q. Other legislators are also subject to rumor and gossip from time to time, are they not?

A. Yes. Yes, all the time, in fact.

Q. To some extent at least this is one of the conditions of political life, isn't it?

A. Yes, it is.

Representative Richard Morphis, another Republican and operator of a Spokane nursing home, quoted Goldmark as having said, "Oh, pro-America. American Legion. Those super-patriotic groups, they give me a pain in the neck."

The defense was proceeding slowly, with plodding, methodical examination of every witness. The sheer passage of time—the widening distance between the jury and our evidence—could hurt us. There were signs that the delay was intentional. Christmas recess lay ahead, and the defense lawyers told the court they would probably ask for an unusually long one—a continuance of the trial—because their out-of-state witnesses were prevented by the holiday rush from getting airplane reservations to the Northwest. That night I telephoned a travel agent in Seattle and next morning reported the results in open court: between Seattle and New York, Chicago, Denver, and Los Angeles there was space available on every flight of every airline through the month of December. Nothing more was heard about a continuance.

Harmon offered the film *Communism on the Map* into evidence. "I think we have a right to show 'Communism on the Map,'" he argued, "for the very reason that the Communist Party is itself opposed to it . . . and I think it is one of those small factors that might well be probative in the minds of these jurors in making the determination whether either Mr. or Mrs. Goldmark are or are not communists." Defense lawyer Kimball added that "every challenged statement has been documented and researched and we will present what we feel is proof that it is factual."

We objected. The film was notoriously potent in stirring up irrational fear; numerous authorities had criticized it as inaccurate; therefore, no inference could be drawn from the Goldmarks' criticism of it. "I suggest respectfully," I said, "that the motive for offering it is to try to convince this jury not that the Goldmarks are communists but there is a creeping communist threat in every country in the world, including this one, and to get this jury exactly in the same frame of mind that many people were gotten into in 1962 here in the county."

Judge Turner compromised. The defendants could place in evidence a transcript of the sound track, but not the film itself. Both sides could present evidence "within reasonable bounds" on the accuracy of the sound track's content.

Harmon called the name of Hazel Niendorff. A tiny, pale woman came forward carrying a bundle of documents. She was the widow of a Seattle newspaperman. Before her marriage, she said in a soft voice, she had done "library and research work." In 1961 she grew interested in the controversy over *Communism on the Map* and set out to learn the truth for herself. "I got a tape recording of the commentary and then taking it paragraph by paragraph I started searching for the documentation on it through reports of Congress, government investigation committees, government publications, books on the subject, newspapers and periodicals and so forth."

The study consumed all her time for six months. She had numbered each paragraph of the sound track transcript and then laboriously compiled footnotes listing "sources" for it.

Her work possessed the trappings of scholarship, and the judge allowed her to testify as an expert.

Painstakingly, one statement at a time, Mrs. Niendorff testified that each assertion in *Communism on the Map* was true, and cited sources. Many of the statements were wildly inaccurate and the "sources" meaningless; but would the jury know that?

I cross-examined her gently. The sound track said, and she confirmed as true, that "undoubtedly United States recognition saved the USSR from financial collapse."

> Q. . . . I will ask you if it isn't a fact that the United States was the last important country in the world that gave recognition to the Soviet Union?
>
> A. I can't answer that without looking it up.
>
> Q. Do you not know that before the United States recognized the Soviet government it had already been recognized by Germany, Italy, France, Great Britain, Japan, China, Norway, Austria, Sweden, Greece, Turkey, Denmark, Mexico and other countries; do you know whether that is true or not?
>
> A. I still think it was up to us.
>
> THE COURT: He didn't ask you what you still thought. He asked you whether the facts asserted in his question were correct.
>
> THE WITNESS: I couldn't answer that without looking it up.

The film, and Mrs. Niendorff, treated socialist and communist regimes as being indistinguishable. Did she recall that six countries that joined in forming the NATO pact in 1949—Britain, Belgium, Iceland, Denmark, Norway, and the Netherlands—all had socialist governments at the time? "I haven't checked that angle on it," she said.

> Q. Do you not think that the overall effect of this film is to give people the idea that the United States is

encircled by communist countries and almost-communist countries?

A. Yes.

Q. Including our own allies?

A. Yes, I would say that situation is presented, yes, and I think it is true.

The defense called the news director of radio station KPQ, Wenatchee. As a public service KPQ had broadcast "Know Your Enemy," a daily five-minute talk by one Hurst Amyx of Tucson, Arizona. "It was a commentary on what he purported to be the threat of the communist influence to world freedom and American freedom, as well," said the news director. Amyx mailed the tapes up free of charge. The program went on for three weeks; then Sally Goldmark sent in a letter whose "general tenor was that the program was not something that could be carried as a public service, that it was not a factual program, that it had a tendency to create hysteria, and she asked that it be withdrawn." Similar letters came in from other people, and the program was dropped. The judge allowed into evidence the first twenty-one scripts in the series.

Waiting in the hall was Barbara Hartle, one of the country's best-known ex-communists. For years she had been a star government witness in Smith Act prosecutions and before the House Committee on Un-American Activities. The Goldmarks had never met her; she would testify not about them but as an expert on communists and their "party line."

We knew that witnesses of this nature would paint a terrifying picture of the Communist Party as a deadly apparatus whose secret agents were everywhere. By creating an atmosphere of subversion and peril, the defense would seek to frighten the jury into suspicion of John Goldmark. While the jury waited upstairs, the lawyers presented their arguments over whether such evidence should be received.

"The burden on the defense in this case," I told the court, "is to establish the plaintiffs are communists or at least they are communist sympathizers or agents or something of that nature. That is the issue in this trial. As I understand their approach they intend to try to do this by having some aspects of this so-called Communist Party line listed by a witness and then show that some beliefs or past actions of the plaintiffs conform to that. This is not a permissible way to prove that somebody is either a communist or a communist sympathizer and has never been done, to my knowledge, in any trial whether civil or criminal in the United States."

But the plaintiffs, Harmon replied, "are not quite in the same position as every other American, including Your Honor and everyone else in this courtroom. It is an admitted fact that Mrs. Goldmark was a member of the Communist Party for a substantial period of time." Furthermore, the testimony would cover not just adherence to the "party line" but the nature of life in the communist organization, the restrictions on marriage, and the methods of ending a Party membership.

Judge Turner ruled that the evidence would be admitted. The door was open to a repetition of the fright campaign of 1962.

The jury was brought in. Barbara Hartle entered the room and was sworn. Her deeply lined face implied some of the agony she had been through. We expected Mrs. Hartle, who had wildly named hundreds of people at federal committee hearings in Seattle some years earlier, to be a nervous and perhaps hysterical witness. Instead she spoke with a weary calmness, mechanically but with intelligence, peering steadily at counsel through thick eyeglasses. She was impressive.

As a young woman, she said, she had graduated Phi Beta

Kappa from Washington State University. In 1933 she joined the Communist Party at Spokane; she was then in her mid-twenties. She remained in the Party for twenty-one years, leading a life of dark duplicity. She had become a full-time paid organizer, and then organizational secretary of the Party's northwest district.

"What was the historic mission of the Communist Party," Harmon asked, "during this period from 1935 through 1943?" These were the years Sally Goldmark had testified she belonged to the Party.

The mission, said Mrs. Hartle, was and still is "to achieve world communism through the methods that had been developed specifically by Lenin and Stalin of achieving the proletarian revolution. . . ."

Mrs. Hartle had been a Party official when the Canwell Committee on un-American activities in the state of Washington began its work in 1948. "The attitude of the Communist Party," she said, "was to mount an all-out campaign for the defeat of the Canwell Committee and later Mr. Canwell himself." She herself had organized a picket line around the building where the committee's hearings were held. "It was to be a very large and a very noisy picket line which would attempt with its very size and noisiness to make it impossible to hold the hearings." In later years she had gotten to know Canwell. "And I found him to probably know as much about communism and communists in the State of Washington as anyone I had ever talked with and certainly a good deal more than I knew after my years in the Party."

Harmon asked a startling question. "What are the facts with respect to whether you ever met in Communist Party meetings in which Professor Melvin Rader was in attendance?"

The case of Melvin Rader, above all else, had hastened the Canwell Committee's downfall. Professor Rader was a

140

member of the philosophy department at the University of Washington. At the 1948 committee hearings one George Hewitt, a witness from New York, testified he had met Rader at a secret communist training school in New York State in the summer of 1938. Rader took the stand, denied the charge, and worked diligently to prove his innocence beyond any doubt. Bit by bit, through the records of a dentist, an optician, and the university library, and through the memories of friends, he assembled proof that he had spent the entire summer of 1938 in Washington State. One piece of evidence was missing: Rader and his wife had spent several summer days at a mountain retreat called Canyon Creek Lodge, and the crucial pages were missing from the lodge's guest register. A diligent *Seattle Times* reporter traced them to the Canwell Committee itself. Canwell, questioned by reporters, first denied knowing where the pages were, but, after many evasions and pressure from other state officials, finally produced them. They showed the Raders registered at the lodge at the time in question.

Rader was proclaimed innocent by the university president. Hewitt, the witness from New York, was charged with perjury but was never returned to the state to face trial. The *Times* reporter, Ed Guthman, won a Pulitzer Prize for his investigative reporting.

Canwell, in political eclipse, had lived for years with the frustrating memory of the Rader case, insisting it was "still open." After fifteen years he now sought to redeem himself through Barbara Hartle's testimony.

We objected: the jury was here to try the Goldmark case, not the Rader case. But Melvin Rader had served as state chairman of the American Civil Liberties Union, and on this basis Judge Turner allowed the testimony. Did Mrs. Hartle attend closed communist meetings with Professor Melvin Rader? "Yes, I did," she answered. "I knew Melvin Rader to be under Communist Party discipline. He was talked of and known to be a member of the Communist Party in the circles of the district that I was active in in Seattle." The significance of a closed Party meeting, she said, "is that the business of the Communist Party is taken there and the persons who are there are members of the Communist Party, all of them."

Melvin Rader, having gone through the ordeal of proving himself innocent, again stood accused.

Mrs. Hartle went on with her life story. In 1950 she dropped out of sight and joined "the underground Party." She lived in hiding, moving from one town to another. In 1952 the FBI arrested her at Eugene, Oregon, on a charge of violating the Smith Act. She went to trial in Seattle with six co-defendants; one committed suicide before the verdict; five, including her, were convicted.

While out on bail after the trial, Mrs. Hartle went to the FBI and said she would cooperate with it. Her cooperation was thorough; since 1954 she had testified repeatedly at Smith Act trials, deportation hearings, and congressional committee hearings.

"In your opinion," Harmon asked, "would it be possible for any person to have been a member of a secret underground cell in Washington, D.C., or anywhere else in the country from 1935 to 1943 and not be totally committed to communism?" Our objection that the question invited the witness to guess at the state of mind twenty-five years earlier of another person whom she had never met was overruled. "No, it wouldn't be possible," said Mrs. Hartle; all communists at that time were under rigid discipline.

Point by point, answering hypothetical questions, Mrs. Hartle testified that Sally's account of Communist Party life was "impossible." There was no such thing as an underground cell which had no action program. There was no such thing as leading a normal life while belonging to a cell with members engaged in espionage (an assumption which the court allowed Harmon to include in his questions). It was impossible to quit simply by dropping out or ceasing to attend meetings; the communists would force the member to come back by whatever means were necessary. It was impossible to be in an underground cell without learning that the Party aimed at destroying the United States government.

"In your opinion," asked Harmon, "could any person who was a member of a secret, underground communist cell in Washington, D.C. or elsewhere from 1935 to 1943 with Communist Party members then engaged in espionage have been married in December, 1942 without Communist Party approval and then have remained a member of the same secret, underground cell for almost another year without Communist Party approval?"

The question was designed to brand John Goldmark a communist at the time of his marriage.

"No," answered Mrs. Hartle. "A Communist Party member, especially in any type of underground cell or special work, or even in another branch of the Party, does not get married without the approval of the Party; certainly doesn't get married against the wishes of the Party."

She elaborated: "In the event the person had married someone that the Party thought was not suitable for the Party—a danger to it or someone who would take them away from the activity of the Party, then disciplinary measures would be taken."

If the jury believed this, our cause would be lost.

The film *Communism on the Map,* Mrs. Hartle said, was "basically accurate about the progress that communism had made in the world." *Operation Abolition* she knew even better: she had been in San Francisco as a House Committee on Un-American Activities witness when the anti-committee riots depicted in the film occurred. She saw a former Party colleague leading the protesters. The film was "as absolutely totally accurate as it possibly can be and not be the action itself in front of your eyes."

The Communist Party currently opposed the showing of both films, said Mrs. Hartle; it argued falsely that they were inaccurate and tended to create hysteria.

Was communism at present a serious internal threat to the United States? The court allowed an extended answer. The Party's program is "aimed at the overthrow of our government and is a part of an international conspiracy to set up communism on a world scale." Its members are still disciplined. "And even a relatively small number of communists will accomplish with their discipline and their system of organization and their activity a great deal more than the average person organized in average organizations."

At last the direct testimony ended. Mrs. Hartle had faced cross-examination many times; she had the knack of remaining cool whatever happened.

> Q. Mrs. Hartle, did I understand you to say that you had never met Mr. Goldmark?
> A. Yes.
> Q. And that you have never met Mrs. Goldmark?
> A. That is right.
> Q. You were a member of the Communist Party for twenty-one years, was it?
> A. Yes.
> Q. During several of those years you were an officer of the Communist Party here in the Northwest, is that right?
> A. Yes.

By her own testimony she had remained a communist through the harshest times of the cold war.

Q. . . . Whose side were they on in the Korean War?

A. The communists?

Q. Yes.

A. Well, they were on the sides of the communists—the North Koreans, the Chinese and the Soviet Union.

Q. And that is the side you were on yourself then?

A. Yes, it was.

Q. That is, you wanted the North Koreans and the Chinese communists to defeat the American troops in Korea?

A. Yes.

Q. Then you were still in the Communist Party as a professional member of it in 1952, is that right?

A. Yes.

Q. And in that year you were arrested and charged with violation of the Smith Act?

A. Yes.

She had claimed a desire to leave the Party long before the FBI picked her up. The sequence of events suggested otherwise.

Q. And at the end of the trial the court imposed a sentence on you to be confined in the penitentiary?

A. Yes.

Q. And that was in 1953?

A. Yes.

Q. Then were you still a communist after that sentence was imposed?

A. Yes.

Q. And were you still a communist still into 1954?

A. Yes.

Q. Then in 1954 you decided that you would cooperate with the FBI?

A. Yes.

I took up her charge against Melvin Rader. In 1954 she had appeared before the House Un-American Activities Committee in Seattle and named hundreds of people as communists. Her prolific testimony had gone on for days and caused a sensation at the time.

Q. At one point in your testimony you were asked to state how many people you had named up to then and you said that your estimate was more than 300 and then you went on to name a considerable number more, isn't that so?

A. Yes, that might—that may be so, I don't remember exactly.

Q. At the time you gave your testimony you were aware that Mr. Canwell had previously accused Mr. Rader of being a communist, were you not?

A. Yes, I think I was aware of it.

Q. You knew generally that Mr. Rader had resisted the charges against him and that there had been a controversy about it; you knew that, didn't you?

A. I didn't know it generally; I knew it specifically.

Q. One of the things you were to tell was people that you had attended closed meetings of the Communist Party with, isn't that right?

A. Yes, I was to name persons whom I could recall having met in closed meetings with.

Q. Yes. And despite the fact that you named several faculty members at the University of Washington, you did not name Professor Rader did you?

A. I don't think that I did.

I handed her a thick printed volume which contained all of her committee testimony, and asked her to search the index for Rader's name. It was not there. She had not mentioned him although his name, if he had in fact been a communist, would have been important above all others.

I asked for details about the "closed Party meeting" she claimed to have attended with Rader. Mrs. Hartle was vague; it took place, she said, in 1937 or 1938 at a house in either the Interbay or Ballard district in Seattle.

At noon Judge Turner ruled on a legal question he had been considering for two days. The film *Operation Abolition,* offered by the defense, would be received in evidence. When court resumed, the room was darkened and the motion picture shown to the jury. It showed militant witnesses shouting abuse at the committee while demonstrators surged and rioted outside. All opposition to the Committee on Un-American Activities, the film asserted, stemmed directly or indirectly from the Communist Party. It closed with a shot of the committee chairman, standing before the capitol building, urging Americans to awaken to their peril.

The motion picture undoubtedly frightened and disturbed the jury. But when I started to question Mrs. Hartle about who the film's critics were, I was cut off by a ruling from the bench: only the bare fact that it was "controversial" could be shown. Luckily the defendants had placed in evidence an ACLU pamphlet containing a *Washington Post* editorial on the film, which I now read:

"The movie presents a mendaciously distorted view of the demonstrations staged by a group of college students when the committee held hearings in San Francisco last May. This is a flagrant case of forgery by film. The film warps the truth in two important respects.

"First, it suggests as its main thesis that the demonstra-

tions were communist inspired and communist led. Diligent
inquiry has led us to a conviction that this charge is wholly
unjustified. . . ."

The editorial went on to quote the sheriff of San Francisco County as saying: "There was no act of physical
aggression on the part of the students." The witness on the
stand disputed the editorial; but it was now before the jury.

Mrs. Hartle would blandly admit contradictory testimony
given in earlier cases. She had sometimes offered a much
different version of the Party than the picture of unrelenting
evil she painted in Okanogan. In a 1955 deportation case
she had said that the Party in the 1940s had not advocated
forceful overthrow; that she had been free to disbelieve the
works of Marxism-Leninism she read at the time; and that
in the early forties the Party's support of the United States
Constitution was "unqualified."

> Q. Did you so testify?
> A. I might have. It sounds reasonable.

She tried to explain such conflicts by saying her earlier testimony referred to the Party's fluctuating "line," not its basic aims.

She had told the federal judge who was about to pass
sentence on her in 1953: "Never at any time did I understand that my work was designed to contribute in any way
to the overthrow of our government." Yes, she recalled
making that statement to the court. "And I must explain
that it was a Communist Party lawyer who helped me draw
up that statement—came up into the jail and had a conference with me in a conference room there and helped me to
draw that up and urged me to do so. . . ."

> Q. Was the statement you made to Judge
> Lindberg true or false?

A. It was true as the current political line of the Party was concerned. And it was false as far as the basic doctrines of the Party were concerned.

She acknowledged a similar statement to the federal judge: "I have always had a deep faith in our democratic institutions and the democratic heritage of the American people."

These words clashed sharply with her present account of herself as an iron-willed conspirator while in the Party. Harmon drew her explanation on redirect examination:

Q. Those statements that Mr. Dwyer just read you were made you say by you in court while you were still a member of the Communist Party, is that right?
A. Yes.
Q. They were just a Communist Party lie?
A. Yes.

Here was the essence of how professional ex-communist witnesses established credibility. It amounted to saying: "My admission that I used to be a liar proves that now I am telling the truth."

We had cross-examined Mrs. Hartle to bring out her professional witness standing, her unreliability, and the emotional makeup which had placed her first at one extreme, then the other, of the communist controversy. But we were uncertain how much we had gained; and more such witnesses, we knew, were coming.

CHAPTER **11**

ASHLEY HOLDEN was back on the stand. His jaunty
air had been banished by his lawyers. In subdued
tones he told his life story. The son of an old Okanogan County family, he started a weekly newspaper at the
little town of Chesaw in 1914, and married a hometown
girl. He was then a "Jeffersonian Democrat," he said.

Holden volunteered for the Army in World War I and
was on military police duty in Seattle during the 1919 strike
started by the "Wobblies," the Industrial Workers of the
World. He went on to be a newspaperman in Spokane.
Covering the Washington legislature in the thirties, he said
he saw communist cell meetings held under the capitol dome.
Busloads of communists had come down to stage unruly
demonstrations.

Later, in 1945, Holden covered the meeting that founded
the United Nations in San Francisco. "I saw Alger Hiss
turning the pages for Edward Stettinius, the Secretary of
State," he said, "standing at his elbow and putting the words
almost in his mouth when he addressed the conference of
the United Nations."

Holden was one of the state's most experienced political
reporters. He had returned to Okanogan County four years
earlier, and now published the weekly paper at Tonasket.

Defense lawyer Kimball read aloud Holden's articles on
Goldmark, pausing at the end of each paragraph to ask the

150

defendant's basis for writing it. Every word, Holden testified, was true:

> Q. . . . what was your opinion when you said ". . . all the while carefully concealing his true political philosophies which make him the idol of the pinkos and ultra-liberals which infest every session of the legislature"?
> A. He certainly had concealed from the voters of this state the fact that his wife had been a member of the Communist Party and the fact he was a member of the American Civil Liberties Union. Nobody knew that, strictly speaking.
> Q. What made you say he was the idol of the ultra-liberals which infest—
> A. . . . He would become the center of not only the left-wing lobbyists but those who were advocating left-wing policies at the legislature. He was the focal point. They rushed in on the floor to confer with him.

Goldmark had supported "legislative proposals and the program advocated by this monstrous conspiracy which has threatened the freedom of our country." He had "done everything he could to obstruct" the showing of *Operation Abolition* and *Communism on the Map,* two films "which would alert the people to the menace of communism."

Holden's new, temperate demeanor eroded when Mansfield began cross-examining. What had Goldmark done to obstruct showing of the films he named? Holden could think of nothing. What in Goldmark's legislative record showed communist sympathy? Surprisingly, Holden failed to improve on his first performance. Goldmark favored a graduated net income tax for the state of Washington—but so, he admitted, had every Democratic platform for years past. Goldmark had opposed the American Heritage Bill—but so had many others.

Q. What measures in the Washington State Legislature, Mr. Holden, were advocated by the communist conspiracy?

A. I will have to ask for clarification on that question. I covered sessions of the legislature for twenty years and I couldn't possibly answer that question.

Q. Just take the ones that Mr. Goldmark was in.

A. It is impossible to answer that.

Q. Why is it impossible to answer it, Mr. Holden? Is it because you don't know or because they didn't?

A. I can't again answer that yes or no. Do you ask me because he didn't or—I don't know.

Q. Yesterday you said Mr. Goldmark was sympathetic to the program advocated in the legislature by the communist conspiracy. Now what was the program advocated in the legislature by the communist conspiracy?

A. I don't recall any such testimony.

Q. You don't think you said that?

A. No.

Mansfield had forced an important retreat, but our troubles were compounding. A gray-haired, handsome man with a deeply lined face had been sitting in the audience. Harmon now called the name of John Lautner, and the man came forward to the witness stand.

Lautner was a former high official of the American Communist Party and, later, the principal ex-communist witness for the United States Department of Justice. He responded to questions with a strong voice and great assurance; speaking in a marked foreign accent, he attacked his job with the relish of a professor expounding his favorite subject. Within moments the jury was transfixed.

Lautner said he was born in Hungary in 1902. He came to America as a small child and became a naturalized citizen. In 1929 he joined the Communist Party in New York and remained in it for twenty-one years, most of the time as a professional functionary. In the 1930s he served as a communist organizer among Detroit auto workers, on a Cleveland newspaper, among the Hungarians of Canada, and among Manhattan's poor. Then he had been the Party chairman in West Virginia. It was the time of the "popular front." "The Party exploded during that period in the battle against fascism," said Lautner. He startled the jury with his position in World War II: while a communist he had served in American counterintelligence, "assigned to General Eisenhower's headquarters in Algiers in the psychological warfare branch and then later on transferred to Marshal Alexander's headquarters in Italy."

After the war Lautner rose in the Party hierarchy: he became a national committeeman and a member of the Party's national review commission. "That is the disciplinary arm of the Communist Party," he testified. "It has a responsibility to safeguard purity, Marx-Leninist purity of the Party to prevent any alien infiltration into the ranks of the Communist Party, to ferret out so-called enemy agents. . . . It is like the FBI of the Communist Party."

Lautner described the Party's structure in the nation's capital. "There were two separate organizations and there were Party members who worked in the federal government within one structure and open Party members in D.C. within an entirely different structure. They don't mingle."

In 1950 Lautner broke away from the communists when he was falsely accused of having become an FBI informant. It was a dramatic story that had spellbound many courtrooms. "I was assigned to go to Cleveland, Ohio," he said, "and to help the Midwest underground in its activities because, according to the information they gave me, they were far behind the organizational phase that we had in New York. I went to Cleveland. Instead of finding and meeting the coordinator there I find myself in a cellar. I was abused. I was undressed, stripped naked. I was accused of being an FBI agent and I practically ran from the place with my life in my hand—and that is how I got out of the Communist Party."

Lautner was expelled. He asked for a Party hearing to establish his innocence, but received no answer. His wife, who remained a communist, left him. For a few months he thought things over; then he volunteered his services to the FBI. He soon became a full-time government witness with his own office in the Justice Department building in Washington. For nine years he testified in Smith Act prosecutions, congressional hearings, grand jury proceedings, and Subversive Activities Control Board matters—about ninety cases in all. Now a lecturer and writer on communism, he spoke at colleges and seminars throughout the country.

By this time even Judge Turner appeared to be entranced. Lautner's expertise was established.

Harmon turned to life in the Communist Party. The communists, said Lautner, use any tactics they can get away with, without regard to morals or truth. "What helps the Party is the truth, is good." Anyone in the Party from 1935 to 1943—as Sally Goldmark had been—was under "very severe" discipline. A member could not just resign or drop out. One who argued with those in authority would be warned, punished, or even killed. Private lives were controlled—"at no time did the Party tolerate an anti-Party person associating with a Party person"—and political marriages were common. Lautner himself had married, on orders from the Party, a woman he had never met.

Harmon asked the question aimed at tying John Goldmark to the Communist Party in 1942.

Q. In your opinion could any person who was a member of an underground cell in Washington, D.C. or

elsewhere in the United States from 1935 to 1943, with
Communist Party members who were then engaged in
espionage during a part of that time, have been married
in December of 1942 without Communist Party approval,
and have remained a member of the same underground
cell for another year still without Communist Party
approval or disapproval?

An objection was unavailing.

> A. . . . First of all, I have to assure the Party
> and I have to go out of my way to do that, that the
> person I am associating with is sympathetic to my views
> and my activities and give every guarantee to my
> organization that there will be no difficulties out of this
> relationship as far as the Party is concerned. I have to
> give that assurance. And that assurance has to be very
> convincing.

Did the Communist Party still operate through fronts?
Yes, Lautner answered, and they were numerous. "Any organization that in the estimation of the Communist Party
can be used to advance the tactical line of the Communist
Party today is called a united-front organization." Similarly, being a communist today was not a question of membership. "Being a communist is a state of mental condition.
There is no Party membership anymore, since '48. There
are no books. Now you judge a person by what they do,
what they say and what is their background. You judge
their affinity toward an ideology or their rejection of an
ideology on the basis of their activities and what they say."
The communist menace today, Lautner testified, "is much
stronger than it ever was before." The external and internal
threats could not be separated. "The objective of the worldwide movement is the same for every communist." These
adversaries of our country "will endorse for technical reasons all kinds of noble issues that a lot of people are con-

155

cerned with"—but meantime they are "killing our soldiers in Vietnam [and] kidnapping people in Bolivia. . . ." In the United States "communist leaders can roam all over the country, invited to universities and speak to students. They are accepted in the labor movement again."

The "spearhead of this worldwide communist movement is a terrifically developed armed force that is a constant threat to our country," said Lautner. Peace was but a communist tactic. "They are beating for time." If subversion does not work in America, they "will use non-peaceful methods, force and violence."

Harmon asked about current Party projects. A major one, said Lautner, was to destroy the House Committee on Un-American Activities and the Senate Internal Security Committee. If that could be done, "they could have the road wide open again for communistic activities without any legal recourse." To this end the Party sought to discredit the film *Operation Abolition* and the anticommunist study groups which had sprung up across the country. Orders to implement this line in the United States had gone out from Moscow.

There was only one way to make a genuine break with communism: absolute cooperation with the FBI. And the defector must go to the agency, not vice versa. "When the Bureau has to come after you there is something wrong there already. You demonstrate. You go out of your way. You come to the authorities. 'Look, fellows, I made a mistake. I am sorry. I want to make amends for my mistake. What I did, I don't like it; I hate it. I want to do whatever I can against it. What can I do to you—what can I do to help you?'"

Only when that approach is taken, said Lautner, is the break with communist ideology complete.

The defense had subpoenaed books from the Goldmarks'

home library. Harmon placed one of them, *A Quarter Century of Un-Americana,* before the witness. It was the recent product of a communist-run publishing house, Lautner said, "a classical application of communists working together with other left-wingers in trying to destroy and ridicule a congressional committee." Harmon offered it in evidence; I objected, then leafed through the book quickly and changed my mind. "I think the way it has been characterized it would be more fair if the book were admitted, and we withdraw our objection."

The 1962 Democratic state platform was in evidence. Harmon pointed out to Lautner its planks favoring the elimination of loyalty oaths, amendment of the McCarran-Walter Immigration Act and of the McCarran Internal Security Act, and the ending of political restrictions on travel. Each of these planks, said Lautner, was the same as the Communist Party's position on the issue. Was communism, then, a political threat or not? "They used deception, fraud, cheating, lying," said the witness. "Anything goes as long as they can further their aim. That is the threat."

We had done advance research on the country's leading ex-communists. Of all of them Lautner was the least vulnerable to cross-examination based on his past life and earlier testimony. Professor Herbert Packer of Stanford, in his book *Ex-Communist Witnesses,* described Lautner as essentially a bureaucrat; when expelled from the Party he lost a job rather than a calling. He quickly got a job on the opposite side as a Justice Department witness. Lautner had faced cross-examination scores of times.

"Now you say," I asked him, "according to the communists that any organization is a front which can serve as a vehicle for the Communist Party to project its tactical program at the present time?" "That is correct," he answered.

Q. Those were your words?

A. That is correct.

Q. So by your words the Parent-Teachers Association could be a communist front?

A. If the communists can decide so and they can get away with it, why not?

Q. And the Grange could be a communist front?

A. Of course.

Again we had shown that the defense attack could be directed not just against John Goldmark and the ACLU, but everyone.

I read to the witness a description of the Communist Party given by Justice William O. Douglas of the Supreme Court: "It is safe to say that the followers of the creed of Soviet Communism are known to the FBI, that in case of war with Russia they will be picked up overnight as were all prospective saboteurs at the commencement of World War Two, that the invisible army of petitioners is the best known, the most beset and the least thriving of any fifth column in history. Only those held by fear and panic could think otherwise."

Lautner disagreed. "That is not thinking," he said. "And Justice Douglas also falls into this tendency to make a separation between the domestic variety of communist so-called, and the other communists, as such."

About half a million people, Lautner admitted, had passed through Communist Party membership since 1919, chiefly in the 1930s when the party appeared to be a champion against poverty, unemployment, and fascism.

Q. . . . . You are not asking the jury to believe that you can look into the minds of all of these thousands and thousands of people that belonged to the Party and tell what they were thinking or what their ideas were?

A. I didn't convey that. If you think that, then it shouldn't be. I judge them by their activities, what they say, what they do and what their past associations—these are the contributing factor in making the judgment.

Was not peaceful coexistence, condemned by him as a communist trick, the policy of our government under Presidents Truman, Eisenhower, Kennedy, and Johnson? Yes, said Lautner, but he disagreed with that policy.

It happened that John Goldmark's positions on world events had ordinarily *not* coincided with those of the Communist Party. I carefully drew from Lautner testimony describing the communists' position on major issues and events of the last quarter century. Then I asked a question based on the facts of John's public career:

Q. Now a man who was an adult for the last, let's say, twenty-five years, who was opposed to fascism and Nazism even during the Hitler-Stalin Pact, who was in favor of Lend-Lease to Britain at all times, who has always praised rather than criticized our economic system, called it "free enterprise" rather than "monopoly capitalism," who was in favor of the Marshall Plan, who was in favor of the Truman Doctrine, in favor of NATO, was against the communists in the Italian elections in 1948, was in favor of our intervention in the Korean War, was in favor of our side in all of the Berlin crises, was in favor of German reunification, was critical of Castro, was against the Progressive Party in the Wallace campaign and supported President Truman, would have been dead against the Communist Party line in each one of those points, isn't that true?

A. If he was an open and known communist by necessity he would have to support this line, all these actions that you enumerated. But as I said before if the person for—

Q. I am not asking you about a communist. I am

asking you about a man. Wouldn't such a man be against the Communist Party line on each and every one of those points?

A. Yes, generally speaking—if he was not a communist.

The answer exposed the utter fatuity of "communist line" reasoning: one who followed the Party line was procommunist; one who took opposite stands was a possible secret agent.

I read to Lautner a passage written by J. Edgar Hoover in 1961: "It is therefore almost inevitable that on many issues the Party line will coincide with the position of many non-Communists. The danger of indiscriminately alleging that someone is a Communist merely because his views on a particular issue seem to parallel the official Party position is obvious. The confusion which is thereby created helps the Communists by diffusing the forces of their opponents." Would he agree with that statement? "Of course," said the witness. "That is what we were talking about all morning."

I set out to show Lautner's pecuniary interest in communism, which had been the source of his income, one way or another, for three decades. Had he himself been a convinced communist on our opponents' side during part of the cold war? Yes. And he was expelled from the Party in 1950 against his wishes? Yes. But for the expulsion he might still be in the Communist Party? Perhaps. But Lautner was saving an unexpected blow against us.

Q. But one way or another, either by working for the Party or testifying in cases you have made your living off communism ever since 1929?

A. If I would have considered that, sir, I would be on your side today sitting here for a thousand dollars.

I had no idea what he meant. Lautner went on to say that he had been offered "a big fee" by a New York lawyer to testify for the plaintiffs. He gave a name which none of us recognized.

      Q. Have I ever communicated with you, Mr. Lautner?
      A. No, not you.
      Q. Has Mr. Mansfield?
      A. No.
      Q. Mr. Goldmark?
      A. No. It was a New York law firm trying to entice me to come out over here to testify in this case in behalf of the plaintiffs.

Lautner said he had come to help the defendants for patriotic reasons; no fee had been mentioned. I pursued this, counting on his reluctance to waive payment in the defendants' presence, and won an admission. "Well, I made certain sacrifices to come out here," he said, "and I expect to be recompensated for those sacrifices, that is for certain."

Later we learned what had happened. A friend in New York, trying to help us find experts on communism, had enlisted the well-intentioned help of a lawyer in that city. The latter approached Lautner and mistakenly mentioned a fee—often paid to expert witnesses, but not by our side in this case. All the experts we later used appeared without compensation, and Lautner in any event would not have met our standards for an impartial expert. Lautner had apparently declined the invitation; we knew nothing of the conversation until it came out at trial. Now the excommunist's testimony was before the jury, and it must have been impressive and frightening.

The defendants called Father Emmet Buckley, the Jesuit priest who had inspired anticommunist study clubs throughout the district. Their aim was to show that Buckley and a citizens' group he organized—not the defendants—were responsible for the 1962 attack on Goldmark.

Father Buckley appeared to be a changed man. At his pretrial deposition he had made wild accusations, lapsed into Latin, invoked Aristotle, and insisted that he wanted to rescue Mansfield and me from the hell-fire we would face if we kept on representing the Goldmarks. "The real danger is to Mr. Mansfield and yourself because you stand in danger of being unmanned," he had said. ". . . At the end of your life you go into what is called 'the second death which is called damnation.' And is described later on by Christ as being 'exterior darkness where there is only weeping and the gnashing of teeth.'" Instead of answering questions he had retreated through a thicket of term defining. "What do you mean by the word 'Russians'?" he had asked me. "What do you mean by 'talks'?" "A 'Communist,' would you explain that a little more?" And even, to defense counsel, "What do you mean by the 'whole truth'?" But now, at the trial, he appeared chastened and reasonable.

The priest had begun his study of communism, he said, while serving as chaplain at the Tonasket Hospital. He read the writings of J. Edgar Hoover, Whittaker Chambers, other ex-communists, and FBI plants within the Party. Alarmed, he enlisted citizens in study groups and supplied them with materials and tape recordings.

Father Buckley became an admiring acquaintance of Albert Canwell's. From Canwell he learned of John Goldmark, and that Mrs. Goldmark had belonged to a communist "underground or crypto-apparatus, which apparatus was involved in—at least its members were involved—in penetration of the government." He embarked on what he called his "second program"—that of "bringing to the people at this time a knowledge of the background of John Goldmark because of the degree of success of what we call, or is commonly called, 'psychological warfare' that is being waged against the American people." The Communist Party, said the priest, made it a practice to send agents "into a remote area where they can be elected cheaply and with little difficulty." He had found that the Goldmarks were carrying out the Party line: ". . . I became convinced and had no doubt that they were operatives. And in view of that I felt a very grave moral responsibility to act according to my capacity to help the fellow citizens and the whole country against this very pressing and very grave menace."

Members of Father Buckley's group had distributed many of the leaflets and tapes which we now claimed were libelous. It was a "moral matter," he said, not a question of politics.

The next morning brought a grim surprise. To the stand came Donald Jackson, a seven-term California congressman who had recently retired after long service on the House Committee on Un-American Activities. Ex-communists were one thing; to an extent their own pasts weakened their testimony. Here was a man with experience on the government side of the "communist problem."

Jackson settled into the witness chair and answered questions with a theatrical fluency. He had left high school after two years, he said, enlisted in the Marines as a private, and served in an expeditionary force to Nicaragua. Back in civilian life, in the 1930s, he worked as a ditchdigger, dishwasher, truck driver, and newspaper reporter. Reentering the Marine Corps after Pearl Harbor, he served in the South Pacific and attained the rank of major.

In 1946 Jackson ran for Congress in Southern California and was elected. After fourteen years of service he had voluntarily left the Congress—chiefly, he said, "from a desire to return to what is sometimes called the grass roots of America for the purpose of continuing the fight I had carried on for many years against what I considered to be the greatest threat against the liberties of free men since the time of Genghis Khan—the international communist conspiracy."

He now ran a commercial radio and television program on the communist threat.

Jackson told of long experience with communism while a member of Congress. He had seen communists at work in Greece, Turkey, and Colombia. He had served ten years on the House Committee on Un-American Activities. The job of that panel, he said, "is to act as a watchdog committee over matters which involve the infiltration of our national institutions of labor, of education, of youth groups by any organization which is deemed to be subversive in nature, which is controlled from abroad and which there is reason to believe advocates the overthrow of the government of the United States by force and violence."

Jackson described the committee's work in glowing terms. Its bipartisan membership worked with the aid of a trained professional staff; its file room was used by the FBI and other agencies. It conscientiously held "investigative hearings" at which Jackson himself had observed hundreds of communists as witnesses. Its work had produced important legislation including the Smith Act, the Communist Control Act, and part of the Taft-Hartley Act. Every session the committee was reapproved by the House, with few dissenting votes. "Which reflects, I believe," said Jackson, "a widespread public support as expressed through the elected representatives of the people of the House of Representatives."

"Congressman Jackson," asked Kimball, "have there been communists in high places in our government?"

We objected; the conduct of individual people was not a subject of expert testimony, but of eyewitness testimony, and Jackson was not an eyewitness. What he was about to say was drawn from the uncross-examined testimony of others before the committee; often Jackson had not even been present when the witness appeared. Jackson's testimony, we argued, would be inadmissible hearsay. Judge Turner disagreed because the witness was giving his opinion as an expert; the evidence was allowed to come in.

    Q. Do you know whether or not there have been communists in high government positions in this country?
    A. Yes, there have been.
    Q. And can you give us the name of just a few of them and their positions, as you recall?

    A. There was Harry Dexter White in the Treasury Department. Lauchlin Currie had a desk at the White House. Nathan Witt. Jacob Abt, the lawyer. Nathan Gregory Silvermaster, who headed a cell of communist sympathizers in government.

Kimball asked about the two men who had led Sally's group: what did the witness know about Victor Perlo and Charles Kramer? "I know from my reading of the transcripts of testimony," Jackson answered, "that Victor Perlo and Kramer headed one of several cells in Washington, D.C. Communist Party branches. The membership of which comprised employees of the United States government. . . . the cells were organized for the purposes of obtaining from the various agencies and departments of the United States government information, information which was to be transmitted to the Soviet Union and was, in fact, transmitted to the Soviet Union."

His knowledge, Jackson said, came from "sworn testimony as recorded in the official reports" of the committee.

For weeks the defense had dwelled on "espionage." Now they had gotten before the jury evidence that Kramer and Perlo—the two leaders of Mrs. Goldmark's group—had been the leaders of an "espionage cell" in Washington. The implication was that they had headed but one cell and that she had belonged to it.

And what wretched evidence this was! In effect Jackson was allowed to give his "opinion" that certain facts were true because he believed what someone else had testified to years earlier at the other end of the country, in a forum where the accused had no chance to cross-question the accuser. By this means the evil of such testimony could be compounded indefinitely, with no one ever having a chance to question the person originating the charge.

Jackson had read the transcript of Sally Goldmark's testimony before the committee. In his opinion had she "cooperated fully"? He thought not. "I would term the statement inconclusive and incomplete. And had I been chairman of the sub-committee would have so stated at the termination of that hearing." The group to which Sally belonged could not have been a study group, said the witness; the purpose of the Party cells in Washington, D.C. was espionage.

The communist threat continued today, said Jackson.

Q. And in your opinion how serious is the threat from within, first, and then, from without?
A. Well, in the first instance it is almost

impossible to separate the two because they constitute in the final analysis an identical instrument designed to destroy us. The threat from within, I think, was demonstrated on last November 22nd in Dallas, Texas, when a self-admitted Marxist fired a shot that killed the President of the United States.

This was the defense's first overt use of President Kennedy's assassination.

I had been watching Jackson closely as he testified. He spoke in a radio announcer's voice, and on the surface his testimony was damaging, but there seemed to be something deeply wrong with him. His suntanned face twitched at times, he often shifted in his chair and stared at the ceiling, his flowery answers grew pompous. I began the cross-examination with his unmitigated praise of the House Committee on Un-American Activities.

> Q. Now you realize, do you not, that this is a matter of great controversy and continuing controversy in the United States?
> A. No one recognizes it better than one who has served on that committee.
> Q. And you are not meaning to suggest, are you, that people who dislike the House Committee are communists?
> A. No.
> Q. Or sympathizers with communism?
> A. No.
> Q. Or are the dupes of communism?
> A. In some instances, yes.
> Q. Some of them are dupes and some are not, is that it?
> A. Well, it has been said that some were dupes and some were dopes.

At hand was the book *A Quarter Century of Un-Ameri-*

cana, from the Goldmarks' home library, placed in evidence earlier by the defense. It contained quotations about the committee from distinguished Americans.

> Q. Well, let's see which way you would classify this man, as a dupe or a dope, and I will read you a quote from Exhibit 174. "The Committee is . . . flagrantly unfair and un-American," President Franklin D. Roosevelt. Dupe or dope?
> A. I would probably classify that as a dupe statement.
> MR. KIMBALL: Would you like to take a look at this exhibit?
> THE WITNESS: It isn't necessary; I am sure counsel would not misquote.
> Q. Now I will read you another quote. ". . . House Un-American Activities Committee is the most un-American thing in America," Harry S. Truman. Dupe or Dope?
> A. Misinformed.
> Q. Misinformed. Here is another one. "Unscrupulous demagogues have used the power to investigate as tyrants of an earlier day used the Bill of Attainder," Senator John F. Kennedy?
> A. I would think uninformed.

We had placed Jackson's stand, so unarguably patriotic on the surface, at odds with three American presidents.

The most frequent charges against the committee, Jackson conceded, were that it punished people for beliefs rather than actions, and punished them summarily, without a trial. Again we were able to use a defense exhibit. They had placed in evidence, as proof of the ACLU's perfidy, a booklet on why the committee should be abolished. It contained quotations from various newspapers.

> Q. I will read you another part of this Exhibit.

This is an article from the *San Francisco Chronicle,*
April 24, 1960. Are you familiar with the *San Francisco
Chronicle?*

A. I am.

Q. . . . the headline says "FACED DOWN ON
SLANDER. To report that a member of the House Un-
American Activities Committee had launched a new
contemptible slander against a respectable group of
American clergymen is no shattering novelty. Among the
fanatical vendettas which the Committee has never let up
on is its long-standing effort to blacken the name of the
National Council of Churches. Representative Donald L.
Jackson . . ." That is you, of course?

A. Yes, it is.

Q. ". . . Republican of Los Angeles, is the latest
Committee member to take up the smear brush and go to
work. Well protected, of course, by his immunity from
libel. Jackson, who will retire this year at no very great
loss to California's reputation in Washington, charged the
National Council of Churches with promoting obscene
books written by Communist sympathizers. When
Representative Edith Green of Oregon faced him down
with this denunciation, Jackson was unable to name one
book on any list of the National Council that had been
found obscene by the Post Office Department."

You recall this incident that this refers to?

A. Oh, yes, very well.

Q. Is it true that you charged the National
Council of Churches with promoting obscene books
written by Communist sympathizers?

A. I did indeed and reiterate it out from under the
cloak of immunity at this time.

I turned to the heart of Jackson's testimony. He had identified communists in Washington and accused them of espionage, all with the prestigious stamp of a congressman
who specialized in the field. It was vital that we expose the
ramshackle, irresponsible nature of these charges.

Q. . . . . Now you have testified about communist penetration of our government and I want to be sure I understand the basis of your testimony. First of all, you were talking about things that you didn't witness yourself, is that right?

A. That is correct.

Q. Second, you were talking about the testimony of witnesses that you didn't even hear testify, is that correct?

A. That is correct.

Q. Third, you are talking about the testimony of witnesses that you didn't hear testify who weren't cross-examined by anybody?

A. That is correct.

We did not have time to unravel every charge made by Jackson and the defense on this basis. As an example I took up the case of Lauchlin Currie, a former White House staff assistant named by Jackson as a communist.

Q. And you testified . . . that he was a communist in our government, is that right?

A. That is correct.

Q. And you have one basis for saying that, don't you, Mr. Jackson, which is that he was named by a communist—a woman by the name of Elizabeth Bentley?

A. That is correct.

Q. And Mrs. Bentley, of course, was not cross-examined, was she?

A. No one is cross-examined in a congressional inquiry of any kind.

Q. No, indeed not. And on the basis of her testimony and hers alone you say that Mr. Currie was a communist in our government?

A. Yes, I accept the evidence.

Q. You accept it. You have read the report where her testimony appears?

A. Yes.

Q. This, of course, is the report you are talking about—the hearings of 1948 of the House Committee on Un-American Activities?

A. May I take a look at it, please?

Q. Certainly. Is this the one?

A. Yes.

Q. Now did it also come to your attention that on Friday, August 13, 1948, Lauchlin Currie appeared as a witness before the committee, explained his career in the government in full, answered every question that was put to him, denied that he had ever been a communist and denied everything that Mrs. Bentley had ever said about him?

A. Yes.

Q. That testimony was given under oath before that committee, wasn't it?

A. It was.

Q. Was Mr. Currie ever charged with perjury?

A. Not to the best of my recollection.

Q. You know he wasn't, don't you?

A. Not to the best—well, I am certain he wasn't because I would have certainly have known about it.

❖ ❖ ❖

Q. So, when testifying here in court today that this man, Mr. Currie—he was a former White House assistant to President Roosevelt, was he not?

A. That is correct.

Q. And testifying here today that he was a communist you are accepting what Mrs. Bentley said about him and rejecting what he, himself, testified to under oath?

A. I am saying that there were people who were so high in the hierarchy of the Communist Party, and unquestionably are today, that there would not be enough

evidence to bring against them any charge of perjury
following an identification of a single individual.

Q. Haven't you told us just a few minutes ago
that the only thing you have against Mr. Currie in that
respect—in the respect of communism is his
identification by Mrs. Bentley?

A. Exactly.

Q. Mrs. Bentley's testimony about Mr. Currie
was based on hearsay, wasn't it; that is, she was
testifying what she understood from somebody else?

A. That is substantially correct.

A. That she had been told by her superiors and
others that he was a member of the Party.

Q. That is an example of what we mean by
hearsay?

A. Yes. Which would be accepted in any
congressional hearing in the form of a statement from the
witness because there is no formal cross-examination.

Q. And, of course, you know that is not accepted
in court?

A. I understand that.

Q. Now, let's take Mr. Currie. She testified—
Mrs. Bentley testified before the committee that she
understood from somebody else that he was a
communist. He showed up and denied under oath that
this was true. And that is all that has happened, isn't it?
Is that right?

A. Yes.

Q. So you are now in court testifying that he was
a communist, on the basis of her having heard from
somebody else who was never produced either before the
committee or before this court, that he was a communist,

when he himself denied it under oath to your very committee, that it was a lie; that is the position we are in, isn't it?

A. Yes. And I revert to my original position on it. Elizabeth Bentley's testimony by and large was ninety-nine percent corroborated. This individual witness may well have been so highly placed in the—in the Party that it was not practicable nor feasible to attempt to bring the evidence necessary to sustain it.

Q. Or, on the other hand—

A. It doesn't rule out the possibility of his being a communist by any means.

Q. Yes, but on the other hand he may have been entirely innocent, isn't that true?

A. He may have been.

The key concession had been won. Jackson had admitted that Currie, whom he named as a communist before the Okanogan jury earlier that day, might have been innocent. Now the witness tried to retract his original answer.

Q. Yes, but you testified under oath here this morning to Mr. Kimball that he was one of the communists in the United States government, haven't you?

A. Said he was communist named, one of those named by Elizabeth Bentley as being a communist.

Q. That was not your testimony, was it; Mr. Kimball asked you who they were and you named him?

MR. KIMBALL: Object to this, argumentative.

THE COURT: Overruled.

THE WITNESS: I believe I was asked—I believe I was asked who were the communists in the government.

Q. Yes.

A. Yes, I believe that was the answer. And I included his name among those as being remembered by me as having been a communist.

I turned to the witness's testimony about Kramer and Perlo; it rested on the same kind of flimsy assumption.

Q. Now this same Miss Bentley was the only witness who ever testified to any alleged act of espionage committed by Victor Perlo, wasn't she?

A. I believe so.

Q. And the same Miss Bentley was also the only witness—

A. There is a possibility that I would have to refresh my recollection as to whether or not Whittaker Chambers testified to this.

Q. We have the book. And the same Miss Bentley was the only witness who ever testified to any alleged act of espionage committed by Charles Kramer, wasn't she?

A. Correct.

Q. And she testified, did she not, that she hadn't even met either one of them until the year 1944?

A. I believe that is a correct statement.

Q. And do you know how many different units or groups or cells Mr. Perlo or Mr. Kramer may have been involved with?

A. I do not.

Q. And there is no way to tell that from the testimony of Miss Bentley, is there?

A. No.

Q. After she testified, Mr. Perlo appeared before the committee and denied that he had violated any laws, do you recall that?

A. Yes, I recall that he appeared. Again, I—in retrospect I could not say whether I was a member of the committee or sub-committee. I would think not. However, he did so appear.

Q. Yes. Well, this was in 1948, so you weren't even on the committee then?

A. That would be correct.

Q. And Mr. Kramer also appeared. Both of them,

by the way, invoked the Fifth Amendment as to whether they were communists, do you recall that?

A. Yes.

Q. Mr. Kramer in his testimony was asked about espionage and he didn't invoke the Fifth Amendment; he said he had never engaged in any espionage, is that right?

A. Again, I would have to read the testimony; that was earlier than my service.

In fact, the Bentley testimony suggested that the communist group she was describing could not have been the same one Sally belonged to. She had identified eight or ten people as being in it—none of whom except Kramer and Perlo, as Jackson now admitted, were in the group described by Mrs. Goldmark.

Jackson had praised Canwell's services as a private investigator of communism. This allowed me to read him a passage from J. Edgar Hoover's book *A Study of Communism*. "In dealing with Communism," Hoover wrote, "citizens should refrain from making private investigations. . . . Moreover citizens should not circulate rumors about subversive acts nor draw conclusions from information which may come to their attention. The information an individual receives may be incomplete or only partially accurate. And by drawing premature or ill-founded conclusions or circulating rumors he can often cause grave injustice to innocent people. Vigilante action weakens our free society. . . ." Wasn't that contrary to his testimony about Canwell? "Not at all," said Jackson; but the point had been made.

The jury may well have felt a revulsion at Jackson by the time he finished. But this case could not be won on cross-examination alone, and we were in trouble.

The shape of the defense's "proof" that John Goldmark

was a communist was now clear. Its main points were these:

1. The Communist Party was a vast conspiracy ruthlessly bent on destroying the United States and enslaving the world. Its secret agents were everywhere—in the churches, the unions, and especially the government. The domestic communists were one arm of a monster equipped elsewhere in the world with rockets and nuclear bombs. Deeply entrenched in American society, they carried out espionage and covertly influenced policy.

2. Sally Goldmark had been in a "secret underground cell" of federal employees for eight years. Perlo and Kramer, the two leaders of the cell, were espionage agents for the Soviet Union. Communist Party discipline was such that Sally must have been a fully committed Bolshevik who could not have married without the Party's approval of her husband's politics—which meant that Goldmark must have been a communist, or at least a sympathizer, when they married in 1942.

3. In Washington State, Goldmark had concealed his wife's past from the voters while gaining political power. Meantime Sally, approached by the FBI and the House Committee on Un-American Activities, had told them less than the truth.

4. Throughout his career John had followed the "Communist Party line." The defense had listed fifteen of his positions on issues which, they said, illustrated this. Most recently the Goldmarks had resisted the new "anticommunist drive" by seeking to suppress *Communism on the Map, Operation Abolition,* Don Caron's columns, the radio program "Know Your Enemy," and the anticommunist study clubs. These efforts matched the current directives from Moscow.

5. There was, finally John's attachment to the ACLU. The Communist Party used as a "front" any organization

that served its purposes, and the ACLU—defender of the communists' constitutional rights—was the country's most potent front.

This complicated indictment was false in every part. Yet the defense's version of communism, however distorted, strongly resembled the one instilled in many citizens by two decades of the cold war. To reawaken it in the jurors' minds might require only a few fresh horror stories; and of these there had been no shortage. An aura of fear and suspicion had steadily worsened in the courtroom. In order to win, the defendants need not prove their argument literally true; it would be enough if they left the jurors in fear and doubt, as they had left the voters in the campaign.

With these problems in mind I drove with my wife and children over the Cascade Mountains, deep in winter, to Seattle for the Christmas recess.

CHAPTER 12

T HE GRUELING weeks of trial had increased my admiration for the Goldmarks. John with his superb mind and dedication to public service, Sally with her fervent concern for justice and indignation at any kind of cruelty or pettiness—these people, I felt, were critically important in themselves. And now there were broader issues at stake, for the sweeping defense attack indicted not just the plaintiffs but liberal democracy itself.

The trial resumed on January 2, 1964, with the defense's incongruous reading of Francis Biddle's deposition. We had questioned the Roosevelt-era attorney general months earlier at a hotel suite in New York City, where he had cheerfully seized and autographed one of his books for the startled Canwell, who had brought it along to study for signs of subversion.

Biddle had served as chief judge for the United States at the Nuremberg war crimes trials and was a former chairman of the ACLU's national advisory council. His testimony strongly supported the noncommunist nature of that organization. But the defendants, it appeared, were reading his deposition in an attempt to show that even the Justice Department harbored communist fronters. Their hero, J. Edgar Hoover, had been obliged to work under the attorney general's supervision. "He was one of my subordinates," said Biddle, "who acted as a service division for all the other divisions."

Defense counsel had argued with the witness over whether the New Deal was infested with communists. Would he not accept the testimony of a former communist under oath that a certain person had been a member of the Party? "Well, of course, it is evidence," Biddle answered, "but I think reformed commies who turn state's evidence are often pretty suspicious characters. They are like crown informers during the eighteenth century in England, so I would have my fingers crossed about their evidence; but it is evidence, but it is not the evidence that I would give much credit to."

A striking couple were sitting in the audience. The woman was attractive and flashily dressed; the man was small, had light curly hair, and appeared to be in his mid-forties. The next morning the defense called the man as a witness; he was Karl Prussion, a former communist and FBI informant. On the stand he smiled frequently and talked with easy confidence.

Prussion had joined the Communist Party in 1933, he said, while a student in Detroit. He had been sent to a Party training school in Michigan, where he was "given a course in insurrection." He had gone on to become president of a United Auto Workers local while a secret communist. In 1947 Prussion had gone to the FBI; he had stayed in the Party thirteen more years, he said, operating as "a counterspy for the Federal Bureau of Investigation." In 1960 he left the Party and surfaced as a witness before the House Committee on Un-American Activities. He was now a lecturer and writer.

Getting out of the Communist Party was not easy, said Prussion. He recalled one member who had been suspected of defecting. The man was summoned to a meeting where he "was pistol-whipped, black-jacked, pummeled and whipped until he bled from the mouth and finally [he] admitted that he was a counterspy."

Once out, Prussion testified, the departing member "will suffer unquestionable economic and social attrition, which is launched by the left-wing liberal movement generated by the Communist Party." The opponents will start vicious rumors and will make it hard for the defector to find work. He himself had been forced to move five times in the three years since his appearance as a committee witness. "And a great deal of this attrition against me," said Prussion, "was directed by the American Civil Liberties Union. . . ."

A former communist was obliged to speak out. "J. Edgar Hoover, for example," Prussion testified, "stated that a person who is a former communist and claims to have left the Communist Party but remains silent is still helping the enemy and therefore is still within the Communist discipline."

What was Communist Party discipline? The witness offered what he said was a quote from Lenin: "A Communist must be prepared to make every sacrifice. . . . He must lie. He must deceive. He must hide his identity, if necessary, to get into unions, political organizations, civic groups and to stay there and do your revolutionary work therein."

The communists were out to destroy us. Their mission was "to set up a Soviet America—a dictatorship—just as they did in Cuba." Through the subterfuge of "peaceful coexistence" they worked to "dismember the rest of the world piecemeal and bring the rest of the world—the free world—within the jurisdiction of the Soviet satellite system." Their tactic was to "take us closer and closer to a strong centralized left-wing government that controls business, professions, workers, farmers and ultimately the individual and the family from the day that you are born until the day that you die." They were achieving this "by infiltrating or joining trade unions, especially political organizations, civic groups, church groups." He himself had infiltrated many such organizations as a secret communist—including the ACLU.

Abolishing the House Committee on Un-American Activities, Prussion testified, was a prime communist objective. "They want to do away with the Senate Internal Security Committee. They want to do away with atomic testing. They want to do away with loyalty oaths. They are very interested in taking God out of our schools, God out of government, and God out of the military. . . ."

Most people in this country wanted to do the right thing. "But the problem we Americans have is that there is a certain claque of scholars and intellectuals, politicians and statesmen who, like a button is pressed, will support all of the communist objectives and fight for them."

The House Committee on Un-American Activities was vitally necessary to expose infiltrators. The committee's work, said Prussion, "is meticulous, it is accurate, it is complete, it is thorough." He knew that the film *Operation Abolition* leaned over backward to be fair.

The heart of current communist work, Prussion said, was resisting "the anti-communist movement." The Party knew that this movement posed "the greatest obstacle that there is to communism or socialism in the United States and other countries in the world. . . ."

Communists lived their private lives under the Party's iron discipline. Marriage was impossible without official approval. "They have to be people of the same ilk." He himself had been directed to marry a girl of the Party's choosing.

Q. From your experience what have you observed

about communists who do marry; do they usually marry someone else in the Party?

A. Yes, or somebody who will be brought into the Party.

Q. In the period of '35 to '43 could a communist have married a person whom the Party did not approve without any action being taken by the leader of the cell?

A. No, this couldn't happen. . . .

Nor, said Prussion, could a member simply drop out and resume a normal life.

The American Civil Liberties Union, the witness testified, "has been the protective coat in the armor plate of the communist conspiracy in the United States." Hundreds of communists belonged to the ACLU. "A good example is very recently the assassination of the President of the United States."

Prussion's frequent smiles and casual, airy answers did not match the deadly business he was describing. There was about him something of a schoolboy reciting a piece for his elders' approval.

On cross-examination I filled in some gaps in his strangely sketchy background. He had spent World War II working in defense plants; during that time he attended no communist meetings, paid no dues, and apparently had no connection with the Party. He had tried five times without success to "get with" the FBI as an informant; the Bureau finally accepted him in 1947. For a time he had operated a construction business which, he said, was a "successful venture until the House Committee appearance disclosed me to the communists. And they caused social and economic attrition which caused it to be thrown into involuntary bankruptcy."

Since then Prussion had made his "meager living" by speaking and writing on communism.

He had insisted that the ACLU was full of communists. But when asked for names, he could name only two who were dropped from membership in 1940, and one California professor allegedly a member of his former Party cell. All the others were "hidden identity communists, nobody knows who they are." He had never attended an ACLU chapter meeting, but merely sent in a few dollars a year and received the literature.

Was the Democratic Party in Washington State also in league with the communists? I referred Prussion to its 1962 planks on the McCarran Act, loyalty oaths, and the House Committee on Un-American Activities. "I think," he answered, "without the hidden identity, subtle activity of the communists, within the conventions of the various Democratic clubs, that these conditions would not prevail."

The witness had spoken of communist-generated measures to centralize governmental power. Would Social Security be an example of this? "I think that Social Security has always been a trend," he answered, "a drift toward the type of socialist government the communists are working for. . . ."

Socialism and communism, Prussion had testified, "in the final analysis are the same."

> Q. Now let's see if we can find out if there is any differences between them. For many years there was a Socialist Party here in the United States, wasn't there?
> A. Yes, sure.
> Q. It used to run a man for President every election, his name was Norman Thomas?
> A. That is right.
> Q. The Socialist Party has never been listed as a subversive organization by any government agency, has it?
> A. No, it hasn't.

Nonetheless he insisted the two were identical. The difference between them and free enterprise rested with belief in God. "We have laws which try to implement the Sermon on the Mount. And socialism does not believe in this." Was the Socialist Party of Great Britain an example of one that denies the existence of God? Yes, Prussion answered.

The witness had spoken of a "claque" of professed liberals who supported the fight for communist objectives in the United States.

Q. And in this group there are, this claque—there would be a lot of professors and scholars and people like that?

A. And politicians.

Q. And politicians. And one of the politicians, I suppose, would be the governor of your own state, Governor Brown?

A. Very definitely.

Q. And another one in this claque would be the Chief Justice of the Supreme Court, Earl Warren?

A. I think so, yes.

Q. Another one would be Justice Black of the Supreme Court?

A. Well, name the rest of them.

I asked Prussion if he knew that one of the foreign policy positions he had described as communist inspired had been shared by the national administration in office from 1952 to 1960. "Yes, I know this, sir," he answered. "And, may I say something, that same administration gave Castro his full support in the so-called agrarian reform movement and actually carried out, if you please, a communist-generated objective in the United States and we have Castro there today as a result of your administration policy of that period. . . ."

The answer completed Prussion's political isolation. He had now condemned the Eisenhower administration along with the Democrats.

At hand were some of Prussion's writings that showed the use to which he put his patriotism.

Q. Do you publish a magazine?

A. I certainly do. It is called *Heads Up*. I would like to have you subscribe to one.

Q. Have you written a book too?

A. Yes, I have written a book. I have it right here for you. It is called *The California Dynasty of Communism*. It might be an interesting book to read for you.

Q. In your book did you refer to the Attorney General of California, Stanley Moss, as a collaborator, appeaser and consistent supporter of communist objectives in the state?

A. Yes, I did, sir.

Q. By the way, is Mr. Moss a Democrat or Republican?

A. He is a Democrat. If he would have been a Republican I would have said the same thing.

Q. Did you also call Attorney General Moss "A leading national figure in a subversive web which attacks patriots while protecting subversives"?

A. That is correct, sir.

Q. And the distribution of your book was enjoined by the Supreme Court of California on the ground that it is libelous and spurious, wasn't it?

A. There was an injunction gotten out against the book by the Democratic Party and by Governor Brown, who sued me for half a million dollars.

Q. Who issued the injunction—the governor or the court?

A. I think the injunction was issued at the request of the Central Committee of the Democratic Party through General Wyman and was granted by the courts.

The patriotic reformed communist had been restrained as a libeler.

Prussion was on the stand a full day. By the end of it, we thought, he was destroyed as a defense witness; the jurors must have detected his airy contempt for the truth, his wild use of the communist label. Yet we had undergone another day of submersion in the communist threat, and the atmosphere of suspicion had thickened.

One morning the courtroom was packed with a defense cheering section. Folding chairs had been set up in the aisles, and people stood around the walls. They had come to hear Herbert Philbrick, the most famous of the FBI "counter-spies" within the Communist Party. Philbrick had written a popular book called *I Led Three Lives,* and a dramatized version of his life was a current television series. He was a boyish-looking man of forty-eight, with curly hair, a bland face, and a ready smile. He could have passed for an articulate, rising corporation executive.

Philbrick told of his youth in New England. As a college student he had joined the Cambridge Youth Council, thinking it a Christian pacifist organization; he found it was a communist front, and promptly went to the FBI. This was in the spring of 1940. The FBI suggested he stay in and keep it posted on what was going on. Philbrick agreed, joined more front organizations, then the Young Communist League, and the Communist Party itself in 1943. He held various Party offices, and kept always in touch with the FBI. At last, he said, he became a member of the "so-called 'pro-group' section, which is the most deeply underground section of the communist apparatus. And it was here that I found the real leaders, the brains of the communist apparatus."

Meantime he held a normal job with the advertising department of Paramount Pictures. These were his three lives: his ordinary working and private life, his Communist Party life, and his FBI-informant life.

Philbrick had ended his Party membership in 1949, when he appeared as a prosecution witness in the Smith Act trial of eleven communist leaders in New York. Since then he had written for the *New York Herald-Tribune,* published his book, and outlined the television series; he made his living by writing and speaking about communism.

Philbrick claimed thorough knowledge of the American Civil Liberties Union. Its executive secretary in Massachusetts, he said, had been a fellow member of the communist underground. "In my opinion, because of the widespread good reputation in the minds of many people for the American Civil Liberties Union, this was most effectively used by the communists as a front behind which they could move in directions they wanted to go." Unfriendly witnesses before the congressional committees "were represented by members and those on the payroll of the American Civil Liberties Union." In his own work across the country, "I find that not only am I attacked by the Communist Party but also attacked by the American Civil Liberties Union."

Philbrick had known Albert Canwell for at least fifteen years and held him in the highest esteem. "I have found his information to be always accurate, factual and true, and very fair. I know that this is the reputation that he does enjoy in the field among competent investigators and researchers in the field of communism in Washington, D.C. and other places."

What was meant by the terms "floaters" and "sleepers" in the Communist Party? Harmon asked. A "floater," Philbrick answered, "is a communist who, although he continues active in communist duties and responsibilities, he does not attend a cell meeting. He does not pay dues to the Communist Party. All links and ties with the communist apparatus are broken off except for one or two and usually only one courier or contact person who keeps in touch with that individual." A "sleeper" was a person "who would go 'on ice' completely. He would be separated to all intents and purposes totally from the communist apparatus." He added: "Now as a matter of fact, the Rosenbergs in the Rosenberg spy case were sleepers. . . ."

Here was a tacit comparison of the Goldmarks to the Rosenbergs, executed after the most publicized cold war espionage trial.

Getting out of the Party "is a very difficult process," said Philbrick. Of the communists he knew the only ones who got out successfully did so by going to the FBI. To its members the Party is "a religion to which they are deeply and totally dedicated." They knew what awaited them if they tried to break away: "[O]ne of the favorite examples was Leon Trotsky who had an axe buried in his skull. . . ." The Party would do anything to prevent defections from an underground cell, "and this would include assassination itself, if necessary."

A communist was taught to lie and betray without qualms because "he was totally dedicated to exterminating the enemy." No one could belong several years to an underground cell and not be totally committed to the Party. Marriage to a nonsympathizer would be unthinkable:

> Q. In your opinion could any person who was a member of a secret underground cell anywhere in the United States for a period of some seven or eight years be married in December of 1942 after some seven years of membership in the Communist Party and then have remained a member of the same secret underground cell for almost another year without Communist Party approval of such a marriage?

188

A. This couldn't possibly take place, and this I can testify from my own personal experience. In my own instance in order for me to become a communist it was necessary for my wife to become a communist as well. . . .

The current drive against the "anti-communist program" in this country, Philbrick said, had been launched at a Moscow meeting in December 1960. It was "an all-out campaign to crush and destroy the only anti-communist movement in the United States." Patriots were being "labeled by the communist apparatus as extremists, as extreme right-wingers, as extreme right-wing radicals." Harmon asked him about the tapes, films, and pamphlets used by the anticommunist study groups in Okanogan County. Philbrick described them as "excellent," "reliable," "brilliant," "factual." He himself had shown *Communism on the Map* to PTA meetings, and he knew *Operation Abolition* to be "a most accurate illustration of communist tactics in stirring up mob hysteria and violence."

What was the relationship between communism and socialism? The communists themselves "do not make a distinction," said Philbrick. To "establish in the United States a socialist system—this would be a step towards the ultimate communist system." Communists were constantly working to increase the power of government and to raise taxes—a prelude to their final seizure of power.

He was shown the 1962 Washington State Democratic platform.

Q. Does the Communist Party have a position with respect to the McCarran Internal Security Act?
A. Yes, they have.
Q. Is there any relation or correlation to the position taken in this platform?
A. Yes, here there is a complete agreement,

not only in the position taken but even in the language used. . . .

The planks on loyalty oaths, immigration, and travel restrictions all resembled Communist Party positions.

Philbrick, a prestigious witness, talked persuasively. By the time Harmon released him he had made a strong impact on the jury. Fortunately a good cross-examination tool was at hand: the book *I Led Three Lives,* written years earlier before he had become a full-time professional anticommunist. The book contradicted the picture of a Depression-era and wartime Communist Party fiendishly bent on destroying capitalism. I read him a passage from it referring to the 1940s:

> Q. [*Quoting*] "It was a time of abnormal Communist activity. The Party cooperated willingly and enthusiastically with the constitutional authorities, eschewed . . ." Eschewed means stayed away from?
> A. Uh-huh.
> Q. ". . . eschewed all obstructionist tactics and with singular purpose aided in the prosecution and winning of the war." And that was the case at that time, was it not?
> A. That was the case all the way even to—even to urging the communists, for example not to strike in any defense plants no matter how bad the provocation on the part of the industry. The rights of the workers were relegated to a minor position and the waging of the war was given a major position.
> Q. Yes, and you wrote in the next sentence: "Browder laid down the national Party line and held out hope of collaboration with capitalism not only in war but in peace as well."
> A. That is right.

Cross-examination can aim chiefly at destroying the witness's credibility or at drawing favorable answers. With Philbrick the prospects for the latter seemed good.

> Q. In the '30s it was true, was it not, that many thousands of Americans were induced to join the Communist Party?
> A. Yes, I think that would be true.
> Q. It had a considerable popular appeal then which it doesn't have now, is that right?
> A. Yes, that is right.
> Q. And it preyed upon the desire of people to overcome poverty and overcome the Depression, did it not?
> A. In part, yes.
> Q. And in part it preyed on their desire to combat Hitler's Germany?
> A. Right.
> Q. And Mussolini's Italy and the fascist governments in general?
> A. Well, part of the time, yes.
> Q. Then of those thousands who joined in the 1930s the great majority of them have left the Communist Party long since? They became disillusioned and they left?
> A. That is true.

Philbrick estimated the number of these at about a hundred thousand.

> Q. . . . the great majority of those people have settled down and are leading normal lives, isn't that so?
> A. That is right.
> Q. And the great majority of that hundred thousand or so do not spend their time either lecturing or giving talks or making tapes about their Communist Party experience, do they?
> A. No, I think that would be true.
> Q. And the great majority of the hundred

thousand have been rehabilitated and have talked to the FBI at some time or another and have renounced what they formerly were duped into doing, isn't that so?

A. I would say that is true, yes.

In his testimony he had mentioned the House Committee's *Guide to Subversive Organizations*. It proved useful regarding the ACLU.

Q. This book, *Guide to Subversive Organizations*, published by the House Committee is kept up to date by new editions from time to time, is it not?

A. Yes.

Q. I will ask you if it isn't a fact that the American Civil Liberties Union is not listed anywhere in that book?

A. That is true, the American Civil Liberties Union has never been cited either by the House Un-American or by the Attorney General as a communist or subversive organization.

Q. Yes, and it is not listed in this book which includes citations by state legislative committees too?

A. That is right.

We placed the book in evidence. Philbrick tried to argue against the effect of the ACLU's absence from it.

A. I might point out for example that the "Fair Play for Cuba Committee" has never been cited by the Attorney General or by the House Committee as a communist front organization.

Q. When did that come into existence?

A. In 1960.

Q. When did the ACLU come into existence? 1920?

A. Around that time, yes.

Q. You think they haven't had time to get around to it yet?

A. No, it has never been cited.

I returned to Philbrick's own book and read him a passage in which he expressed resentment over a communist effort to infiltrate what he described as "the liberal, non-communist Civil Liberties Union."

Q. It angered you because you knew it wasn't a communist organization, wasn't that the reason you were angered?

A. That is right.

Q. And yet in dispute of that in your talk in Omak in March, 1962 you called the ACLU a "dirty red," didn't you?

A. That is right.

We had shown Philbrick's metamorphosis to meet the rising demands of the anticommunist market. He was now willing to attack organizations he had praised a few years earlier.

Q. You also said that the position on the McCarran Internal Security Act is a communist position, Mr. Philbrick. Do you not know that the McCarran Internal Security Act was vetoed by President Truman?

A. Yes, it was.

Q. And do you not know in his veto message he said it was a threat to freedom of thought and expression in the United States?

A. I recall that statement.

Q. And do you recall—

A. In fact it has been quoted many times by the communists in support of their position.

Q. Does that make it wrong? Does the fact that the communists quote it make it wrong, Mr. Philbrick?

A. Well, the communists have used the quote in support of their position.

Q. All of these things that you have said the communists are for, does the fact that the communists are for something mean that everybody else has to be against it?

A. Not at all. In fact you can take almost any position of the Communist Party, you can take any position of the Communist Party and you can find numbers of people who will agree with one or more of parts of the Communist Party platform.

Q. Then how do you tell a communist from anybody else?

A. It is impossible.

Here was the essence of the irrational right. In the end, there was no way to tell a communist from anybody else. The corollary was that no evidence was needed; suspicion would be enough.

Yet in his book several years earlier Philbrick had included an appendix headed "The Communist and the Liberal," in which he listed sixteen differences between the two. I placed the list before him. "A Communist," he had written, "interprets and misinterprets history for his own purposes; a liberal studies history honestly and learns from it." Yes, that was a distinction. "A Communist uses the ills and defects of the capitalist system to foment anger and class strife; a liberal points out those ills but tries to cure them." That also was true. "A Communist, although he pretends to be independent always takes orders from above; a liberal makes up his own mind." The description of "liberal" on each point could as readily have been applied to "conservative" in the true sense of that term; and the words in each instance described John Goldmark.

I questioned Philbrick respectfully but caught him with his own writings often enough to make him feel that his safest course was to answer favorably. He was intelligent, and his mood changed as the examination went on. The answers became temperate and reasonable. On direct examination he had praised the House Committee and denounced the supposedly communist-inspired attacks on it. Again his book moved him to our side.

> Q. In your book you have a sentence here that says: "Blanket condemnations such as those of the House Un-American Activities Committee which blacklist entire organizations because of the presence of a few Communists frequently harm innocent persons." Is that still your view of it?
> A. Yes, it is.
> Q. And you go on to say: "Guilt by association merely strengthens the hands of agitators in their attacks upon the infringement of civil liberties."
> A. Right.
> Q. That is still your view of it?
> A. Yes, right.
> Q. You would agree, I guess, that opposition to the House Un-American Activities Committee does not necessarily indicate any communist sympathy?
> A. That is right.

On redirect questioning by defense counsel Philbrick, as if reawakened to his duty, resumed full militance. "It is my prayer indeed," he said, "that all of the American people come to recognize the extreme danger from the far left before we have more assassinations and more killings in this country."

CHAPTER **13**

THE DEFENSE unexpectedly called John to the stand and put a long series of questions attacking his truthfulness on details of his past life. Goldmark answered patiently but with growing restrained anger. In 1945 he and Sally had visited Charles Kramer at the Agriculture Department in Washington before heading West. Defense counsel hammered away at this fact. Had he not known then Kramer was a communist? No, he had not; their talk had been about farming.

> Q. Did Mr. Kramer say anything to you or anything in your presence when you met with him in Washington, D.C. about your wife resuming her activities for the Communist Party?
> A. No.
> Q. Did Charles Kramer give either you or your wife any instructions to be carried out on behalf of the Communist Party when you met him and talked with him in Washington, D.C.?
> A. Of course not, Mr. Harmon.

The defendants tried to minimize Goldmark's Naval Reserve service, but pressed too far.

> Q. Now as a matter of the clearance itself, other than changes in the Naval Reserve manual, you have access to no secrets basically other than that, do you?

A. Oh, certainly. We go on tours of the installations in the area, Air Force, Army. We go to places where we have to have a secret clearance to go.

Q. Isn't it true that many, many other people do that?

A. No. We go to a place as a Naval unit, as an official tour. Our commanding officer assures the Air Force personnel or whoever is involved that every member of the unit has been cleared for secret. We are given a briefing as to what is involved. We saw the Atlas and the Titan launching sites and we have been up at Geiger on the radar, the Air Defense Command. We have done all this kind of thing to keep ourselves abreast and they all require secret clearance.

Q. And that was simply a matter of going in and observing these various sites, is that right?

A. No. We are told what the program is, what the strategic mission of the place is; our questions are answered.

John had made speeches on the radical-right movement to audiences around the state. The defense saw the speeches as another communist tactic.

Q. You have made reference to the fact that they are hurting someone. Now who is the far right hurting?

A. They are hurting the common bond of trust and unity in our national institutions that Americans should have one with another.

Q. Do you consider that they are hurting the far left?

A. Not particularly. This is also an objective of the far left, is to destroy that same thing.

Had he referred to the current anticommunist movement as "un-American"? "Yes," said John. "When I sat in the American Legion hall meeting and heard that crowd, a majority of whom were members of the far right, say to throw

Senator Hallauer out because he suggested that the procedure was unfair, that was about as close to a lynch mob as
anything I have come [across] in the United States. And I
didn't like that feeling."

Defense counsel pored over more of Goldmark's legislative stands. One was an atomic test ban memorial; as before, John was incisive.

> Q. It is a fact, Mr. Goldmark, is it not, that the
> memorial as introduced and as amended does call for
> unilateral halting of the testing of atomic and hydrogen
> weapons, is that so?
> A. No, I don't think that is a fact, Mr. Harmon.
> The committee amendment changes the character of it
> decisively. It declares a trial moratorium as long as all
> other nations adhere to a like policy of the suspension of
> such explosions. This is, in fact, what the Eisenhower
> administration did about two years afterwards.

The defense recalled Sally, and at once attacked an in-
consistency in her testimony. In her deposition she had
mentioned working evenings in a soup kitchen run by the
Eastside Unemployed Council in New York. Her trial testimony contradicted this; she now said she had only helped
publicize the project. Which was correct? The latter, said
Sally. "My best recollection is that I did not work in the
kitchens, that I just helped to do some promotional work
in connection with them." The events had taken place thirty-
two years earlier.

The defense lawyers had subpoenaed books from the
Goldmarks' home library. One was *Proletarian Literature
in the United States,* issued in 1935 by a communist publishing house.

> Q. And how does it happen that you still have it

in your personal library twenty years after you have testified you left the Communist Party?

A. Oh, I kept quite a few of my old books and that is just one I kept, that is all.

Q. Well, was this book and other books you obtained while you were a member of the Communist Party available in your personal home library where your children could read them if they wished to during the years they were growing up and going through school?

A. Certainly.

Q. And did you make any effort to see that your sons either did or didn't read this particular book and others of the same nature?

A. I don't think they even know it is there. But if they wished to look at it it is there.

Q. Did you ever warn your sons of the dangers of communism to the United States prior to the time that this lawsuit was commenced?

A. I don't think I ever discussed communism with them in any shape or form.

Recently Sally had joined the Prometheus Book Club. Its proprietor was the publishing house of Marzani & Munsell, described by defense experts as a communist publisher. Was not Mrs. Goldmark aware of this? She had no idea, Sally answered; she had subscribed simply because some of the books listed in a mail solicitation looked interesting. Harmon approached her with the book *A Quarter Century of Un-Americana,* distributed by that club.

Q. How did that particular book happen to be in your personal library?

A. It was sent in the mail to me.

Q. Well, is it your book or your husband's book?

A. It is my book.

Didn't she recognize the book as a communist publication?

"I wouldn't have any idea if it is or not," said Sally.

The defense interrupted Sally's testimony to call to the stand a woman whom they had brought from a distant part of the state. She was a farm wife who had once lived on the Goldmark ranch while her husband worked as a hired man. "Did you and Mrs. Goldmark ever have any discussions regarding your respective beliefs in God?" Harmon asked. An objection was sustained. "I think there is more danger of this matter being given an improper effect," said Judge Turner, "than would compensate for any value it might have."

Resuming with Sally, Harmon sought to raise the religion issue through her request that "Know Your Enemy" be taken off the air. Her objection was that the program, offered as a public service, was attacking the churches. Was she herself a member of any organization connected with the National Council of Churches? She was not. "But I feel that I am a deeply religious person," she added.

On cross-examination I read from one of the "Know Your Enemy" scripts. "Some leaders of the Federal Council of Churches had a long record of Communist affiliations," it said, "and a few of them were hard core members of the Communist Party. Most of them were bitter opponents of the free enterprise system and through their infiltration of the theological seminaries and the subtle brainwashing campaign throughout the ministry they were able to establish a socialist philosophy that was alien to our way of life." This was the kind of statement, Sally testified, that she had in mind in saying the program unfairly attacked the churches.

We presented a complete inventory of the Goldmarks' home library. The defense had offered a tiny sampling of the books. There were more than four hundred others: novels, poetry, biography, books of history and politics, books on farming and aviation. Among the authors represented were General Eisenhower, Judge Harold Medina, and J. Edgar Hoover. The Bible was there. Why had Mrs. Goldmark left this varied collection open to her children? "I think that education should be access to all types of books," she said, "all types of learning, and all types of information."

A day later, after one of the defendants' expert witnesses finished his testimony, Harmon recalled Sally for a further attack on the religion issue. Hadn't she told the hired man's wife that she did not believe in God? And that religion was not to be discussed in the presence of her children? She had not.

The questioning compelled us to develop the subject. Sally had been raised in the Dutch Reformed Church, we brought out, but currently had no church affiliation. The Goldmark children had been sent to Sunday school. She and her husband occasionally attended services.

The defense again offered the testimony of the woman who had once lived on the ranch. Judge Turner responded by ruling the whole issue of religion out of order. It should never have been raised in the first place, he said; and he instructed the jury to disregard what they had heard on the subject.

Albert Canwell, his reputation bolstered by earlier defense experts, came forward as the last witness for his side. His job was to clinch the case that Goldmark was a communist. With him the defense intended to reach its summit.

Canwell retold the story of his life and work. This time he seemed confident and voluble. The state was full of reds in the thirties and forties, he said. "I remember Barbara Hartle. There is little resemblance to the gal you saw on the stand. She was a pretty wild and violent communist at that time."

He had begun keeping records. "[L]ike some men play

golf I collected information on the communists. It became a way of life with me." After his wartime sheriff's job ended he ran for the legislature. In the 1947 session he wrote the bill creating the state un-American activities committee, became its chairman, and presided at public hearings. Canwell told this in a chatty, reminiscent way, yet it was clearly the central experience of his life.

"What happened when you ran for re-election?" Harmon asked. Canwell slid into a long speech about his misfortunes. "Lying pamphlets were distributed the night before the election. . . . The communists did not want me to return to the legislature because they did not want a continuation of the investigation into communist activity by someone who would do it professionally. And they pulled all stops."

As a private investigator, he said, he possessed "one of the extensive libraries in the field." He supplied information to "the FBI, the military intelligence branches," and other agencies. He maintained "contacts with undercover operators in the Communist Party." Canwell spoke with pride of "knowing almost all the top ex-communists."

The defense had offered into evidence six reports issued by the House Un-American Activities Committee and the Senate Internal Security Subcommittee. Their titles implied their inflammatory contents: *The Communist-Led Riots Against the House Committee on Un American Activities in San Francisco; The Truth About the Film Operation Abolition; The New Drive Against the Anti-Communist Program; Interlocking Subversion in Government Departments; Expose of Soviet Espionage; The Communist Party of the U.S.A.;* and *Communist Target—Youth*. The reports consisted largely of uncross-examined testimony and untested narratives by authors whose qualifications were not shown. Their contents were alarming and often irresponsible. While we knew that a congressional committee can print anything it chooses, we were astonished to read these sorry examples. Judge Turner ruled the reports were hearsay and would be excluded, remarking that in any event their substance had already come into evidence through live testimony.

But a defendant is entitled to show the sources he relied upon in writing an alleged libel. Although the reports would not go to the jury room as exhibits, Canwell was allowed to read excerpts from them on which he said he had relied. The reports supported his charges of vast espionage rings serving a Communist Party whose secret members had infiltrated every segment of society.

There were other sources. On the ACLU, Canwell pointed to the 1931 report of the Fish Committee of the U.S. Congress, and to statements by legislative committees in New York, Massachusetts, and California. In substance these charged that the ACLU was a communist front. In addition, Canwell said, ACLU lawyers represented committee witnesses "who repeatedly were in almost every case defiant and took the Fifth Amendment, who were contemptuous of the committee, who were rude and conducted themselves in a manner that should not be tolerated anywhere in a court or hearing. . . ."

Harmon read from ACLU press releases describing sixteen recent projects involving the rights of communists, contempt of Congress, the internal security laws, and similar subjects. On each point Canwell said the Communist Party's position was identical. The ACLU wrapped "a flag around their activities—they are able to do something that the Communist Party could not possibly do in open court and for that reason are far more effective than the Communist Party itself would be in court."

He had also relied on numerous American Legion documents. "The American Legion has consistently over many years been demanding an investigation of the American Civil Liberties Union." The Communist Party openly admired the ACLU, he said; he possessed a file of forty *Peoples World* stories mentioning the ACLU in 1962 alone.

Canwell went through the libels in detail, testifying that each statement was true and identifying his sources for making it. He punctuated his testimony with speeches about the communist menace. ". . . I am still of the opinion that had the disclosures that came about through Whittaker Chambers and Elizabeth Bentley and similar ex-communists not been made, that the communists could well by this time have completely penetrated and taken over our government."

The "Perlo-Kramer cell," he said, "was devoted to espionage and precisely that on the highest level of government." It was "completely impossible" for Mrs. Goldmark to have belonged to that group without being part of the espionage apparatus.

Canwell concluded by listing recent actions which, he said, betrayed the Goldmarks' guilt. They opposed the showing of *Operation Abolition* unless another side was presented, "which was precisely the Communist Party position on that film." They opposed the showing of *Communism on the Map*. Mrs. Goldmark telephoned Don Caron's superiors to complain about his anticommunist newspaper articles, and asked a Wenatchee radio station to take an anticommunist program off the air. Goldmark opposed and obtained the defeat of a Grange resolution supporting Don Caron's right to publish his articles while on the government payroll. Another resolution was offered to outlaw the Communist Party in Washington; Goldmark brought about its defeat. In 1962 he went out of his way to address the Methow Grange, telling the members that concerns over communism "should not be handled by the people but should be left to the FBI." He "advocated the Communist Party line" by urging diplomatic "recognition of Red China," and "reiterated that communism is not a serious internal threat in America." In 1962 when the Gold-marks met with friends to explain her Communist Party past they did not tell them the truth.

In opposing the "anti-communist movement," Canwell said, the Goldmarks followed a policy directed from Moscow. "At the time this line was laid down and immediately after undercover communists all over America responded like puppets on a string. The line was that the right wing and conservative movement in America should be opposed by all means."

To Canwell these recent events tied in with a long history of guilt. "All of these things and many others add up to the observation in my mind that they are and have been and are still today under Communist Party discipline."

Harmon turned him over for cross-examination. Canwell had begun smoothly, but the long strain of the trial was telling on him. He had developed a facial tic, which wors-ened during cross-examination. I was quickly able to trans-fer his attacks from Goldmark to the Department of De-fense.

> Q. Don't you know that both of those films [*Communism on the Map* and *Operation Abolition*] were banned by the Department of Defense in being shown to soldiers?
> A. Yes. And I know the circumstances under which that occurred.
> Q. You say it was done by communists?
> A. I think they had a lot of influence on the confusion and deceptiveness in using the various means of propaganda and influence that they have, which are

startling and frightening that they were able to place influence upon the Department of Defense.

He had complained that Goldmark's eloquence swung the Grange vote to defeat a resolution calling for a state statute to outlaw the Communist Party.

> Q. All of those members that voted against it were following the Communist Party line, is that your testimony?
> A. Not necessarily. They were influenced by a very able speaker, an orator, a man of considerable prestige. Graduate of the Harvard Law School.
> Q. Mr. Canwell, you know, don't you, that that meeting where Mr. Goldmark was, was not a meeting where there was any voting on this resolution?
> A. I don't remember the precise details of the thing.

We reviewed the details. At length he admitted the truth. The resolution was defeated by majority vote at a Grange meeting at which John did not speak.

Wasn't the resolution unnecessary in any event, since the state already had a law on the books of the very kind it called for? Canwell was confused over what statutes existed and what did not. Finally he admitted that a 1951 Washington State law made it a crime to belong to an organization whose object was to overthrow the government.

Supporting the aggressive defense, Canwell had testified he believed Goldmark and his wife to be under communist discipline at the time he wrote the libels. This was necessary to make out the defenses of truth and good faith—but it conflicted with his pretrial testimony. I now read this aloud. "Do you maintain now that John Goldmark is a communist?" he had been asked. "No, I do not," he had answered. "You maintain that Mrs. Goldmark is a commu-

206

nist?" "I do not. I do not know and that is why I am continually seeking the answer."

He further admitted saying two years earlier that he had no evidence that Goldmark was a communist. Yet all this, he insisted, was consistent with his current testimony. "I don't know under what influences they respond to Party discipline. It could be membership, it could be blackmail."

In all his talk of selfless dedication to anticommunism and of lack of income which would require the filing of tax returns, Canwell had never mentioned a salaried job. "Did you not have a job in 1961," I asked him, "in which you were a manager at the Sharon Arms Apartment of Spokane at a salary of $400 per month?" We had learned of this during the trial; Canwell was visibly surprised. It was "an interim accommodation job" for his brother, he said.

> Q. Did you have the job I described in 1961?
> A. I did. I believe that was the year. I spent—I don't know, a month or two up there.
> Q. Did you not have that job in January, February, March and April up to April 20th?
> A. I don't remember the precise dates. I did fill in there during some of that time and during that same time I carried on my other activities.
> Q. It wasn't one month; it was about four months.
> A. I don't know what the precise time was; it wasn't very long; if you say that is the amount of time, it could be.
> Q. And was that salary $400 a month?
> A. I can't remember that; maybe it was some such figure.

He had blamed criticism of the Canwell Committee on the Communist Party. Was it also responsible, I asked, for the *Seattle Times*'s charges that the committee had wrongly concealed records pertaining to Professor Rader? "Yes," said Canwell, "very definitely in this particular instance." "That was Ed Guthman, was it?" "Yes, he was the one I have in mind."

When he wrote the libels was he familiar with the statements of Presidents Truman and Eisenhower praising the ACLU? "I know they were alleged to have been made and I gave them the approximate weight that they deserved—I just disregarded them." Did he know that neither Kramer nor Perlo, whom he had accused, was ever charged with espionage or any other offense? "Yes, it is unfortunately true; that is why we can't leave the thing entirely to the executive department of the government. . . ." Was he familiar with J. Edgar Hoover's warning against private investigations of communism, with his statement that "vigilante action weakens our free society"? "I am familiar with the statement," said Canwell. "I heartily agree. I am certain that Mr. Hoover did not mean me. I know him. He is aware of what I do. . . ."

The defendants rested their case. We had again shown their reckless use of the "communist" label. But they had placed before the jury evidence—in the form of "expert opinions"—from which the jury could find all the libels were true. To us that evidence seemed disgracefully shoddy and irresponsible. It could nonetheless carry the day unless we succeeded in banishing suspicion from the courtroom.

CHAPTER **14**

WE SET out to change the pace of the trial. The defense had proceeded with agonizing slowness, keeping experts on the stand for days at a time. The feeling was that of sinking into a morass. We wanted to counter with a swift and pointed rebuttal case.

Over the nine-day Christmas recess I had worked up our response. We knew we would have to restore confidence in John, show the true nature of the Communist Party and the radical right, and place American politics in perspective. I telephoned and wrote to people all over the United States. The response was magnificent. Many had been following the trial, there was concern over a revival of McCarthyism, and nearly everyone I talked to wanted to help.

The defendants were startled when our first rebuttal witness entered the Okanogan courtroom. He was Harry P. Cain, former United States senator from Washington and, in earlier years, a political ally of Canwell and Holden. Senator Cain's story was well known in the state. A conservative Republican, he held office from 1946 to 1952. After losing his Senate seat he was appointed by President Eisenhower to the Subversive Activities Control Board. But he gradually became disillusioned with the government's loyalty programs and deeply concerned over the preservation of civil liberties. A brave and independent man, Cain spoke and wrote against the system's abuses while still in office. The "Cain mutiny" became famous; of course, he was not reappointed. He was now a Florida businessman.

Cain's wiry figure, creased face, and rasping bass voice implied vigor and authority. He told of his early life in Tacoma, of becoming the city's mayor, and of World War II service as a military government officer in Africa and Europe. After his postwar Senate term he joined the Subversive Activities Control Board in 1953.

The SACB was established by the Internal Security Act of 1950. "Its sole function," said Cain, "was to adjudicate the merits in cases where the Attorney General of the United States alleged that organizations in America were dominated, controlled and directed by either the world communist movement or the Communist Party, U.S.A."

The American Civil Liberties Union had never been listed by the Attorney General as an organization believed to be communist or subversive. While on the board Cain had made extensive inquiries into the ACLU, discussing it with Justice Department officials, the FBI, and congressmen. His investigation "disclosed a total absence of any justification" to have the organization listed.

We had tried to locate the surviving former members of Sally Goldmark's Communist Party group, but could find only two of them. One of these confirmed to us by telephone that Sally's description of the group was correct but refused to "get involved" as a witness; the other was so fearful of publicity that he would not even consent to an interview. We would have to rely on experts to prove the truth about the Communist Party of the thirties and forties.

Harry Cain was an expert. While on the SACB he had heard much testimony from former communists and held "countless numbers of conversations with them officially and unofficially."

Could a member between 1935 and 1943 argue at cell meetings and feel less than total dedication? I asked him. Yes, said Cain. Could a cell be without work assignments and spend most of its meeting time in discussions? That "often happened," he answered. Was it possible for a Party member to marry someone who wasn't a communist at all, with no repercussions? Yes.

There were many former communists in the country and most of them said nothing about their past mistake. "As related particularly to the period of time to which you have made reference," Cain said, "it would be my judgment based on everything I think I have grown to know that a large number of members of the Communist Party of that period left by one means or another to resume what we would call a perfectly patriotic, normal life without ever, for reasons that I consider to be both obvious and understandable, mentioning a word publicly about the Communist Party."

The direct examination was finished in an hour; we turned Cain over to the defense. Defense counsel tried to buttress John Lautner's testimony by bringing out that he had appeared before Cain's SACB. Didn't Cain consider Lautner an authority on life in the Communist Party? "My memory," said Cain, "is some of what he said we took to be true and other portions of what he said we took to be invalid."

Q. Do you mean that seriously, Senator?
A. I do.
Q. Don't you know that John Lautner was the chief expert on communism for the Department of Justice for a period of years, including the entire period you were with the Board?
A. Yes.
Q. Are you telling me that you believe the Justice Department made a mistake in relying on him as its

principal witness in a number of cases involving communism?

Cain pondered the question. "Well, at this point, Your Honor, I am thinking of a Mr. Lautner who was a witness as a former member of the Communist Party before the Board." "Yes," said Harmon. "Then," said Cain, "my answer remains what it was."

Wouldn't it be impossible, Harmon asked, for a woman in a cell with other communists engaged in espionage to marry an outsider and leave the Party? Quite the contrary, Cain answered. "[S]uch a person could marry while a member of the Communist Party and leave that Party and take off to build a completely new life without any repercussions or acts of intimidation being exercised . . ."

Cain headed back to Florida, leaving behind a powerful impact on the trial.

Peter, the Goldmarks' younger son, took the stand to describe his parents' politics as expressed in their home. A high-spirited boy of seventeen, he had lived his whole life on the ranch until he left for college a few months earlier. Never, he testified, had he heard any discussion of communism by his parents or any of their friends. The defense wisely asked no questions.

The defense had pictured Goldmark's legislative record as radical. We called Payton Smith, who, as counsel to the speaker of the Washington State House of Representatives, had kept track of pending legislation and worked with members of both parties. John Goldmark's tax policies "were either long-time recommendations of his party or of the budget recommendations of the governor," said Smith. Neither Goldmark nor anyone else in the legislature had been on the extreme left.

The Democratic Party's state platform, attributed to John,

had been repeatedly attacked in court. Roberta Morical, chairman of the platform committee, now testified that Goldmark had nothing to do with it; he did not even speak before the committee. The Democratic State Central Committee, she added, had adopted in early 1962 a resolution criticizing the John Birch Society, the Christian Anti-Communist Crusade, and similar organizations. "Mrs. Morical," Harmon asked on cross-examination, "you are a personal friend of John and Sally Goldmark?" She replied with spirit, "I am a very good friend and proud of their friendship."

Paul Holmes, a Grange official, had served with Goldmark in two sessions. John "voted and acted very much in accord with all the regular Democrats," he said. There were no radicals in the legislature. "They all believe in the free enterprise system, to the best of my knowledge, and in the freedom of the individual."

In the defense case, public life had been reduced to a polarized struggle between the communists and their adversaries. We had to sweep away this fiction and repopulate the political landscape with real, varied, and complicated people. To the stand came Raymond Muse, chairman of the history department at Washington State University at Pullman. Coming from the eastern Washington wheat country, a stocky, soft-spoken man with a distinguished war record, Muse was an ideal expert witness in Okanogan. His field was American history.

"What in your opinion," Mansfield asked him, "is the political importance of the Communist Party today?" "I think it is nil in political importance," Muse answered. ". . . I cannot think of a single piece of domestic legislation that the Communist Party has had anything to do with the initiation of or the carrying out of insofar as the legislative process is concerned."

Muse compared the attraction for communism felt by many in the 1930s to the current right-wing surge. Both arose from frustrations. "It seems also that each movement—very different though they are—is in some extent a result of our impatience to get simple solutions for rather complicated problems."

Mansfield read a list of fifteen positions on issues concerning civil liberties and relations with communist countries. All had been attributed to Goldmark and stigmatized as communist inspired. The likelier basis for these views, Muse explained, was concern for our historical tradition of individual rights. "[A]s a matter of fact I think the great majority of American persons are very much dedicated to these rights, to this tradition which I have tried very briefly to indicate to you."

Professor Muse was personally acquainted with John.

> Q. Have you ever at any time observed in Mr.
> Goldmark any indication of communist influence?
> A. No.
> Q. —politically or otherwise?
> A. Neither.

Defense counsel cross-examined aggressively. Was not the Communist Party a peril despite its small numbers? No, said Muse, simply a nuisance. "The Party is absolutely— it is a dud." Did he deny that communists had taken over other countries? "I do not know of any country in which this has happened in which you could make a logical comparison between the state of the United States, powerful, impregnable, with majestic defenses, with a—in my opinion—a perfectly excellent espionage service, and about one hundred and ninety million persons dedicated to our system."

As the defense lawyer challenged him, Muse answered

temperately at every point. His moderation seemed to goad the cross-examiner on. Shouldn't ordinary citizens be concerned about communism? Yes. What should they do about it? "The best thing that they can do about it," Muse answered, "is to be loyal to the American constitution . . . [and] insist that we maintain our parliamentarian processes or arriving at solutions to problems in this country, and that we do not take quick, snap, easy answers to complex problems. . . ."

Which was the greater menace, defense counsel demanded, the communists or their far-right opponents? "My own inclination," said Muse, "is that they are both outside the American tradition."

The winter was deepening, but the tiny Okanogan airstrip remained open. Every day more rebuttal witnesses were flown over the mountains from Seattle by a pilot friend of John's, and every night we worked late preparing their testimony.

A tall, massive, handsome man with curly blond hair and a beard came to the stand. When he gave his name, it was familiar to everyone in court; he was Sterling Hayden, the motion picture actor. Hayden was at a high point in his career; *Dr. Strangelove* had been filmed, and his successful autobiography *Wanderer* had just come out.

Years earlier Hayden had been a friendly witness for the House Committee on Un-American Activities, naming people with whom he associated during a brief period of Communist Party membership in Hollywood. Some of those he named lost their jobs. Hayden was conscience-stricken about the harm he had caused. A troubled, decent man, he was unsatisfied by the usual rewards of a movie star's life.

Hayden told of going to sea as a boy, of becoming a film actor, and of a spectacular World War II career. He had

215

run an ammunition schooner in the West Indies, and then had served with the OSS in Southern Europe. He had been in the mountains of Yugoslavia with Tito's partisans. There he had become interested in communism. ". . . I began to think and I began to connect it with the things I had observed during my years at sea, because I had been all over the world and I had seen there were two levels only really, there seemed to be poverty and wealth. . . . I began to read, which I had really never done when I was going to sea. And I continued this after the war."

Q. And then after the war did you join the Communist Party in the United States?

A. Yes, I joined in May or June of 1946.

Q. Whereabouts was that?

A. Hollywood.

Q. And what kind of a group or cell did you belong to?

A. Frankly, I don't know how I would define it. It was composed primarily or I guess exclusively of what were referred to in the industry as "back lot" workers, people who were technicians, they were not in the front office and they were not in the limelight, they were not actors or directors or writers.

Q. They were people employed in the motion picture industry?

A. Yes, sir.

Q. Did the group have meetings?

A. Yes, there was a meeting every week.

Q. What went on at the meetings?

A. Usually there was an agenda. As I recall it was split into three components. There would be discussion of world affairs for perhaps an hour, maybe a little more, and then there would be a discussion of the situation within the industry. There was a strike on at the time. And finally there would be a discussion, a theoretical discussion, of Marxism, socialism, capitalism, political science—the whole thing.

Q. Did you pay dues?

A. I did.

Q. Were those collected regularly at the meetings?

A. They were.

Q. And was there a leader of the group?

A. Yes, there was.

Q. And, generally speaking, what did he do?

A. He was just the moderator. He set the tone. He conducted the meeting.

The defense had pictured a Communist Party which exerted iron rule over every detail of its members' lives and which would do anything—even to the point of murder—to prevent a member's breaking away.

Q. Did the Communist Party ever make any attempt to run your whole personal life?

A. Not in the least. As a matter of fact, I guess I should say I—because I mentioned a book that I wrote—I made the statement that I was perhaps the only person who ever bought a yacht and joined the Communist Party in the same week.

Membership was secret. After six months Hayden had simply stopped going to meetings. Had there been any reprisals by the Party over his dropping out? "No, no. I had a phone call from a person whom I knew and she said, 'Are you sure you are doing what you want to do?' And I said, 'I am sure.' She said, 'Do you realize if you go through with it you will never be able to get back into the Party?' And I said, 'I do' and that was the end of it. I have never heard another word on it."

Hayden had come from San Francisco with a thoroughly qualified expert on communism. He was Paul Jacobs, a former Trotskyite official and labor union organizer, now a well-known writer and staff member of the Center for the Study of Democratic Institutions.

A short, bald, dynamic man with a strong voice and piercing eyes, Jacobs quickly summed up his manifold activities. He was currently on the staff of the University of California while writing a book on unemployed workers; director of a trade union project for the Center for the Study of Democratic Institutions; correspondent for the *Economist* of London; contributor to numerous other magazines; and consultant to the Peace Corps, for which he had just returned from Southeast Asia. He had been a lecturer to Air Force officers on communism, and consultant to the McClellan Committee in its probe of union racketeering. His book *The State of the Unions* had recently come out. He now held a security clearance. As a writer his chief concerns were labor unions and communism.

Jacobs had joined the Young Communist League while a student in New York in 1933. He took courses at the Workers' School—the same one attended by Sally Goldmark—which the defense had wrongly pictured as a training center for illegal activities. "It was more of an adult education center, in a way," Jacobs said. The school, the Party headquarters, and the bookstore all operated openly.

Jacobs soon switched to the Workers' Party of America, a Trotskyite organization. To the Trotskyites the Communist Party had betrayed the true revolution. "[W]e considered ourselves," said Jacobs, "to be the heirs of Lenin and Trotsky and of Marx and Engels."

He spent five years as a full-time Trotskyite official and organizer in New York and the Midwest. There was constant warfare with the rival communists. "One of the great difficulties of being a Trotskyite was that you had to be better educated about the nature of the Communist Party than the communists themselves."

He broke away from the Trotskyites in 1939—because, he said, "I began to understand that the solution which was proposed by the Bolsheviks—and I considered myself a Bolshevik—was no longer what I believed to be the proper solution for the problems of America."

Jacobs became an organizer for the International Ladies Garment Workers' Union; served in the wartime Army; worked after the war for the American Jewish Committee; and returned to the labor movement as an organizer for the Oil Workers' Union. He prosecuted the CIO's intraunion case which led to expulsion of the Longshoremen's Union as a communist-dominated organization. His final report was published by the Senate Labor Committee.

Since then Jacobs had written about communism for leading periodicals. No friend of the Soviet Union, he was denounced as a "hooligan" for an article he published following a visit to that country.

As an expert on the Communist Party, Jacobs confirmed the reasonableness of Sally Goldmark's account of her life in the Party and departure from it. It would have been possible for a secret cell member in 1935–43 to be less than fully committed, to argue over ideas, to marry anyone she chose, and to leave the Party freely. Would the answers be any different if Charles Kramer and Victor Perlo were in the group? "No," said Jacobs, "not for the ordinary Party member."

The period from late 1935 through the end of the war, Jacobs testified, was the "people's front" period. "It was during this period that the Communist Party put up such slogans as 'Communism is twentieth-century Americanism' and touted Thomas Jefferson and Abraham Lincoln as the communists' heroes." Once the war started, the atmosphere in the United States "was one of tremendous support for the Soviet Union and for everything Russian, as one of our allies." Most who had ever belonged to the Communist Party had both joined it and left it during the years 1935–45.

"Communist Party discipline," Jacobs said, "would be observed very carefully and very rigidly on people who considered themselves or were considered to be a person like myself, a hardened Bolshevik type. We were expected to observe Party discipline and we did. However, the great mass of Party members were not expected to observe such discipline because if the Party had tried to impose a kind of heavy discipline upon them as it did upon its hard-core members, they would have simply run in terror from the Party." The hard-core group had probably comprised less than one percent of the communists.

Did the Party ever send people into rural areas to run for office? "I never heard of such a practice," Jacobs answered. "It would be contrary to the theory of the Communist Party. . . . It would be a waste of good talent, they would think—I would."

The direct examination was over in less than an hour. We hoped for a strong defense attack, and were not disappointed.

> Q. Mr. Jacobs, you testified on direct, speaking of yourself and others in your Trotskyite cell, "We considered ourselves to be the true communists in America." You are speaking of the period of time while you were in this cell, is that right?
>
> A. Yes.
>
> Q. And do you still feel that way, that the Trotskyites are the true Communist Party in America?
>
> A. I think that the Trotskyites were closer to the standard and patterns set down by Lenin than the communists were.
>
> Q. In other words, that the real—what we refer to as the Communist Party, U.S.A., had departed further

from the theoretical communist pattern than the Trotskyites had?

A. Yes.

Q. Is that still true?

A. It is very difficult to talk about the Communist Party of the United States today. It doesn't really exist.

Q. Well, the Trotskyites group still exists, does it not, Mr. Jacobs?

A. About the same rate as the communists do, very tiny and without any influence.

Harmon turned to Sally's past membership in a secret group.

Q. Now you said that it was possible for someone to be in a cell with Perlo and Kramer and not know who they were. On what do you base that possibility, Mr. Jacobs?

A. The way the Party operated, the way Party membership operated, was that you had at the bottom a kind of a mass base of people whose commitment and whose attachment to the Party varied considerably. Some came in for personal reasons; some came in for political reasons; some came in because they thought they were going to find girls they could go out with—lots of reasons why people joined the Communist Party. That was kind of a big mass of people. Included in that mass of people were some people like Perlo and Kramer who were much more devoted and much more committed communists. . . . And the ordinary rank and file Party member in the normal course of his Party career, which might extend over a period of many years, might never know that some of the people in the unit in which he belonged were actually higher officials in the Party than they said. . . .

Some placed the Party above their private lives, said Jacobs. "There were others who fell in love with people who weren't communists, married them and left instantaneously, suddenly discovering that perhaps this was what they had been looking for all the time they were in the Party."

Were the communists' aims during the "popular front" period really different from those of any other time? "Yes, I believe that is one period in which both the membership and most of the leaders of the Communist Party of the United States believed, sincerely believed, that it was going to be possible to achieve their objective somehow in the United States by making alliances with liberal organizations, by working in all kinds of groups that weren't communist groups, and actually believed that it was going to be possible to defeat fascism in this way." During those years, Jacobs added, the communists "supported Wendell Wilkie, supported Franklin Roosevelt, supported a whole series of people who at earlier times they had denounced as enemies and who they denounced as enemies later on—the very same people."

Didn't communism present a serious threat today? "Yes, I believe that world communism represents a threat to freedom all over the world and that obviously includes the United States. I think that the American Communist Party does not represent the threat to the United States at the present time. . . ."

Q. Well, isn't the American Communist Party part of the overall worldwide communist movement and as such a part of the total threat?

A. No. The world communist movement has many national parties in it. There is a Communist Party of Holland, for example, but the Communist Party of Holland represents no threat to the Dutch society. On the other hand, there is a communist party of some significance in certain South American countries. They do represent an internal threat.

As Jacobs talked, the complex, real world replaced the defense's simplistic battleground. Exasperated, Harmon invoked his clients' highest authority.

Q. Mr. Jacobs, would you consider J. Edgar Hoover an authority on communism?

A. Yes, I think Mr. Hoover is an authority. I disagree—authorities disagree among each other—but on the whole I think Mr. Hoover is a reasonable authority.

Q. You disagree with his belief which has been reiterated a number of times including recently, that the Communist Party of the United States is a serious internal threat, is that it?

A. Yes, I disagree with that belief. I believe that the FBI is more capable than Mr. Hoover seems to believe it is.

Harmon's questions frequently spoke of "underground espionage cells." But there is no such thing, Jacobs testified. "Anybody engaged in espionage for the communist movement or indeed for espionage for any movement never is part of a cell. . . . The espionage agent never knows more than perhaps one or two other people, usually only a courier or a contact man. So that the concept of doing espionage, or having an espionage cell, is utterly destructive of the very idea of espionage. . . ."

Yet Elizabeth Bentley had placed Perlo and Kramer in her espionage group, Harmon insisted. By now even the judge appeared fascinated as Jacobs replied: ". . . I must confess with regard to Miss Bentley, I have found, along with others in this field including Professor Packer who made a detailed study of her testimony, I find of all the witnesses who testify about their activities during this period that Miss Bentley is considered by most people not directly involved in testifying themselves, to be the least reliable witness."

Perlo and Kramer, he added, "both denied under oath the charges that she had made. They have not been prosecuted for perjury. They have not been prosecuted at all. They have never been brought up, despite Miss Bentley's charges, on any charge of espionage. So on the basis of that fact alone I would tend to regard Miss Bentley's testimony with a good deal of doubt."

"You also know," Harmon asked, "that both J. Edgar Hoover and the Department of Justice during the period of time when Alger Hiss was being prosecuted disagreed with your analysis of Miss Bentley and the reliability of her testimony, don't you?" "Yes, I do," Jacobs answered. "They do disagree. And I disagree with them."

The sweeping cross-examination opened new ground for us on redirect. Since the defense had invited Jacob's views on ex-communist witnesses, I named the ones who had appeared at the trial and asked his view of their credibility. None of them, he answered, was fully reliable. "My greatest complaint against these people is that they obscure the real problem of the communists and the communist menace with these kinds of notions of being surrounded on all sides by enemies who in most cases don't exist. And I would finally say that the more a witness testifies in such hearings as a professional witness, the more his story—which is the product that he is selling—gets tailored to meet the specific demands of the customer in any given trial. . . ."

Jacobs stimulated everyone in the room. We followed him with Dr. Gabriel Almond, director of the Institute of Political Studies at Stanford University. A quiet, scholarly man, Almond was a leading expert on political parties, a former officer of the American Political Science Association, and a current consultant to the State Department's Bureau of Intelligence and Research.

Dr. Almond had directed a research project which ex-

224

actly suited our needs. In a three-year study, researchers in the United States and four other countries interviewed a wide spectrum of people—workers, intellectuals, professional men and women—who had belonged to the Communist Party. Their aim was to discover why people joined the Party, and why they left it. Almond's book, *The Appeals of Communism,* reported the findings. His answers now on the witness stand were like concise essays on the history of communism in America.

Most people who joined the Party in the thirties and forties, he explained, were neither "hard-core," nor "indoctrinated," nor "militant." In fact, the "whole idea of the 'popular front' was to get out of this isolation, to form alliance with other groups and movements, trade-union movements, intellectuals, professionals, and the like, in an effort to build the biggest possible coalition so that the Soviet Union, which was then menaced by Japan on one side and Germany on the other, would not be isolated. . . . The tactic of the Party, you see, was to advocate popular causes, to assume a character that would make it easy for people, let's say, to join the Party."

Recruitment and discipline had followed "a deliberately lax policy. In order to be able to reach out and draw in people of this kind it was very important not to put the heat on."

Was espionage carried on by Communist Party cells? "No, espionage is not a group activity. Groups, cells, do not carry on espionage. Units do not carry on espionage."

I put to him a hypothetical story like Sally's. Was it possible? Yes, one could belong without full dedication, join a group which did nothing but talk, argue against the leadership, marry a noncommunist without repercussions, and leave the Party simply by dropping out. Would his answers be different if the cell included Victor Perlo and Charles

Kramer? "They would not be different. I would give the same answer."

There were several hundred thousand ex-communists in the country. What did his study show about their lives after leaving the Party? "This was one of the aspects of the American communist movement that we were most interested in. What we discovered was, on leaving the Party, most—the great majority of people sought to, you might say, re-establish a private and safe and secure existence. Most of them had a feeling of having been disillusioned, of having been, you know, of having been sold a bill of goods, and having been involved in something that had left them with a feeling of having been contaminated. This was the common feeling among most of the people whom we talked to and their every impulse was to try to reconstruct, you know, some existence of which they could be proud, re-think their values, develop their family life and this kind of thing." Many had changed locations in the country in order to find "some part of the world where they could be taken for their own merits."

Defense counsel challenged Dr. Almond's study. Those interviewed had not been placed under oath. The interviews had been conducted by assistants, not by the witness himself. The defense saw the intellectuals as forming the Party's militant hard core.

> Q. . . . Isn't it the intellectual class from which that group is recruited?
> A. No, not even in the American Communist Party which had more intellectuals proportionally than most communist parties. The real hard core consisted of pretty tough guys. Intellectuals aren't usually—they don't usually have those qualities that are needed, you know, they are a little bit too nervous, too skittish, too

sensitive. They are too troubled. They suffer from conflicts, guilt and the like. . . .

How many of the ex-communists interviewed had entered into active political life? Almond could not recall the number, but some had. It was common for them "to change and to become quite moderate liberals in their views. This was the most frequent pattern."

Almond's scholarly manner was in sharp contrast to Jacobs's fiery temperament, but he was equally persuasive.

CHAPTER **15**

Professor Melvin Rader came to Okanogan to answer Barbara Hartle's charge that she knew him to be a communist because she had attended a closed Party meeting with him in about 1937. He could have responded simply by reminding the press that a similar charge against him had been exploded fifteen years earlier; instead he chose to defend himself in full measure.

A tall, lanky, thoughtful man with glasses and a shock of gray hair, Rader was at first uneasy in the courtroom. He told of growing up in Walla Walla, where his brother was still a farmer; of attending the University of Washington; and of serving on the philosophy faculty there since 1930. "Now, Doctor Rader," I asked him, "are you now a member of the Communist Party?" "I am not," he answered.

> Q. Have you ever been a member of the Communist Party?
> A. I have never been a member of the Communist Party.
> Q. Have you ever been at a closed meeting of the Communist Party, that is a meeting at which only Communist Party members were present?
> A. No, I have never been at a closed meeting of the Communist Party at any time, anywhere.
> Q. Have you ever been under the discipline or control of the Communist Party?

A. No, I have never been under the discipline or control of the Communist Party.

Q. As far as you know have you ever met a woman named Barbara Hartle?

A. So far as I know I have never met her. I haven't any idea what she looks like.

Q. Have you been accused of being a communist at any time before this trial?

A. Yes, I have.

Q. And when and where did that happen?

A. During the Canwell hearings in the summer of 1948.

This was the famous Rader case which epitomized the Canwell Committee's methods. A witness imported from New York accused him from the stand; the committee permitted no cross-examination and immediately spirited the witness out of the state. During a long ordeal of uncertainty and suspicion, Rader gathered evidence which finally proved his own innocence.

The defense lawyers appeared surprised that Rader had come. They had apparently thought he would defend himself from the safety of his home in Seattle.

During the thirties, Harmon asked, had Rader belonged to "organizations which have been listed as communist fronts by governmental agencies?"

A. That is eventually and later listed by the Attorney General?

Q. Yes.

A. Well, there was the American League Against War and Fascism. There was the Friends of Spanish Democracy . . .

He named a few others. Had he known that some of the other members were communists? ". . . I think that was fairly general knowledge. There were many communists in

practically all liberal organizations in those days. . . ."
Rader's nervousness vanished as he talked, and his honesty
became unmistakable.

Q. During the period of time about which we are
concerned . . . in the late '30s, it is a fact, isn't it,
Professor, that you wrote a book entitled *No
Compromise*?
A. Yes, I wrote such a book.
Q. And isn't it a fact that you classed Soviet
Russia as a democracy?
A. It is not a fact; that is false.
Q. Let's see, you are a member and past
president of the Washington Chapter of the American
Civil Liberties Union, aren't you?
A. I am very proud to say so.
Q. It is true, is it not, Professor Rader, that while
you were president of the state ACLU you were bitterly
opposed to teaching any courses in the public schools of
this state which would include material derogatory to the
Soviet Russia brand of communism?
A. That is not true at all.

On redirect examination I asked him to explain why he
had joined organizations along with communists in the 1930s.
"This was a time of deep Depression," Rader said, "when
there were millions—a good many millions unemployed and
desperate poverty on the part of a great number of people
who were losing their farms and their homes. It was also
a time when Hitler and Mussolini and the Japanese fascists
were very much on the march. And there was a great movement toward a world war. Under these circumstances it
seemed to me that it was extremely important for all the
people who were opposed to this sort of thing to unite and
to try to prevent and to try to keep us from having a third

world war. These organizations publicly were dedicated to this purpose. . . ."

Rader explained why he had always been opposed to the communists' ideology. "[A]s a philosopher, I think that dialectic materialism is a crude and dogmatic philosophy. As an American I believe in the Bill of Rights, in the fundamental constitutional liberties and human rights written into our Constitution. And I don't believe the communists believe that and respect that." The Marxist theory, he added, "is very lopsided in its emphasis upon economic causes to the exclusion of all other causes. That seems to me a very great misreading of history."

We obtained the court's leave to reopen Barbara Hartle's cross-examination. A witness may be impeached—that is, his credibility questioned—by proof of a "prior inconsistent statement" contradicting his sworn testimony. The cross-examiner must first ask the witness if he made the earlier statement; if the witness denies it, then the person who heard it may testify. By telephone to Washington we had discovered a remarkable statement Mrs. Hartle had made about Melvin Rader nine years earlier.

She resumed the stand. "Mrs. Hartle," I asked her, "during the time that you were a witness before the House Un-American Activities Committee in Seattle, did you tell . . . Edwin Guthman in a conversation between you and him that Melvin Rader had never been a communist or a member of the Communist Party; that you knew that the Communist Party had tried to get him to join on several occasions, but that you also knew that their efforts had always met with failure?"

"No, I did not," she answered.

We called Ed Guthman. A dark-haired, athletic-looking newspaperman in his forties, Guthman had won a Pulitzer

231

Prize for his *Seattle Times* articles on the Rader case. Now he was serving with the Johnson administration as Special Assistant to the Attorney General for Public Information; his immediate superior was Robert Kennedy.

Guthman testified that he had graduated from the University of Washington in 1941, served as a reconaissance platoon leader in North Africa and Italy in World War II, and joined the *Times* after the war. In 1948 he covered the hearings of the Canwell Committee. He was present when the committee's imported witness accused Melvin Rader of having been at a communist training school in New York State, and when Rader took the stand to deny that charge. Over the following several months Guthman made an investigation to find out who was telling the truth. It ended with a series of articles setting forth the proof of Rader's innocence and recounting the committee's suppression of evidence. In later years he remained interested in the case.

Q. And in that regard, and directing your attention to the 1950s, did you make any effort to talk about Professor Rader to people who were then in the process of leaving the Communist Party?

A. Yes, I did.

Q. Was Mrs. Hartle one such person?

A. Yes, she was.

Q. And if you recall a conversation with her about that subject, tell us when and where it was and what was said by both of you, please.

A. I covered the hearing—the House Un-American Activities Committee, both hearings at which Mrs. Hartle testified, 1954 and 1956. My recollection is that in 1954 I asked her during a recess whether Professor Rader had ever been a member of the Communist Party. I recall that she answered to me that he had not been; that they had sought to recruit him into the Communist Party and that he had refused to join.

Q. How clear or how certain are you about this conversation with Mrs. Hartle?

A. I am very clear.

Harmon was coldly angry as the cross-examination began.

Q. Well, I suppose it is a fact, isn't it, Mr. Guthman, that this was very gratifying to you to find that your judgment was right on this subject of Mr. Rader.

A. It was.

Q. As a matter of fact it was quite a—quite a news story, wasn't it?

A. What, Mr. Harmon?

Q. On verification from the communist who was in charge of the picketing the Canwell hearings, that Mr. Rader in fact was not a member of the Communist Party at the time he was accused, wasn't that a news story?

A. No, it wasn't.

Q. It wasn't.

A. We had written that in 1949. And I never wrote a word of it.

Q. You are telling me, Mr. Guthman, that you never wrote a word about this story?—

A. I didn't.

Q. —that Mrs. Hartle gave you when you had solicited the interview through the Marshal's office?

A. That is right.

Q. Wasn't it a scoop of the first order?

A. I didn't consider it so.

Q. Oh. Private satisfaction, is that all you were interested in?

A. I had asked many people who had come out of the Communist Party following the incident with Professor Rader as to whether he had been a member of the Communist Party. And Mrs. Hartle was the highest ranking former communist that I had ever talked to on that subject and so had confirmed what I had heard from others, so I—

Harmon lost his temper and pounded the table with his fist.

Q. Mr. Guthman, I was a newspaperman for ten years, and isn't it a fact that that was a scoop of the first water? Here was the communist who was in charge of picketing those hearings who told you that it was true that it had been a lie told by the witness from New York about Mr. Rader; wasn't that a scoop of the first order?

Guthman remained cool; the contrast was devastating.

A. I can only tell you, Mr. Harmon, what I did.
Q. Yes. You didn't print it.
A. We had printed it in 1949.
Q. Mr. Guthman, did she tell you what you say from the witness stand?
A. Certainly she told me.
Q. Why didn't you print the story?
A. We had printed it in 1949.
Q. Oh, and this would be merely verification of what you said in 1949?
A. Not what I said, Mr. Harmon.
Q. All right, what the *Times* had said in its story?
A. Not what the *Times* had said, Mr. Harmon.
Q. All right, what would it be a version of?
A. What Professor Rader had said and what Doctor Allen, the President of the University of Washington, had said.
Q. And it was not a news story?
A. Well, I didn't write it.
Q. Yes, I know you didn't write it; but did it happen?
A. Certainly it happened.

With his quiet courtesy in the face of a violent attack,

Guthman had destroyed Mrs. Hartle's testimony about Rader, and the impact would go beyond the immediate question of the professor's innocence.

Our experts on communism had refuted the defense's argument that John must have been a Party member or sympathizer when he married Sally in 1942. Now we called a witness who knew him at the time. Henry Reuss, a distinguished congressman from Milwaukee, a vigorous man with a powerful frame who spoke decisively and to the point, had been assistant general counsel for the Office of Price Administration. John Goldmark, just out of law school, worked for him a year beginning in the summer of 1941. The work was so intense, Reuss said, that "I spent almost all of my time during almost all of that year with Mr. Goldmark that I wasn't either at home sleeping or eating some place."

The OPA lawyers often discussed politics and world affairs, including communism. "The belief that both Mr. Goldmark and I expressed during that period on that subject is that communism is an evil thing, that it denies the basic human rights of freedom of speech, freedom of religion, freedom to conduct one's affairs; that Soviet communism was a dangerous form of world imperialism."

Goldmark went into the Navy, and Reuss visited him and his wife and newborn son in January 1944, the evening before John left for the South Pacific. "They seemed very happy, very affectionate toward each other."

The two men met again as delegates to the 1952 Democratic National Convention. They had talked about John's move to the West. Harmon objected that this was not proper rebuttal. "Now do the defendants concede," Judge Turner asked, "that there is no issue on the purpose of the Goldmarks' coming west?" They would not concede; the objection was overruled. In 1952, Reuss testified, "I asked him how he was doing out in Washington and he told me he and his family loved it out there; that it was just what he wanted and he thought it was the wisest decision he had ever made, not to practice law in the East but to come out here. And he told me something about the country here. . . ."

Reuss qualified as an expert on American politics. I listed for him fifteen positions, described by the defense as "communist," which John had taken, including support of a ban on nuclear testing in the atmosphere, support of trade with some communist countries, opposition to the Smith Act and portions of the McCarran Act, support of a state income tax referendum, criticism of the current "anti-communist movement," and support of the American Civil Liberties Union. "Can you tell us whether or not all of these positions are held by substantial numbers of American citizens who have no connection or sympathy with communism?" "Yes, they are," Reuss answered. ". . . I think reasonable and patriotic Republicans and Democrats alike hold to these positions."

We called Richard H. Riddell, a well-known lawyer who was current president of the Seattle-King County Bar Association. Riddell and Goldmark had attended law school together. As friends they saw each other daily during a critical period in history—September 1939 to June 1941, the time of the Hitler-Stalin Pact. The defense had proved that during this interlude the communists, reversing an earlier stand, had argued that Americans need not arm and must not intervene in the European war. Goldmark, Riddell testified, had taken the opposite tack; he favored commencement of the draft and a buildup of the American armed forces. John had seen "that our interests were inextricably bound up with the democracies in that fight and that sooner or

236

later this country would be drawn into the conflict on the side of the western democracies."

During the war Riddell served as an Air Force intelligence officer in England. Back home in the late forties, he joined the Young Democrats and led a struggle for power against a communist faction in King County; Goldmark, though outside the county, helped.

The defense had attacked the Young Democrats during Goldmark's presidency as "soft on communism." Riddell had attended most of the state board meetings of the time. Goldmark and the organization "were strongly in favor of President Truman's decision to jump into South Korea with full force when the communists invaded from North Korea."

Had he ever known Goldmark to do or say anything that would in any way suggest sympathy with communism? "Never, quite the contrary." The same was true of Mrs. Goldmark; he had been shocked to learn that Sally was a former communist. "It was totally contrary to every discussion of politics, international affairs, that had been participated in in her presence and in mine through the years during which I had known her from '47 on."

The jury knew John held a security clearance but had little idea what this meant. We called Marvin Durning, a reserve lieutenant in Navy Intelligence who practiced law in Seattle. A former Rhodes scholar and teacher at Yale, Durning had served on a destroyer in the Far East, with a counterintelligence unit in Germany, and with the Office of Naval Intelligence in Washington, where he had been "assigned to a group which dealt with sabotage, espionage and subversive activities." He had extensive experience in evaluating security files on Navy personnel, and was familiar with the governing standards.

A security clearance such as Goldmark held would not

be granted or kept in force, Durning testified, if there was the slightest doubt about the loyalty of either the officer or his wife. What would Navy Intelligence do in the case of an officer known to be married to a former communist? The benefit of a doubt always goes to the government, said Durning. "[T]hey would overwhelmingly have to convince themselves that the wife in question was no longer a communist, no longer sympathetic and that the person in question was in no way sympathetic." If any question existed as to whether the officer's spouse had ever been involved in espionage, there would be no security clearance under any circumstances.

In a long trial there usually comes a point where one side seems to pull ahead for good. Sentiment shifts, the weaker side almost visibly falls apart. In our rebuttal case we seemed to have reached this point. Our witnesses had been superb. Yet the feelings of the stoical jury remained unknown; for all we knew the case may have been hopeless from the start.

At a weekend recess we welcomed a personable trial lawyer from New Jersey, William F. Tompkins, who, as Assistant United States Attorney General in charge of the Internal Security Division in the Eisenhower administration, had been one of the top security officers in the country. None of us had met Tompkins before. At Christmas I had written to him describing the case and asking him to come; he readily agreed to interrupt his practice and cross the country to help us.

Tompkins came to the stand, a pleasant, informal man with a prominent nose, a ready smile, and a quick wit. He had taken his law training at Rutgers, joined the infantry, learned Chinese, and served as an officer in charge of war crimes prosecutions in Saigon and Singapore. Back to practice in Newark he became a Republican state legislator,

United States Attorney for New Jersey, and, in 1954, Assistant Attorney General of the United States.

His division, Tompkins explained, "had general supervision in the Department of Justice over the statutes relating to espionage, sabotage, the Smith Act, the Internal Security Act of 1950, the security program internally in the Department of Justice and the coordinating basis with other agencies throughout the government. We had charge of the foreign agents registration, operation. We had a function on the planning board of the National Security Council; I was a member of it. And generally we had also jurisdiction over certain violations of the Atomic Energy Act and generally all of the statutes dealing with subversive activities."

Tompkins was in charge of all espionage cases. He had personally prosecuted several, including that of Rudolf Abel, the Russian spy who was convicted, sentenced to prison, and later exchanged for the American U-2 pilot Gary Powers.

He served until 1958. The Justice Department exercised "a general coordinating function between agencies" on security clearances; Tompkins was thoroughly familiar with the standards used. An executive order by President Eisenhower required that clearance be awarded only when "clearly consistent with the interests of national security." Tompkins had the regulations before him, and read from them. Under Defense Department rules the cleared person must be of "unquestionable loyalty." John Goldmark's clearance had been granted in 1956 and kept in force ever since. I put to Tompkins the hypothetical case of a Navy man whose wife had been in a Communist Party cell while a government employee.

Q. Now if the Navy had any doubt about whether or not the Navy man in question was a communist or communist sympathizer would the clearance be granted?

A. It certainly would not.

Q. Would it be retained if any doubt arose?

A. It certainly would not; it would be cancelled immediately if there was the slightest doubt.

Q. If there was any doubt as to whether the man was under communist discipline in any sense of that term would security clearance be granted?

A. It would not. In evaluating security information your first interest is the protection of this country, so the doubts would be resolved against the individual you have mentioned.

Q. If the man had any sympathetic association with a communist front organization or other subversive organization would the clearance be granted?

A. That is part of your criteria; the clearance would not be granted.

Q. Now with regard to the man's wife, if there were any doubt as to whether his wife were loyal to the United States, would the clearance be granted?

A. I would certainly say it would not.

Q. If there were any doubt as to whether she were a communist or pro-communist, would it be granted?

A. You are talking at the present time?

Q. Yes.

A. No, it would not be granted.

Q. If the evidence indicated that she had ever at any time had anything to do with espionage against the United States government, would the clearance be granted?

A. No, I would say it would not.

Q. If the evidence indicated that the wife had lied to the FBI or to the House Committee or both, would the clearance be granted or would it be retained after such event?

A. It would never be granted if there was a false statement made and that is also part of your criteria.

Former Congressman Donald Jackson had attacked Sally's testimony before the House Committee on Un-American Activities. Now we could reply. Part of Tompkins's job in Justice had been to review the testimony of committee witnesses to determine whether the transcripts should be presented to a grand jury for possible perjury charges.

> Q. Have you read the transcript of Mrs.
> Goldmark's testimony before the House Un-American Activities Committee?
> A. Yes, sir, I have.
> Q. And from your knowledge of the field and your reading of the transcript do you see anything in it which appears to be untrue or inconsistent or false?

Harmon objected that this would not rebut any of Congressman Jackson's testimony. The question to him had merely been whether Sally had cooperated with the committee. "I would think that telling the truth would be cooperation," I responded. But I rephrased the question:

> Q. Can you make a judgment as to whether she cooperated with the committee?
> A. I can.
> Q. What is your judgment?
> A. I would say that she had.

Defense counsel, cross-examining, tried to restore prestige to private investigators of communism. Wasn't it true that governmental agencies sometimes used their files? "I will be very frank with you, sir," Tompkins answered. "I know of no information from private agencies concerning the operations of the Communist Party, any of the internal operations, any of their underground operations—I have never seen any information supplied by a private agency

241

that was not already in the possession of the Federal Bureau of Investigation."

Had not Alger Hiss enjoyed a security clearance? Tompkins doubted this; the system was devised later. Wouldn't the conflicts in Sally Goldmark's testimony change his opinion that she cooperated? ". . . I would want to review it, sir, but it would have to be material and substantial and not just a minor error in recollection." It was customary to question a witness more than once if there was any doubt. "And I would say the fact that the committee didn't recall her would be also very strong evidence to me that they were entirely satisfied with her cooperation and with her testimony."

Again we rested our case.

There was a short surrebuttal by the defense. Ford Elvidge, a prominent Seattle lawyer and former governor of Guam, had served as special assistant to the state attorney general when the state un-American activities committee was founded. He helped the chairman devise questions and procedures. "And Mr. Canwell followed my advice in that connection, as a consequence of which, subsequently, there were prosecutions and conviction for failure to answer questions." The State Supreme Court upheld the committee's constitutionality. Elvidge himself had read the transcript of Canwell's University of Washington hearing. "Yes, I would say that he conducted it in accordance with legal procedure, fairly and ably and intelligently and certainly in accordance with the law, as I viewed it."

The defense recalled Barbara Hartle. This was a brilliant move. Talking in her flat, mechanical way, as if Guthman's testimony had made not the slightest impact on her, she recaptured the jury's attention by telling more stories of life in the Communist Party. The Party did infiltrate candidates into rural areas, she said, and "in some districts, including

rural districts, communists were elected to the legislature."
She calmly denied ever telling Guthman that Rader had refused to join the Party.

Albert Canwell came once again to the stand. He had
turned up "governmental documents" describing Paul Jacobs as a communist front member, an inaccurate writer,
and a member of the Fair Play for Cuba Committee. These
consisted of statements about Jacobs in reports of various
federal and state legislative committees, which the defense
offered into evidence. Our objection was sustained; the
documents were hearsay. Jacobs had returned to California.
The defense lawyers requested a "continuance of perhaps
a week" to take his deposition through written interroga-
tories. That evening I telephoned Jacobs at San Francisco
and asked if he would fly back to Okanogan the following
day. Although busy with other work, he agreed to come.
We reported this to the defense: a deposition would be unnecessary, they could question the witness in person. Faced
with another bout with Jacobs, the defense lawyers dropped
the attack.

There was one more witness, a minor federal official from
Spokane who described Canwell's reputation for truthfulness as "very good." The defense rested.

The judge gave the jurors a day off so that he and the
lawyers could finish work on the instructions which would
tell them the rules of law they should apply. "Don't discuss
the case among yourselves or with others," he reminded
them. "Please do not read any newspaper articles about the
case. Try to keep fresh in your mind what you have heard
and try to avoid making up your minds. . . . Counsels'
arguments to you in this case are going to be of the greatest
value."

CHAPTER **16**

A TRIAL JURY hears the evidence first and the law afterward. Only at the end does the judge give the detailed legal rules which the jurors must follow in deciding the case. Both sides had presented dozens of requested jury instructions and argued them to the court; Judge Turner was now ready with instructions which spanned fifty-seven typed pages. They contained, we believed, the widest escape hatches ever given libel defendants in a Washington court.

The courtroom was full and the jury attentive as the judge read in his dry, quiet voice.

"It is the duty of the court to instruct you as to the law governing the case," he said, "and you shall take such instructions to be the law. . . . You shall not permit sympathy or prejudice or public opinion to have any place in your deliberations, for all persons are equal before the law and all are entitled to exact justice."

"Every man has a right to have his good name maintained unimpaired," the judge went on. "To publish a false and unjustifiable statement which assails the reputation of another is a wrong, for which the law provides a remedy. . . . A libel is a false publication which tends to expose a living person to hatred, contempt, ridicule or obloquy, or to deprive him of the benefit of public confidence or social intercourse, or to injure him in his business or occupation."

The jury was to decide "the meaning of the statements sued on, and whether or not they are of a defamatory nature or character. To charge in express language that another person is a communist, or that he is guilty of a crime, is defamatory as a matter of law, and if false, is libelous. However, where the statement does not contain such an express charge, but contains language from which the reader might or might not infer that such a charge was intended, then the actual meaning of the language is a question of fact for the jury. . . ."

He came to the defenses. "Truth is a complete defense to an action for libel or slander based upon a claim that the defamatory statement is false in fact." But the alleged libel might not be an assertion of fact. It might be an expression of opinion; in that event, the fair comment privilege could provide a defense. "A 'privilege,' in the law of libel and slander," said the judge, "refers to the protection which the law gives in certain situations to a person who makes a defamatory statement about another person, where it is more important that the statement be made freely, without fear of liability, than that the other person be compensated for the injury to his reputation." So it was with a candidate for office. An attack upon him, "even though it is defamatory," was ordinarily privileged and immune to suit if it represented the critic's actual opinion.

The judge gave the privilege an expansive breadth. "The comment or criticism need not express an opinion with which any person of reasonable intelligence and judgment could possibly agree. It is immaterial that it might not be reasonable warranted by the facts upon which it is based. If the public is to be aided in forming its judgment upon matters of public interest by a free interchange of opinion, it is essential that honest criticism and comment, no matter how foolish or prejudiced, be privileged. The fact that the criticism is fantastic is immaterial, and an extravagant form of expression is unimportant."

There were two qualifications. A publication "made solely from spite or ill will or for the purpose of causing harm" was not privileged. The word "solely" helped the defense; earlier cases had held spiteful defamation unprivileged regardless of the presence of other motives. And the privilege "applies only to defamatory comment and opinion. It does not afford protection for the publication of false defamatory statements or insinuations of fact about public officials and candidates for public office."

These instructions could easily bring a defense verdict. The way was open for the jury to find that everything the defendants had said simply represented their opinions about communism, the ACLU, and a public official, and was therefore privileged.

There was a further escape hatch. "A statement of fact contained . . . in an official report of a committee of Congress or of a state legislature, even though not true in fact, is a privileged statement and is not actionable. . . ." Anyone could freely repeat such a committee statement "without being subject to liability on that account, even though the statement be false and defamatory." This could apply to the defendants' charges against the ACLU, in support of which they could point to legislative committee reports.

If the jury found the defendants liable, the judge went on, then it should consider the question of damages. An award could be made only for real injury. "By the law of this state, neither damages by way of punishment . . . nor damages by way of an example to others . . . are allowable, and you cannot include in your verdict any sum for either of these purposes." If the jurors found liability but "no substantial injury or damage, then the damages awarded should be nominal only."

The reading of the instructions took half a day.

I rose to begin the closing arguments.

All of us were in the courtroom, I told the jury, because "a man's good name has been attacked, destroyed, vilified, dragged through the mud, not once, not twice, but practically every day for a period that is now going on to be two years. The man, of course, is John Goldmark."

The jurors knew that reputation is at the heart of our existence. "In fact, it is no exaggeration to say that life without a good name is hardly worth living." The law of libel was not a matter of legal technicalities. "The Ninth Commandment in the Bible is that 'Thou shalt not bear false witness against thy neighbor'. . . . people recognized then, as they do now, that the power of the written word and the power of the spoken word is really the power of life and death over a man's existence."

In the community where Goldmark had chosen to make his life and bring up his children, he had no choice but to sue. "He has to fight for his good name, not only for his sake but for the sake of his family."

The libels put out by the defendants were of the worst type. "A man who is called a communist is called a traitor to his country, an enemy to his country." One so condemned would be followed everywhere by a cloud of ill will and suspicion; nor would his children escape it. "These are the reasons that this case had to be tried here in Okanogan County and not in Seattle and not in Spokane and not anywhere else. Because it is here that the Goldmarks' reputation is for good or bad. This is their home."

Once in court, the defendants had repeated the charge over and over again—but without ever proving it. I reviewed the evidence, wedding it at each point to the judge's instructions on the law. The defendants had planned the attack on Goldmark for years. "This was not something done in the heat of a political campaign. It was something that was conceived by 1961 at the latest and perhaps even earlier than that." Canwell, Holden, and Gillespie knew of Sally's past in 1956. They did nothing about it until six years later.

"Why? The reason why, I think, is that these men knew that this fact in and of itself was not important and they knew further that the voters of this county would not regard it as important since it was a thing of the past. It had never had anything to do with Mr. Goldmark; and Mrs. Goldmark had done whatever she could do to make good her mistake.

"They saved that information for a time when they could use it, not to tell the truth about it, but to tell lies about it with the greatest maximum effect. And that chance came in 1962."

Step by step I took the jury through the libel campaign, to breathe life once again into the hateful words. First there had been Canwell's and Holden's *Vigilante* pamphlets with innuendos about unnamed communist infiltrators. Then came Holden's July article on John's candidacy announcement, impliedly linking him with communism. Canwell put out his tape-recorded interview, which was circulated through the county by people who relied on Canwell's word as an "expert." Printed in the so-called *American Intelligence Service*, the interview was delivered on election eve to every voter in the district. In the meantime Gillespie, Canwell, and Holden had planned and carried out the American Legion hall attack on the ACLU. I reminded the jury of their false claim that this was a nonpolitical meeting; we had exploded this with proof that the meeting was planned as part of the effort to defeat Goldmark. Holden had followed with his editorial branding John "the tool of a monstrous conspiracy." At every stage the defendants had disguised their purposes and concealed their financing.

"Now there is nothing about any of this, I think, that would appeal to anyone as being an open, above-board, American political campaign. At every step of the way there was an effort to disguise what was being done, from Mr. Gillespie's check made out to the American Legion right up to the last payment of the last bill on the *American Intelligence Service*. Nothing was open. Everything was concealed. And the way these were distributed was similarly not open. These were sent out to the extent of thousands upon thousands of copies in unmarked envelopes through the mail—anonymously."

In all this the defendants were "determined to brand Mr. Goldmark as a communist in the eyes of his fellow citizens." And they had acted with malice, as shown, for example, by Holden's repeated misstatements of fact and his false claim that he had gained information from the FBI; Canwell's years of file building, awaiting an opportune time to attack; and Gillespie's spreading of vicious rumors through the county. None had acted in the public interest; all set out to destroy.

There could be no doubt that the libels charged Goldmark with being a communist. "Insinuations of fact," under the court's instructions, were equal in law to explicit charges. I traced the innuendo of communism through each libel; the meaning was unmistakable.

The defense of truth was a charade. What had the defendants produced to support their accusation? Nothing but a spurious argument over the "Party line" and a tortured attack upon Mrs. Goldmark's description of her experience from 1935 to 1943. "Bear in mind, if you would, that this libel case is primarily Mr. Goldmark's libel case. . . . He was the one who was in public life and he was the one that this whole attack was directed against. They were out to get him. They were not out to get a housewife that lives up on a ranch twenty miles out of town."

The attack had been carried out by professional witnesses. "They are willing to come here and say whatever the occasion called for without knowing or caring whose fate or whose reputation or whose life they are dealing with."

I recalled the appearances of Mrs. Hartle, Lautner, Jackson, Prussion, Philbrick, and Canwell. "They are in the business of calling themselves 'the anti-communists.' And anybody who doesn't look at it quite the way they do is not really an anti-communist. They make speeches. They make tapes. They have schools. They testify in cases. They make their living this way." And yet "not one of those six ever had a position of responsibility with the United States government either in the security field or in any other field."

Against their charges stood the testimony of distinguished experts on communism who had held important positions with the government: Senator Cain, Tompkins, Durning, Jacobs, and Professor Almond.

The defendants' brand of anticommunism, I said, finds nonexistent secret agents everywhere. "Has it occurred to you the people that have been named as either communists or communist sympathizers in this trial by the defendants or their witnesses?" I recalled some of them: Governor Brown of California; Stanley Moss, attorney general of that state; Bishop James Pike; Benjamin Kizer, a respected Spokane lawyer; Francis Biddle, former Attorney General of the United States; Lauchlin Currie, a White House aide to President Roosevelt. Secretaries of State John Foster Dulles and Dean Rusk stood accused of having communist "associations." And the slanderous attack on Professor Melvin Rader had been renewed.

With these distinguished people the defense had consigned whole countries to the communist inferno. Norway, Sweden, Canada, Ireland—they claimed that these and many others were virtually in communist hands. They had slandered the National Council of Churches, the Grange, the PTA, and especially the Democratic Party, whose current platform was called communist inspired. "The Democratic Party of our state is not a dupe of the communists and it is not under their influence whatever. You can be sure, ladies and gentlemen, that if Mr. Goldmark happened to belong to our other party, the Republican Party, this wouldn't stop this kind of attack from being made."

The defense view ascribed every national problem, every overseas difficulty, not to hard realities but to communism and treason. They carried the obsession into personal life. "If they are unsuccessful in business that is because the communists drove all the customers away. If they lose a political campaign that is because the communists spend untold amounts of money in one little legislative district."

They would heed the temperate words of no one. They dismissed Presidents Eisenhower, Truman, and Kennedy, and disregarded even J. Edgar Hoover when he warned against vigilante action and private investigations of communism.

The defense had come down to Canwell sitting on the stand at the end of trial, listing positions of Goldmark which he claimed matched the "communist line." The list included statements John had not actually made. "But whether he made them or not they still would add up to zero. . . . What are we supposed to do, ladies and gentlemen, in our lives, are we supposed to spend our time reading the *Daily Worker* like Mr. Canwell does so we can know what the communists are saying and not do it? That would be the silliest example of the tail wagging the dog in the history of the United States. . . . We needn't be so hypnotized and afraid of the communists that we have to read their papers and find out what they are in favor of and be against it. If we did that they would be setting the policy for us."

The dignity and honor of the Goldmarks' lives were proved by outstanding witnesses who had known them for years: Henry Reuss, Peter Asher, Richard Riddell, the two sons Chuck and Peter, and others.

The defense had also pleaded fair comment. I carefully summarized the court's complicated instructions on this defense. It would apply only to defamatory opinion, not to false assertions of fact. I referred to Holden's phrase "tool of a monstrous conspiracy" as an example. "That is not fair comment. That is not a matter of privilege any more than it would be to say Joe Doakes is a murderer and then try to excuse it by saying 'Oh, well, that is just my opinion. . . .'"

I reminded the jury of another limit of the privilege: the comment must not be made solely for the purpose of causing harm to the person being criticized. What had the defendants' purpose been? The answer was provided by the *Vigilante*. The first issue "talks about lynching and the high price of rope and hang the subversives. And the last one from October, 1962, four years later, says that 'Mr. Canwell was the bullet that got John Goldmark.' That was the purpose of these defendants."

The injury was to reputation and good name. Added to this was mental anguish. The jurors would need no help from us to understand the suffering endured by a family attacked in this way.

The Goldmarks, coming to Okanogan County, "expected to build a new life for themselves and their children and be an honorable part of the community that they had chosen to live in. I think the evidence shows beyond any doubt that that is exactly what they did." Beyond the libels and the injury to the Goldmark family was a broader question: "Is this country still the country that we have always thought it was where people can move to a community and settle down and do their best to earn the respect of their fellow citizens and be judged for what they are and what they do and for the work that they do and the children that they raise? Or have we become so afraid and so terrified of the world and the communist threat that we now are willing to turn upon each other out of fear and hatred and destroy each other and in the process destroy the very freedoms which our country has been built on, which we have always cherished, and which is the real reason that we choose to live here rather than somewhere else?"

Glenn Harmon, emphatic, firm, methodical, and deeply convinced of his cause, argued for the defense.

"Plaintiffs are complaining that their reputations have been damaged right up to this trial," he said. "Don't forget for one minute that the decision to come into this court and put the reputations of the Goldmarks in issue was a decision made by the Goldmarks and not by these defendants. We are not here by choice."

That Goldmark claimed the publications were false did not make it so. "You are the judge of what is true and false; no one else."

All the statements sued on were true. "Personally we of the defense sort of enjoyed the attack of the plaintiffs on expert witnesses who were ex-communists. According to the plaintiffs, Barbara Hartle is a tough lady who had never seen the light and there is really no proof that she ever really left the Communist Party. Well, the President of the United States was satisfied with her loyalty when he granted her executive clemency for her valuable assistance to the

Justice Department of the United States. And the United States has relied on John Lautner, Herbert Philbrick and Karl Prussion as a witness on many occasions. As a matter of fact, as I recall the testimony, the plaintiffs must have felt that Mr. Lautner was a reliable enough witness until he showed up as a witness for the defendants. That made him a professional witness by the plaintiffs' standards."

Without the work of repentant ex-communists, and of specialists such as Canwell, the country would be severely weakened in its struggle against communism. Against the word of such experts the testimony of long-time friends of the Goldmarks meant little. "Don't forget," said Harmon, "what Dean Acheson said about Alger Hiss when he was under attack and before he was convicted: 'I won't turn my back on Alger Hiss.'"

Harmon asked: "Did the voters of this district have a right to know? Did they have a right to know of the Communist Party background and associations of Mrs. Goldmark to aid them in judging her husband as an elected public official?" They did. He read from the court's instructions: "Any person is privileged to criticize so much of another's activities as are matters of public concern. . . ." This was the fair comment rule, vital to the defense.

Harmon turned to the alleged libels, shrewdly taking our weakest claim first. Don Caron's newspaper article "Pillaging Parliament" did not mention Goldmark at all. "It is a situation of somebody thinking the shoe fits and putting it on."

Nor was the Legion hall meeting directed at Goldmark. Canwell simply gave his opinion on the ACLU, repeating the contents of legislative committee reports. This he had every right to do; Harmon read the court's instruction on the privilege of repeating the contents of an official document.

"And don't forget for one minute," Harmon added, "the testimony is that the American Legion has agreed for years that the ACLU is a communist front and is giving aid and comfort to the communists. And the American Legion at its annual convention for years has passed resolutions asking somebody to do something about it."

But the ACLU led a charmed life. "It waves a packet of letters from ex-Presidents—politicians and so forth"—which meant nothing. "How much investigation do those people make when they sign a letter congratulating an organization on its anniversary?" The jury should have no trouble seeing that the organization was a front. It had sided with the communists "for so many years that it can now be simply as expected for communists to ask the ACLU to help them when they are in trouble with the law. And they know the ACLU won't let them down."

Now, said Harmon, "it is time to get down to the sixty-four dollar question. What about the Goldmarks and communism? Where do they stand? First let me point out that this is a libel suit and none of the defendants ever published any statement saying either John or Sally Goldmark was a communist at the time of the publication."

Yet the proof of guilt promised in the defense's opening statement had been presented, said Harmon. Sally Goldmark's testimony contained inconsistencies. "Now it may be that a communist can reconcile all of these different and conflicting stories into one true story but, frankly, I don't see how you can, and I know that I can't."

But the case did not rest only on the plaintiff's "association for more than twenty years with a wife he married as a member of the Communist Party, far from it. John Goldmark has lived and advocated the Communist Party line for enough years to create his own image."

Now Harmon dredged up from the record every event in

Goldmark's life that supposedly lent support to the accusation. The argument was well organized and detailed, again revealing the defense's dedication and fierce industriousness. Goldmark had planned a career in politics even while in college. Yet he married a woman who was a communist. "And by his own testimony he made no effort at all to talk her into leaving the Communist Party." She was in a "cell with others engaged in espionage." No one in such a unit "could have married an outsider not committed to the Communist Party without strenuous objections from the Party and from the cell leaders." The plaintiff's own evidence showed there were no such objections.

Afterward his wife remained in the same "underground cell" for almost a year. The testimony that she then dropped out, simply and without difficulty, was belied by the experts. Goldmark, in the Navy, said nothing to his superiors about his wife's affiliation.

The war over, the couple visited Charles Kramer in Washington before heading West. "I don't know what they talked about. It wouldn't be surprising if it included communism."

They moved to Okanogan County and "John Goldmark wasted little time in starting to go into a life in politics." He kept his wife's past a secret. "Why? If he had told about it in the first place, got her off his chest, it probably would have been a political asset but not if she was going to be a left-winger, because then people would ask questions."

In 1949, when the FBI finally came to talk to Sally, Goldmark still did not ask his wife to tell him the details of her past experience. "Seems to me the FBI coming to a man in his house and interrogating his wife about such things as that, he would want to get to the bottom of it. Unless, of course, he already knew."

In 1951 Goldmark led the Young Democrats into Communist Party positions on McCarran Act repeal and relations with Red China. In the mid-fifties he became a left-wing leader in the legislature, denouncing superpatriots and seeking a nuclear test ban. "Again the Communist Party line." In the 1961 session "he helped control the election of the Speaker of the House. And he won for himself one of the top committee positions as chairman of the House Committee on Ways and Means. Now this is a communist pressure tactic of the kind they talk about in *Not a Shot Was Fired,* the type of tactic that they used in Czechoslovakia to make a minority into a majority, get control, get it from the top if you can."

Meantime the Moscow directive of December 1960 had gone out to American communists. Goldmark and his wife began "an almost unceasing campaign against all anti-communist programs. Whether they knew what they were or not. Whether they had read the stuff or not, seen the movies or not, they were against it."

John had spoken to other farmers, telling "those poor people at the Grange how ignorant they were on communism and why they shouldn't pass this thing. And in his speech to the Methow Grange John Goldmark said that the state didn't need a law to outlaw communism since the federal government outlawed communism by the Smith Act, concealing the fact that he personally opposed key parts of the Smith Act, as does the ACLU."

Goldmark had opposed laws directed against the communist menace. He opposed the House Committee on Un-American Activities. "I will say again I don't mean that everybody who takes one or two or three positions that he is suspect on communism. But there is a lot of difference between one or two or three and twenty or thirty or forty. . . . [I]t would be incredible indeed to find someone who by accident was following so many positions being advocated by the Communist Party. I have taken you through a list of forty; and there are more."

This record, taken with his wife's known past, proved Goldmark's guilt.

The security clearance we had placed in evidence meant nothing. "Now do you think for a moment that such security checks are infallible? All one has to do is to recall such incidents as the Alger Hiss case to realize that communists do get security clearances and clearances of the highest order, and we know it when men with the highest security clearance disappear behind the Iron Curtain." John Lautner himself, a leading communist official, had been placed in American counterintelligence during World War II.

Harmon concluded with intense conviction. "If we of the defense have done our job as we should have done it, as I hope we did, it should be easy for you to see where the truth lies in this lawsuit. It should be easy for you to see that the threat of communism not only can reach into your lives and into your county and perhaps even into your school district, but that in this instance the threat has reached out to touch you and yours and me and mine here in the State of Washington."

Joseph Wicks rose to deliver the defense *coup de grâce*. The tall, silver-haired old judge had sat quietly through most of the trial, legs outstretched, eyeing the jury, interrogating an occasional local witness. His great prestige and oratorical prowess had been saved for the summation. As he began, it was clear that he had worked on this address for weeks. He spoke passionately, frighteningly, in a booming bass voice, striding back and forth before the jury, his eyes flashing, his handsome face filled with conviction.

He had learned things during the trial, said Wicks. "I

never knew before that there were these two brands of communism. They give us a choice—we can either take a rattlesnake or we can take a copperhead." Also, it seemed, two brands of anticommunism. "This anti-communist program that Father Buckley set up in this county in these study groups—that's not the right kind of anti-communism, that creates hatred. And hatred for what?—hatred for the things that would destroy you and me and the things that you and I love as free-born American citizens. Sure it creates hatred. And isn't it about time that we had a little hatred for those people that declare that 'We will bury you'?"

For years there had been talk about Goldmark and his wife. Friends warned him, but he did nothing. "Now I don't know, maybe from political expediency I might do some foolish things, I might fail to do some foolish things, but somebody goes starting, spreading stuff about my wife, he is going to be called to task for it. Now you can kick me on the shin if you want to and I can take it, but you are not going to go out and spread stories about my wife!"

Wicks banged his clenched fist on the counsel table. Carried away by his own eloquence, he appeared to be enraged. He shot a fierce glance at John, and thundered on.

"Counsel refers to the Scriptures. Some four thousand years ago there was handed down by God unto Moses among the vivid flashes and awful thunders on Mt. Sinai the Ten Commandments. . . . 'I am the Lord thy God, which have brought thee up out of the land of Egypt, and out of the house of bondage. Thou shalt have no other gods before Me. Thou shalt not make unto thee any graven image, or any likeness of anything that is in the heavens above, or that is in the earth beneath, or that is in the waters under the earth. Thou shalt not bow down thyself to them, nor serve them: for I the Lord thy God am a jealous God, visiting the iniquities of the fathers upon the children unto the

third and fourth generation of them that hate me; and showing mercy unto thousands of those that love me, and keep
my commandments.'

"That is the First Commandment."

Wicks wheeled and pointed toward the Goldmarks. "Now,
would a communist accept that? Does a communist say that
'There is no other god before Me'? What is God to an athe-
istic communist?"

Sally had been trembling as Wicks's vitriol poured out.
Suddenly she burst into tears and ran from the courtroom.
John remained where he was, looking steadily and calmly
at Wicks.

The argument flowed on. Adam in the garden had eaten
the forbidden apple, proffered by his wife. "And for six
thousand years we men have been trying to live down what
Adam did. We are not laying on to our wives something
that we did ourselves. Chivalry in this country is not dead.
Men still protect their wives. They still fight for them. Did
John Goldmark do it? Did John Goldmark call to task anybody who was making these disparaging remarks about his
wife? John Goldmark knew it. Why? Why didn't he call
them to task? Political expediency—true or false? Any man
worthy of the name of being called man will fight for his
mate, but John Goldmark didn't!"

This last was delivered in a bellow. Goldmark kept looking steadily at Wicks.

The defense lawyer launched into a review of "salient
facts" which he claimed proved the plaintiff's guilt and the
truth of everything the defendants had said.

There was a monstrous conspiracy headquartered in
Moscow. "It is a disease with the people who follow it. It
is a religion." The movement's "leaders frankly tell you
that they will bury us, and they mean it." Fifty billion dollars a year was being spent "to protect your home and mine

260

against the threat of this enemy that would destroy us. And then somebody has the audacity to say that there is no internal menace of communism in this country."

The money for defense, Wicks reminded the jury, "came out of your pocket and mine." Yet there were still American citizens infected with communism. "It is argued that what is one mad dog among so many? It is forgotten that a mad dog, one mad dog, can create an epidemic in any neighborhood if he is left to run wild."

Mrs. Goldmark acknowledged she had been bitten. Years later the FBI had interviewed her at the ranch. "I was an agent in that outfit," said Wicks. ". . . I know what agents in the FBI do." Mrs. Goldmark had not truly cooperated because the agency went to her; she had never volunteered.

"Where are the others of this cell of hers that were just discussing philosophical questions? Did they, too, get out of the Party, as she says she did? Were they just people who were disturbed and frustrated? Did they drift back and take up the normal way of American life? If so, where are they?"

Wicks painted a grotesque picture of the Goldmarks' lives. John was the follower and Sally the leader, he claimed, dating from their courtship.

Goldmark had moved west to consummate his political ambitions. "He, the brilliant student of government, of political science and of law, of human nature, settles for a cow ranch in Okanogan County when he didn't know whether apples grew on a tree or on a vine, when he didn't know which end of the cow gave the milk or which end of the cow ate the hay. It is true that he knew nothing about farm machinery or living in the country. But that is of little consequence. 'My ambition is to render public service. I must settle and live among people whom I can convince and persuade that I am the man whom they should choose to serve

261

them in the halls of parliament.' 'These are the simple folk; when they hear me expound my views on government, how they should be represented, they must be convinced that I am their man.'"

Goldmark quickly rose to power. And "in the 1961 Legislature he is in control of the most powerful committee and the most powerful man in the House of Representatives of this state. He is now really rolling. The rural stepping stones have served him well."

But the truth had come out. Goldmark had wrongly believed "that a politician could conceal communistic skeletons in his closet and not have them dragged out. But dragged out they were. And when they were dragged out he was licked."

Goldmark and his wife had become "a little too bold" in following the Communist Party line on loyalty oaths, the McCarran Act, deportations, nuclear test ban treaties, trade with foreign powers, and the entire anticommunist program.

Wicks turned to the ACLU. "I never heard of the ACLU to my recollection until they had this meeting down here in the Legion hall in 1962." This was an amazing remark from one who had served for years on the Superior Court bench. "Now they say they favor freedom of speech for everybody, even for communists. They want the communists to have the privilege of going into your school room, to go on to the campuses of our universities and any other institution that we have, and preach their un-Godly ideology to our people. They favor that and so does every communist in the United States. That is freedom of speech that they are talking about. They want it for the communists. I don't know, maybe you want it, I don't."

Not only Goldmark's plans "but the dreams of every left-winger in the State of Washington have been shattered" by the 1962 campaign. The Goldmarks, Wicks exclaimed, were not the real plaintiffs. "Is it for John and Sally Goldmark? Is this a lawsuit for damages for them? Or is this a lawsuit to protect the organization that has so frequently been referred to in this trial—the ACLU? That comes to the rescue of every communist in this country? Yes, even the man who committed the most horrible deed on the 22nd of November of this year, the man who said 'I want an ACLU lawyer'?"

The affairs of Goldmark mattered little. "The ACLU must be saved"; that was "the meaning of this lawsuit," said Wicks.

Had the jury noticed that the ACLU leaped to protect the rights of those who spread a godless ideology while denouncing those who defended traditional American values? "They say it is wrong to wave that old flag. That is patriotism. And patriotism doesn't set right with the communists. They are the people who say it is wrong to pray in our schools. They are the people who said that we should take the motto of 'In God We Trust' off of our coins lest we offend some member of a godless ideology. That is what this lawsuit is about."

The verdict, Wicks concluded, would be a signal to the world. There was only one right decision, and it was clear. "And when you return with a verdict for these defendants on every count claimed in this case, you will send a clarion that will ring through the corridors of this old courthouse. It will shake the dome of the capitol building at Olympia. It will reverberate through the halls of Congress in Washington, D.C.—yes, it will be heard halfway around the world, even in the Kremlin in Moscow, Russia.

"Then they will know that they cannot, that they must not, and they shall not use the people to further a godless ideology of communism in this land of ours."

It seemed to take a long time for the echoes of Judge Wicks's argument to die away.

We were entitled by law to a short rebuttal. R. E. Mansfield rose and faced the jury box. He spoke slowly, in a quiet, gentle voice; the jurors were still visibly shaken by the defense attack.

"May it please the court. Ladies and gentlemen. It is not a simple matter to respond as I must in some measure to the speech you have just heard. What manner of men are these whose defense must bring to this courtroom the viciousness that we have seen?"

The contrast between Mansfield and Wicks, the two veterans of the Okanogan County bar, could not have been plainer. As Mansfield talked, calm settled over the room. "It will be my hope to restore to this courtroom a measure of reality," he said. "This is a court of law. This is a trial to establish facts. This is what the jury is for."

The interminable defense arguments, said Mansfield, called to mind the Shakespearean line, "Out, damned spot." But no amount of verbal laundering would delete the stain: "Probably not any of those of us here are more than one generation removed, and most of us here are not even that far removed, from people that moved into Okanogan County to find a place to live, to raise their families, to be good citizens, to take advantage of opportunities and to build homes. Who could have believed that what has happened here would happen?"

Never before had there been such a campaign in the county. "Are we to put a stamp of approval on a program of vilification so that the next time a campaign comes around it will be conducted on the same level or worse? Shall we reduce politics to a position where no one will run for office for fear of this type of abuse? There isn't a person anywhere—not one of you—there is not a person anywhere

264

who does not have sufficient basis in his background of error, confusion or mistake that he could not become the victim of the vicious kind of attack that was carried out in this case. . . . John and Sally Goldmark and their boys happened to be the victims this time. They are not the only persons who will be the victims if this is permitted to continue."

Mansfield closed with a quotation from the Book of Proverbs: "'A man that bearest false witness against his neighbor is a war club and a sword and a sharp arrow.' Hasn't it been so? Hasn't it been so with the Goldmarks?"

I spoke to the jury for the last time. They were tired after nearly two days of instructions and closing arguments, but it was necessary to unravel quickly the defense's web of falsehoods.

The defense had argued that John Goldmark looked down upon the people of Okanogan County as "simple folk." Nothing could be further from the truth. "If there is a man anywhere in the State of Washington who treats all of his fellow men as his equals and treats nobody as a superior and nobody as an inferior, either one, it is John Goldmark."

But there was a side in the case that thought of the people as simple folk: the defense side. "They think that simple folk can be scared and persuaded by a lot of highly charged propaganda and loud arguments which do not apply to the issues of the case, and can be stampeded into committing an injustice."

The defense lawyers had repeatedly dragged the name of Alger Hiss into the case. In the end they made no connection between him and the Goldmarks. There was yet a worse example: the assassination of John F. Kennedy, which the defendants had invoked time after time. They knew that John and Sally were among the late President's strongest local supporters. "And yet this event, which was a genuine tragedy for all of us—Republicans and Democrats alike—has been deliberately used in the most cynical manner possible to try to poison your minds against these two people who were among the greatest admirers and supporters of the very man whose death we mourn."

The defense effort to brand Goldmark a communist because of his wife's past membership was a failure. Mrs. Goldmark's experience during the "popular front" period typified that of many thousands of well-meaning citizens who made the same mistake. It was not realistic to expect others who had belonged to the same group years earlier, even if they could be located, to appear in court and testify. "Why? Because if they do then they place the information about their past in the hands of people like these. And you have seen what can be done with that, and they are afraid."

The experts who testified confirmed that Sally's recollection was not only plausible but typical. And the final test was the security clearance held by John. If the government agencies doubted the truthfulness or loyalty of either him or his wife, he would not possess it.

The defense's effort to link John to communism by "Party line" arguments was an absurdity. Every position he had taken was grounded in reason and shared by good citizens of both parties. "And, of course, they have completely ignored Mr. Goldmark's opposition to the real Communist Party line on the cold war issues such as the Marshall Plan, NATO, the Truman Doctrine, Cuba, the Korean War. They have ignored his activities against communism in domestic affairs such as helping Riddell get the communists out of the Young Democrats. They have ignored his anticommunist stands in every respect."

On the ACLU the defendants took refuge behind legislative committee reports. They were not being sued for repeating these, but for themselves falsely calling the ACLU

266

a communist front as part of their defamation of John. "If these people are able now to libel that respected organization as a communist front then tomorrow you can rest assured there will be another respected organization which will similarly be labeled."

I closed by reminding the jury how readily the far right's guns could be turned in any direction. "Their definition of a good American is someone who agrees with them on everything. If this is to be our system, if this is to be followed, our entire government, our society, our freedoms would be destroyed or lost in short order. When any man is destroyed like this it isn't just he that suffers, and it isn't just his family that suffers, but it is all of us, it is everybody. Because we know that life is only good in a community where freedom and justice are preserved for everybody, not just for a few.

"So in this sense I think it is fair to say we are all plaintiffs in this case. The entire community is the plaintiff in this case."

It was late in the day, beyond the usual closing time, on January 17, 1964. The trial had gone on for over two months. The weary jurors, escorted by the bailiff, filed upstairs to begin deliberating in the attic jury room.

CHAPTER 17

T HERE WOULD be no verdict that evening. The jurors were too tired, the issues too numerous and difficult. We tried to relax, talking and laughing over parts of the long trial.

The next morning I went into the cold sunshine and snow to ski, leaving Mansfield in town to appear in court if anything happened. Nothing did. A full day passed, and the jury retired for a second night in the spartan courthouse dormitories.

The next day was Sunday, a likely time for jurors yearning to go home to compromise their differences. In the late afternoon they knocked on the jury room door—but not with the verdict. They had some questions for the judge.

We reconvened to hear them. The questions concerned the privilege defenses; Judge Turner referred the jurors to the written instructions already in their possession. There was one encouraging question. "How much is the plaintiff suing for?" the foreman asked. The judge declined to say; figures had been mentioned in counsels' arguments and would not be repeated by the court.

Emotions held stoically in check during the trial appeared to be breaking through. A women juror, the former cook at the Cariboo Inn, had fallen ill a few days earlier. Her place was taken by one of the alternates, a mill worker who now smiled openly at Mansfield and me.

Monday came and went. We had thought the courtroom session might be followed swiftly by a verdict; instead, silence. The jurors appeared only at mealtimes, walking to and from a private dining room at the Cariboo. They could speak only to each other and the bailiffs.

By now we feared what many onlookers had predicted, a hung jury. Perhaps the trial was too divisive, the public's allegiance too deeply split, for any random group to reach accord. Ten of the twelve votes would suffice, but that was little short of unanimity. Perhaps, worse yet, a defense verdict was imminent. The jurors might strive, at least unconsciously, to reach the most comfortable result. A defense verdict would be safe. It would satisfy many respectable citizens and would be defensible to everyone. The jury could easily find the publications false but "fair comment" under the court's broad definition, thus voting for the defendants without condemning the plaintiff. But it could not do the reverse: a plaintiff's verdict would mean a commitment to the justice of Goldmark's cause, and a juror publicly making that commitment would risk unpopularity and perhaps even reprisal. To gain each vote we not only had to convince that juror of the Goldmarks' loyalty but to persuade him or her to make a personal stand for justice. Could the townspeople and farmers who sat in judgment carry this burden?

If fortunate enough to win at all, we could not expect a large award. Country juries were renowned for tightfistedness. The state's laws forbade punitive damages in any amount, and John, far from losing income on account of the libels, had actually gained financially by leaving the legislature.

Tuesday. In the afternoon, another knock on the jury room door. They wanted to hear again the entire tape recording of the Legion hall meeting. The jurors, counsel, the judge, and court attendants listened silently in the courtroom as the voices of Canwell, Gillespie, and the angry crowd came once more from the machine. Then the jury filed back upstairs.

Wednesday, and unbroken silence from the courthouse. The day inched by like a glacier. By now we had exhausted our ideas for reassuring each other that nine separate findings were required, after all, and a verdict must be near. This was the fifth day of deliberation; the jury must be divided.

But at dinner time came a sign. The jurors cut short their usual trip to the Cariboo and hurried back to the courthouse. We waited through the evening, expecting a call. None came. At midnight we gave up and went to bed. Half an hour later the telephone rang. The verdict was in.

We quickly dressed and walked through the dark and snow to the courthouse. Everyone was soon assembled: the judge, the parties and lawyers at their familiar places, the visibly exhausted jury, a battery of reporters and television men looking on.

Judge Turner smiled. "Ladies and gentlemen," he asked, "have you reached a verdict?"

"Yes, your honor," answered Carl Voelckers, an orchardist who everyone had rightly predicted would be foreman. He handed up the long verdict forms to the bench. The judge examined them, and said: "There will be no demonstrations when the verdict is read." He handed the papers to the clerk, Jane Profit, a blonde, attractive woman whose office was charged by tradition with reading the verdict aloud.

"We, the jury in the above entitled case," Mrs. Profit began in a soft voice, "do find for the plaintiff in the first claim for relief in the amount of twelve thousand dollars."

We had won a major victory. The first claim involved

Holden's backhanded article reporting John's announcement for relection. The amount awarded was very large by state of Washington standards.

Mrs. Profit read on. The second claim involved Holden's "Catching Up With John" editorial. The verdict was for Goldmark in the amount of $13,000. The third was based on Canwell's *American Intelligence Service,* which Holden had printed and Caron helped distribute. The verdict was for $2,900 jointly against Canwell and Holden, $100 against Caron. The fourth claim involved Canwell's tape-recorded "interview"; the jury found him liable for $5,000 in damages. The fifth claim, based on Caron's "Pillaging Parliament" article, brought a defense verdict. The jury had found insufficient evidence that the column, which did not mention John, was intended to refer to him; but this was now a matter of indifference. The sixth and most complex claim concerned the Legion Hall meeting, where Canwell had smeared the ACLU but had not mentioned Goldmark. John could only have been libeled as a member of an organization falsely called a communist front. The verdict was for the plaintiff: $7,000 jointly against Canwell, Holden, and Gillespie. The elusive Gillespie, who helped plan the meeting and then served as master of ceremonies while Canwell did the talking, was held fully liable. Holden was similarly held for helping plan the affair and asking a loaded question from the floor.

The total damages were $40,000. It was the largest libel verdict in Washington history, except one Seattle award which had been reduced to $7,500 on review.

The jury found for the defendants on the conspiracy issue and on the claim that Sally had been separately damaged by Canwell's tape recording and the *Intelligence Service* which repeated it. These findings left the outcome intact. The conspiracy claim had held the complex case together

271

from the start; under the Legion hall claim, Canwell, Holden, and Gillespie now stood branded as collaborators in slander; and the jurors must have accepted Sally's testimony in finding for John on every count.

The vindication of Goldmark was complete. The jury had resoundingly confirmed his loyalty and patriotism. All four defendants were held liable in varying degrees; none escaped.

The ACLU's victory was equally dramatic. Four of the claims involved "communist front" charges against the Union; Goldmark won on all four. The Legion hall claim, involving no explicit charge against John, raised the ACLU's true nature as an inescapable issue. The plaintiff's verdict was a clear adjudication that the organization was not a communist front; the ACLU had sailed through its first and only court test.

The verdict was by a vote of ten to two, the margin required by Washington law in civil cases. Judge Turner thanked the jurors for their long and faithful service, and sent them home. A few minutes later he declared court adjourned.

In the hall we encountered bedlam. Friends besieged us with congratulations, reporters pressed for interviews, cameras flashed. John and Sally beamed with happiness. They had the satisfaction of knowing they had staked everything for justice, and won.

In the following days the verdict was hailed across the country. People who had anxiously followed the trial expressed their relief in a flood of wires and letters. "The verdict was the more remarkable and reassuring," said Edward Morgan over ABC News, "for the fact that in recent months and years the politics of right-wing extremism had made noticeable inroads in various parts of the Rocky Mountains and the Pacific Northwest, including the State of Washington." *Time* devoted its law section to the case. The Portland *Oregonian,* praising what it called the "courageous verdict," wrote: "In a small community such as Okanogan the pressures from a vocal, unresponsible minority can make life miserable for independent thinkers, which the jurors proved themselves to be. Their refusal to yield to such pressures showed that the jury system can work in an atmosphere of prejudice and suspicion. . . . A few more verdicts like the one in Okanogan might restore the nation to the tolerant level where the constitutional freedoms could be exercised as they should be in a free country."

The *Washington Post* summed up the feelings of many in an editorial headed "Vindication":

> The libel victory won by John Goldmark out in rural Okanogan, Washington, is a victory not for himself alone but for good sense, fairness and fundamental decency. The whole country will be its beneficiary. . . .
>
> The long trial was turned into a valuable educational undertaking. The Birchers brought forth from their well-earned obscurity several of those professional witnesses who used to serve the House Un-American Activities Committee with such deadly effect; but to support the Goldmarks, a number of noted Americans, including former Senator Harry Cain, Rep. Henry Reuss and actor Sterling Hayden made long journeys to Okanogan to testify respecting their knowledge of the Goldmarks' loyalty and patriotism, to elucidate the vital distinction between Communism and liberalism and to point out the dangers of reckless mudslinging in political life.
>
> The jury listened, learned, deliberated and rendered a just and thoughtful verdict—a vindication not alone for

the Goldmarks but for the jury system and democracy as well.

But the last act remained to be played. In fact, it remained to be written. The centuries-old law of libel was about to be transformed.

CHAPTER **18**

THE LOSER in a major civil trial usually moves at once for judgment in his favor notwithstanding the jury's verdict. The motion is seldom granted. On all factual disputes the jury's decision is final; its verdict stands unless some vital element of proof was wholly missing from the evidence.

The defendants in the Goldmark case filed the usual motion, which automatically postponed the entry of judgment until Judge Turner could return to Okanogan and hear the lawyers' arguments. We were confident the motion would be denied. The plaintiff's evidence had been strong; many critical trial rulings had gone for the defendants, leaving them little to complain about. The verdict looked safe against any attack.

Yet within a few weeks, before the defense motion could even be argued, the picture changed completely. For months the United States Supreme Court had been deliberating over an Alabama jury's award of damages to a local politician who had sued the *New York Times*. Its decision came suddenly in March 1964, and shifted the foundations of the ancient law of libel. Nine months and several hundred pages of briefs later, the Supreme Court's new rule would cause Judge Turner to set aside John Goldmark's verdict.

The *New York Times* had published a paid advertisement soliciting funds for the work of Dr. Martin Luther King,

Jr. The appeal was signed by Eleanor Roosevelt, Marlon Brando, Sammy Davis, Jr., and other famous people. Describing recent events in the South, the advertisement read in part:

> In Montgomery, Alabama, after students sang "My Country 'Tis of Thee" on the State Capitol steps, their leaders were expelled from school, and truckloads of police armed with shotguns and tear-gas ringed the Alabama State College Campus. When the entire student body protested to state authorities by refusing to re-register, their dining hall was padlocked in an attempt to starve them into submission.

> Again and again the Southern violators have answered Dr. King's peaceful protests with intimidation and violence. They have bombed his home almost killing his wife and child. They have assaulted his person. They have arrested him seven times—for "speeding," "loitering" and similar "offenses." And now they have charged him with "perjury"—a felony under which they could imprison him for ten years. . . .

The advertisement contained minor errors. The police had not "ringed" the campus but had only been deployed near it; nine students had been expelled not for leading the demonstrations but for demanding service at a lunch counter in the courthouse; other students protested not by refusing to register but by boycotting classes on a single day; the campus dining hall had not been padlocked; Dr. King had been arrested only four times, not seven. But none of these errors reached the essential truth of the advertisement: Southern authorities in fact had repeatedly used illegal measures to

276

silence Dr. King and to quell student protests in Montgomery and elsewhere.

L. B. Sullivan was one of three Montgomery city com-
missioners. His duties included supervision of the police
department. Neither he nor any other official was mentioned in the *Times* advertisement. Nonetheless Sullivan sued
the *Times* for libel. His theory was that the advertisement
falsely accused the local police of misconduct, which necessarily libeled him as the official in charge of the police
department.

Alabama allowed punitive damages—a kind of pseudo-
fine—in libel suits. The case of *Sullivan v. New York Times*
was tried in Montgomery before a judge and jury clearly
hostile to the *Times* for its support of racial integration. The
judge instructed that if the jurors found the advertisement
was made "of and concerning" Sullivan they could award
both general damages for harm to reputation and punitive
damages "as a kind of punishment to a defendant with a
view of preventing similar wrongs in the future." No evidence suggested Sullivan's reputation had really been
harmed, and only 394 copies of the *Times* had been circulated in all of Alabama. Yet the jury brought in a verdict
for the full amount claimed, half a million dollars—all of
it clearly "punitive."

It was obvious that by misusing the law of libel in this
way a state court system could force any unpopular newspaper either to leave the state or cease publishing anything
critical of local officials. By 1963 seventeen libel cases
arising from the racial integration struggle, seeking hundreds
of millions in punitive damages, were pending in Southern
courts. Yet the U.S. Constitution's guaranty of freedom of
speech and of the press applied to the states as well as the
federal government.

The Supreme Court was moved to one of its greatest rulings for liberty of the press. It reversed Sullivan's judgment and by implication all others like it.

The country's history, said the Court, reflects "a profound national commitment to the principle that debate on public issues should be uninhibited, robust, and wide-open, and that it may well include vehement, caustic and sometimes unpleasantly sharp attacks on government and public officials." The Bill of Rights guaranteed everyone's right to speak out against the government. The nation long ago abolished the crime of "seditious libel" which had permitted rulers in earlier times to silence their critics. To award damages to Sullivan, who had not even been mentioned in the *Times* advertisement, would be to revive seditious libel in the guise of a civil lawsuit. The law of defamation, the Court said, "may not constitutionally be utilized to establish that an otherwise impersonal attack on governmental operations was a libel of an official responsible for those operations."

This alone would have disposed of the case, but the Supreme Court went further. The common law had made the defamer's good intentions no defense for libelous misstatements of fact; the fair comment privilege protected only opinions. But errors of all kinds, the Court said, are unavoidable in free and open debate. The traditional law was designed to protect reputations by holding responsible those who spread false and defamatory assertions of fact, regardless of the libeler's state of mind. But as applied to cases like Sullivan's, said the Court, that rule would dampen free speech by levying damages on honest debate of public issues: "[T]he pall of fear and timidity imposed upon those who would give voice to public criticism is an atmosphere in which the First Amendment freedoms cannot survive."

To surmount this danger the Court laid down a new rule:

278

where the plaintiff is a public official or candidate for office, a false but honest attack relating to his public life cannot entitle him to a libel verdict. A libel claimant in that category could never win "unless he proves that the statement was made with 'actual malice'—that is, with knowledge that it was false or with reckless disregard of whether it was false or not."

Sullivan's verdict failed the new test. Nothing proved the *Times* had published the advertisement with "reckless disregard" of the truth.

Three of the nine justices would have gone even further. Justice Black, noting that Sullivan's social standing "has likely been enhanced" rather than damaged by the advertisement, urged the complete abolition of libel laws in realms of public discussion. Justices Douglas and Goldberg largely agreed.

When Justice Brennan finished reading the majority opinion, a modern misuse of libel to stifle a free press had been defeated, but much law protecting the good names of citizens holding public office had been swept away in the process.

For the defendants in the Goldmark case the *New York Times* decision came as a gift from the skies. They would have applauded the Alabama verdict against the liberal *Times,* but now embraced the opinion reversing it. That opinion, ironically, had been urged in the Supreme Court by the far right's bête noire, the American Civil Liberties Union, striving as always for unfettered freedom of speech.

Judge Turner pondered whether John Goldmark's verdict could stand in view of the new rule of constitutional law. The problem was that while our jury had been liberally instructed on the fair comment privilege—comment "no matter how foolish or prejudiced," even "fantastic," was protected—they had also been told that the privilege "does not afford protection for the publication of false defamatory statements or insinuations of fact." As to the latter, malice could increase the damages but was not a requisite of liability. The verdict was silent on malice. The large damage award strongly suggested that the jurors had found that element established, but no legal means existed to amend the verdict to reflect the finding. And "malice" under the instructions could have been simply the vicious desire to injure—not necessarily the awareness or reckless disregard of falsity which alone would now suffice.

At length the judge ruled. The verdict, he wrote, "established that the plaintiff John Goldmark was not a Communist, nor a pro-Communist . . . and that the American Civil Liberties Union, of which plaintiff John Goldmark was admittedly a member, was not a Communist front organization. . . . The court must take as established facts that the defendants made false charges that the plaintiff John Goldmark was a Communist or a Communist sympathizer . . . with intent to injure the plaintiff politically, and to cause his defeat at the primary election. . . ."

But since Goldmark was a public official when the libels were published, the *Times* rule must apply. Nothing in the record, said the judge, proved the defendants "actually knew that the statements were substantially false, or recklessly disregarded whether they were false or not." Since the statements although false "were all of a kind which the First Amendment to the United States Constitution protects . . . I conclude that on all the evidence in this case, the state has no constitutional power to enter a judgement for damages for libel. . . ." He set aside the verdict and entered judgment for the defendants.

We thought a higher court might reverse this ruling and order a new trial, allowing the jury to infer the defendants' reckless disregard of the truth from the circumstances of their behavior. But we decided against an appeal. The goal of vindicating Goldmark against the smear campaign had been reached and that victory could not be undone. The jury's finding that the libels were false was undisturbed by the post-trial ruling. A retrial would consume time and money and could bring nothing better than a second probably uncollectable judgment.

John and Sally issued a statement to the press thanking their friends for their support and the jurors for their service. There the case ended. The Goldmarks returned to their ranch. The long trial and the jury's verdict had cleared their good name; life could go on with honor.

CHAPTER **19**

TWENTY YEARS have passed since the Goldmark trial. Okanogan County is little changed, although a few pockets of its great expanse have been carved into tracts for city people, and the street clock in the county seat now keeps electrified time. R. E. Mansfield still practices law there as the admired dean of the local bar.

Peter Goldmark, the younger son of John and Sally, earned a Ph.D. in molecular biology at the University of California, published a brilliant paper, and was doing advanced research at Harvard when he and his young wife, from New York State, paid a visit to the family ranch on the Indian reservation. They decided to stay. Peter and Georgia, now with four children, have run the Goldmark place for a decade and are among the state's best and happiest ranchers.

Chuck, the older son, served with distinction in the Army, graduated from Yale Law School, entered private practice, and soon became a leader in the legal profession. An accomplished mountaineer, he lives in Seattle with his French-born wife, Annie, and two young and bilingual sons.

Sally Goldmark also lives in Seattle, where she has published movie reviews and magazine articles, contributed volunteer work to good causes, and continued to stimulate her friends. Her sense of justice, her gift for spirited and well-aimed indignation, remain unsurpassed.

On a winter day two years after the trial, in 1966, John

Goldmark was bucked off a half-trained horse on the ranch. He landed on frozen ground and broke his right hip. After a long wait in the cold he was found and flown to Seattle, where a doctor tried to rejoin the bone fragments. The operation was a failure. For the rest of his life Goldmark endured pain and one operation after another, five in all, without complaint. Many would have blamed the doctors or fate for this ordeal, but John saw his own momentary lapse as the cause. "I wasn't on the ball when I let that horse throw me," he said, "and I wasn't on the ball again when I landed the way I did." A plastic hip joint was installed in what was then an experimental operation. With his indomitable will to live Goldmark not only walked again but resumed tennis, squash, and hiking.

The Goldmarks moved to Seattle after the accident. John, although twenty-five years out of school, took up the practice of law and did well. He joined a firm specializing in personal injury and malpractice litigation, became a trial lawyer, and brought to opponents and clients alike his buoyant good judgment and unshakable honesty.

Goldmark greeted the lymph cancer which first came to him in 1973 with the same determination that conquered the broken hip. He would not be disabled and he would not die of it. Through remissions and flareups he lived life to the full, practicing law, traveling with Sally, learning Italian, hiking in the mountains, flying to the ranch for a few days' work, reading voraciously, arguing with his friends. There was nothing in him of martyrdom or of conspicuous, clenched-teeth bravery; he simply relished the world and kept the flame alive. He would answer "Fine, just fine," when asked how he felt. In his last year, when he was wasted by the disease, I tested whether his encyclopedic recall of history was still with him by asking, out of the blue, if he could name the obscure Bosnian nationalist who had assassinated the Archduke Ferdinand in 1914. "Princip," John gave the right answer at once. "Gavrilo Princip."

In September 1979 a recognition dinner was held for the Goldmarks in Seattle. A hundred and fifty of their friends came and many spoke at the microphone. "I loved Sally," said Jo Pardee, now the wife of Wilbur Hallauer, "and I had a pretty good idea she loved me, but I did not know that John loved me until the time he let me help with what he called 'weaning the cattle' at the fall roundup. He put me on the chute, and then had the temerity to say to me 'Keep them coming with their heads forward!' And when I told him what their rear ends looked like he said 'Go get some gloves.' And at the end of that day, exhausted, covered with cow manure, we struggled back around the lake, and I fell into a chair, and John came in and said, 'If you exercised like that every day, you wouldn't have so much problem with overweight!' And that's when I knew he loved me, too."

Slade Gorton, who as a young Republican legislator had braved the far right's wrath by testifying to John's loyalty, was now the state attorney general and would soon be elected United States senator. "In 1959, when I first became a member of the state legislature," Gorton told the gathering, "I took it as an article of faith that I would not like John Goldmark, and that we would vote on opposite sides of almost every significant issue which came before the legislature. The last half of that prediction turned out to be all too correct. The first part did not. Because it was from John Goldmark that I learned the most important political lesson of my entire life. . . . That the character and the courage of the individual within our system counted for far more than anything else. That characteristic, that courage, John marked for me when I was a first-term state representative;

marked for me when I was elected attorney general; and will mark for me as long as I live."

Leonard Schroeter, one of Goldmark's law partners, told how "the last living eighteenth-century rationalist" had burdened the firm with his exacting standards of clarity, brevity, and candor. It was a burden that brought rewards. "He enriches us by his knowledge. He leads us by his example. He ennobles us by his character, and I suppose, most importantly, he is the bravest person I've ever known. For me it's been a mitzvah, which in Hebrew means a gift, a rare gift, a gift of God, to have been his partner and to be his friend."

John thanked his friends and gave credit to his wife. "To go through all the things that we've gone through, no person can do it alone. . . . Anything and everything that either of us has done has been because we've been able to do it together."

The Goldmarks went off on a last trip to Italy where they enjoyed the autumn countryside. Two months later John died in Seattle of the cancer which could not be defeated. He never gave up. Among his last words were those he spoke to a doctor who roused him momentarily from his struggle with pain and drugs and asked how he felt. "Oh, fine," said John. "I feel just fine."

By the time the Okanogan libel trial ended, I never wanted to hear the word "communism" again. There had been enough talk of conspiracies, party lines, ideological menaces, and J. Edgar Hoover to last me a lifetime. I was ready for the city and free enterprise. But communism insists on holding our attention, and is the subject of the first of two messages the Goldmark case sends us today.

For nearly forty years we have let our national life be

blighted by a morbid fear of communism. The doctrine finds almost no support in the United States, where civil liberties, private property, and the concept of limited government are cherished. It has prevailed elsewhere only amid desperate poverty and chaos, or where imposed by force along the borders of the Soviet Union. Even in those places its dogmas fail the test of experience. Yet we have allowed one wave of anticommunist hysteria after another to injure innocent Americans and to debase our political life. In foreign affairs we have drifted into the tragedy of Vietnam, foolishly assumed that radicals seeking power in third world countries must be our enemies, and betrayed our own ideals by sponsoring tyrants who proclaim themselves anticommunist while abusing their own people. The results are all too familiar.

We have thrived for two centuries amid ideologies different from ours. We can continue to do so. It is time to get rid of unreasoning fear of communism and to remember that our democratic values can flourish in the world only if we ourselves act in keeping with them.

The second lesson of the Goldmark case concerns trial by jury. That centuries-old democratic institution is now under attack. Two recent statements by justices of the United State Supreme Court sum up the current criticism. Chief Justice Warren E. Burger has said that lay jurors cannot be expected to understand the evidence and decide the issues in long and complicated trials. Such cases, he maintains, "present problems which often only a sophisticated businessman, an economist, or another expert could grasp." Associate Justice John Paul Stevens, while acknowledging his "great faith in the jury system," has pointed to the problem of court congestion and concluded that the jury "is a luxury we may not be able to afford, at least to the extent we have."

These two arguments—that many cases are beyond a jury's grasp, and that the jury is an expensive feature which must yield to the demands of efficiency—underlie a series of changes that have crept into the system over the past few years. Juries of six members rather than twelve have become the rule in many jurisdictions. This change, which forfeits half of the collective powers of observation, memory, and insight the traditional jury has brought to the courtroom, is grounded solely on the desire to save small amounts of money and time. Its constitutionality has been upheld. The Supreme Court has also approved the use of nonunanimous verdicts in state court criminal trials. The idea is to prevent hung juries. Some judges and scholars now urge that juries be confined to criminal trials and that all civil cases be tried by judges. The result, they claim, would be greater speed with no loss of justice.

All of this adds up to the most serious attack on the jury in our history. Is the attack justified? I believe it is not. Trial by jury is the heart of our system of justice. To cut it out in the name of efficiency would be a disaster.

Jurors can and do understand complex cases. Time after time, juries have capably decided cases in such fields as commercial law, antitrust, construction, malpractice, and libel, as well as in the more common areas of negligent torts and criminal law. It detracts not at all from the achievements of the bench to say that nothing indicates that judges would decide these cases any better. The jury brings to the courtroom an ever-renewed freshness and a wealth of community experience that no one person, not even the greatest judge, can match.

When a judge or lawyer says a jury failed to understand a case, usually he is talking about a case that was not well tried. Juries understand even the most complex evidence if it is well presented. And if a case if not well tried, usually nobody understands it—least of all the lawyers who are putting it on.

The Chief Justice, in arguing that juries do not understand, implies that the spectators who watch the trial, the newspaper subscribers who read about it, and indeed the very parties to the case will not grasp it either, since all of them are laymen. Who, then, is deemed able to comprehend? Only the "experts," it would seem—the lawyers at the bar and the lawyers who wear black robes and sit on the bench. There is no reason to think that providence has awarded our profession any such corner on the understanding market.

But the question in any event is not just the elusive one of who decides cases "better." A trial is not merely a way of getting a verdict onto paper, any more than a football game is merely a way of getting numbers onto a scoreboard. Just as important as the end result is how the contest is conducted, and by whom. The power to decide cases is governmental power. It is largely vested in the jury by the state and federal constitutions. To transfer that power, or any sizable part of it, to the judges would involve a major shift in our governmental structure—away from the people and toward their officials. On this score we should remember a remark made by Woodrow Wilson. "What I fear is a government of experts," he said. "God forbid that in a democratic country we should resign the post and give the government over to experts."

The jury, far from causing delay, promotes economy if the judge and lawyers do their jobs well. It encourages brevity in argument and proof. It leaves the judge free to work on other matters while the verdict is being reached. And it decides promptly; no jury has ever taken a case under advisement for months on end as judges, regrettably, sometimes do.

The cost of the jury is infinitesimal. We spend as much each year for pet food, and three times as much for cigarettes, as we do to operate all courts—federal, state, and local. The federal justice system gets by for about one-half of one percent of the defense budget annually. And the jury represents but a tiny fraction of the modest amounts we allow to the courts.

At several turning points in Anglo-American history the jury has interposed its common sense, and its resistance to tyranny, between the government and the powerless individual. In all kinds of cases it has given its members a unique first-hand experience in the workings of government. It has endured because it has worked.

The "glory of English law" is what the eighteenth-century writer Blackstone called the jury system. He was right and his words fit the American jury today. That is a cheering message for democracy. "For only our minds and not our passions," as John Goldmark wrote on the eve of his last campaign, "can find the road to the survival of free men."

Acknowledgments
and a Note on Sources

I STARTED this book in 1966, while living in Spain for a year; put it aside for a long time; and finished it, from what I hope was a wiser and certainly was a longer perspective, in 1983 on Bainbridge Island, Washington. Many friends and associates helped along the way. I am especially grateful to Vasiliki Dwyer, Fred Brack, Barry Farrell, and Leila Charbonneau for suggestions about the manuscript; to Professor Bernard V. Burke for advice on the history of the U.S. Communist Party; to Donald R. Ellegood and his staff at the University of Washington Press for handling the publication swiftly and well; to Susan Gerrard for checking quotations from the court record; and to Phyllis Hatfield for an expert typing job. None of these benefactors is responsible for any errors in the text.

The main source for the Goldmark case is the trial transcript, which is 6,739 pages in length. Copies are available at the libraries of the University of Washington, in Seattle, and Washington State University, in Pullman. Of the many books dealing with general issues raised by the trial, I would especially recommend the following: on the history and nature of the Communist Party in this country, Theodore Draper, *The Roots of American Communism* (New York: Viking, 1957); Harvey Klehr, *The Heyday of American Communism: The Depression Decade* (New York: Basic Books, 1984); and Clinton Rossiter, *Marxism: The View*

From America (New York: Harcourt, Brace, 1960); on the radical right and comparable movements, Richard Hofstadter, *The Paranoid Style in American Politics and Other Essays* (New York: Knopf, 1965), and Daniel Bell, ed., *The Radical Right* (New York: Doubleday, 1963); and on trial by jury, Alexis de Tocqueville's nineteenth-century classic *Democracy in America*; Jerome Frank, *Courts on Trial* (Princeton: Princeton University Press, 1949) (the leading critique of the jury); and Harry Kalven and Hans Zeisel, *The American Jury* (Boston: Little, Brown, 1966). Vern Countryman's *Un-American Activities in the State of Washington* (Ithaca: Cornell University Press, 1951) describes the work of the Canwell Committee. The late Melvin Rader told his own story in *False Witness* (Seattle: University of Washington Press, 1969).